# THE TRANSFIGURATION: A SOURCE- AND REDACTION- CRITICAL STUDY OF LUKE 9:28-36

ISSN 0575-0741

# CAHIERS DE LA REVUE BIBLIQUE

## 32

# THE TRANSFIGURATION: A SOURCE- AND REDACTION- CRITICAL STUDY OF LUKE 9:28-36

by Barbara E. REID, O.P.

PARIS
J. GABALDA et Cie Éditeurs
Rue Pierre et Marie Curie, 18

—

1993

ISBN 2-85021-061-7
ISSN 0575-0741

*To*

*My parents:*

*Charles, in loving memory*

*and*

*Christine, with love and gratitude*

# CONTENTS

# ACKNOWLEDGEMENTS

No work is produced without the inspiration, challenge, and encouragement of countless other people who support the author. Such is the case with the present study. I wish first of all, to thank my family and friends who have formed me in the faith and have supported me in every undertaking. As well, I am grateful for my community of Grand Rapids Dominican Sisters who provided me the opportunity and encouragement to pursue doctoral studies in Scripture.

This study originated as my doctoral dissertation, completed in 1988 at The Catholic University of America. I wish to acknowledge with gratitude the expert guidance of Professor John P. Meier, who directed it through to completion. I am further indebted to Professors Francis T. Gignac and Mary Ann Getty who served as readers of the dissertation and who provided encouragement and suggestions throughout its formulation, and to Fr. Joseph A. Fitzmyer, S.J., whose monumental work on The Gospel of Luke served as a constant resource and inspiration, and whose teaching and mentoring were of inestimable value.

To Jerome Murphy-O'Connor, O.P., Professor of New Testament at the École Biblique et Archéologique Française in Jerusalem, I am indebted for the inspiration to pursue this topic. Moreover, it is he who has guided the refinement of the dissertation into the present work. For his careful critique and enthusiastic encouragement I am particularly grateful.

I want to thank also my colleagues at Catholic Theological Union in Chicago, and members of the Chicago Society of Biblical Literature and participants in the Consultation on NT Prayer in Historical Context of the Society of Biblical Literature, all who have contributed valuable critique in my presentations to them of various portions of the work.

Finally, I am deeply grateful to Dennis Foley, C.P., for his invaluable computer skills, and to Ardis Cloutier, O.S.F., for her generous loan of office space and equipment in preparing the camera-ready copy of the manuscript.

May God's face shine upon you!

# PREFACE

Despite centuries of research the Transfiguration narrative remains the most enigmatic story in the New Testament. Occurring roughly half way through each of the synoptic bospels, it disrupts the normal pattern of Jesus' ministry in Galilee even more decisively than the nature and the feeding miracles.

These two types of miracles make it impossible to interpret Jesus' gift of healing as merely the impact of a profoundly sympathetic personality. Their dramatic character contrasts with the mundane quality of the healing miracles. Nonetheless they are all points on the same continuum. Once a person is chosen by God to be the channel of divine power its gradations are irrelevant.

But is Jesus only a conduit of grace? This is the radical question forced upon us by the Transfiguration. The heavenly light which shines about him on the mountain distinguishes him from such great servants of God as Moses and Elijah. But how great is the difference? Is it qualitative or merely quantitive? Does the radiance come from without or within? Is Jesus God or man?

Such questions underline the extent to which our understanding of the Transfiguration goes to the very heart of the mystery of Jesus. In consequence, the faith committment of the reader, or its lack, is more likely to influence the interpretation of this narrative than any other passage of the New Testament. Inevitably the spectrum of opinions is vast. Their very number betrays the lack of any consensus, and underlines the difficulty of saying something new.

Nonetheless Barbard Reid has succeeded in making an original contribution. In great part this is due to her refusal to assume the blinkers of the two-Source theory of synoptic relationships. The lack of any real progress in the study of this central text has been due to the presumption of Markan priority. Taking up a proposal of Marie-Emile Boismard, OP, to which I gave popular form, she convincingly demonstrates that the most primitive narrative is to be found in the first half of Luke's narrative.

In its present form Luke 9:28-32 betrays the secondary influence of Mark. Once those insertions have been eliminated Luke's primary source emerges. Reid's recognition of its combination of factual and interpretative components enables her to makes a second major, and original, contribution by classifying this source as a predictive angelophany.

The development of this source by material drawn from Mark transformed it into a pronouncement story, which Luke places at a turning point in his gospel. It is the hinge between the Galilean phase of Jesus' ministry and his journey to Jerusalem. Reid's clarity regarding the configuration of the sources available to Luke enables her to offer valuable new and controllable insights into his redactional methodology. This necessarily leads to a more precise and profound perception of the evangelist's theological intentions, particularly as regards Christology and discipleship.

More recently developed forms of criticism have much to contribute to our total understanding of the Bible. Certain presentations, however, may give the impression that these replace older approaches to the text. To highlight how mistaken such views are is a most important by-product of this book. This exemplary treatment of the interplay of source-criticism and redaction-criticism admirably illustrates the perennial value of these venerable approaches to the New Testament.

Jerome Murphy-O'Connor, O.P.

# ABBREVIATIONS

| | |
|---|---|
| AB | Anchor Bible |
| *AJT* | *American Journal of Theology* |
| AnBib | Analecta Biblica |
| AnOr | Analecta orientalia |
| ASNU | Acta seminarii neotestamentici upsaliensis |
| *AsSeign* | *Assemblées du Seigneur* |
| ATANT | Abhandlungen zur Theologie des Alten und Neuen Testaments |
| *ATR* | *Anglican Theological Review* |
| BAGD | W. Bauer, W. F. Arndt, F. W. Gingrich and F. W. Danker, *A Greek-English Lexicon of the New Testament and Other Early Christian Literature*, 2d ed. Chicago: University of Chicago, 1979. |
| B.C.E. | Before the Christian Era |
| BDF | F. Blass, A. Debrunner, and R. W. Funk, *A Greek Grammar of the New Testament and other Christian Literature*. Chicago: University of Chicago, 1961. |
| BETL | Bibliotheca ephemeridum theologicarum lovaniensium |
| *Bib* | *Biblica* |
| BibOr | Biblica et orientalia |
| *BJRL* | *Bulletin of the John Rylands University Library of Manchester* |
| *BR* | *Biblical Research* |
| *BSac* | *Bibliotheca Sacra* |
| *BTB* | *Biblical Theology Bulletin* |
| *BVC* | *Bible et vie chrétienne* |
| BWANT | Beiträge zur Wissenschaft vom Alten und Neuen Testament |
| *BZ* | *Biblische Zeitschrift* |
| BZNW | Beihefte zur *Zietschrift für die neutestamentliche Wissenschaft* |
| C.E. | Christian Era |
| *CBQ* | *Catholic Biblical Quarterly* |
| CBQMS | Catholic Biblical Quarterly Monograph Series |
| CGTC | Cambridge Greek Testament Commentary |
| DJD | Discoveries in the Judaean Desert |
| *DRev* | *Downside Review* |
| EBib | Études Bibliques |
| *EstBib* | *Estudios bíblicos* |
| *ETL* | *Ephemerides theologicae lovanienses* |
| *EvQ* | *Evangelical Quarterly* |
| *ExpTim* | *Expository Times* |
| FB | Forschung zur Bibel |
| FRLANT | Forschungen zur Religion und Literatur des Alten und Neuen Testaments |
| HKNT | Handkommentar zum Neuen Testament |
| HTKNT | Herders theologischer Kommentar zum Neuen Testament |
| *HTR* | *Harvard Theological Review* |
| HTS | Harvard Theological Studies |
| ICC | International Critical Commentary |
| *IDB* | G. A. Buttrick (ed.), *Interpreter's Dictionary of the Bible* |
| *Int* | *Interpretation* |
| *JBL* | *Journal of Biblical Literature* |
| JBLMS | Journal of Biblical Literature Monograph Series |
| *JR* | *Journal of Religion* |
| *JSNT* | *Journal for the Study of the New Testament* |
| JSNTSup | Journal for the Study of the New Testament—Supplement Series |
| *JSOT* | *Journal for the Study of the Old Testament* |
| *JTS* | *Journal of Theological Studies* |

| | |
|---|---|
| KB | L. Koehler and W. Baumgartner, *Lexicon in Veteris Testamenti libros* |
| LSJ | Liddell-Scott-Jones, *Greek-English Lexicon* |
| *LumVie* | *Lumière et vie* |
| *McCQ* | *McCormick Quarterly* |
| MeyerK | H. A. W. Meyer, Kritisch-exegetischer Kommentar über das Neue Testament |
| *NAB* | *New American Bible* |
| NCB | New Century Bible |
| *Neot* | *Neotestamentica* |
| NIC | New International Commentary |
| *NJB* | *New Jerusalem Bible* |
| NJBC | R. E. Brown, *et al.* (eds.) *The New Jerome Biblical Commentary* |
| *NovT* | *Novum Testamentum* |
| NovTSup | Novum Testamentum Supplements |
| *NRT* | *La nouvelle revue théologique* |
| *NRSV* | *New Revised Standard Version* |
| NTAbh | Neutestamentliche Abhandlungen |
| NTD | Das Neue Testament Deutsch |
| *NTS* | *New Testament Studies* |
| PTMS | Pittsburgh Theological Monograph Series |
| *RB* | *Revue biblique* |
| RechBib | Recherches bibliques |
| *RevExp* | *Review and Expositor* |
| *RevThom* | *Revue thomiste* |
| *RHPR* | *Revue d'histoire et de philosophie religieuses* |
| *RHR* | *Revue de l'histoire des religions* |
| *RSR* | *Recherches de science religieuse* |
| *RTP* | *Revue de théologie et de philosophie* |
| *SBAW* | *Sitzungsberichte der bayerischen Akademie der Wissenschaften* |
| SBLDS | SBL Dissertation Series |
| SBLMS | SBL Monograph Series |
| SBS | Stuttgarter Bibelstudien |
| SBT | Studies in Biblical Theology |
| SE | Studia Evangelica |
| SJLA | Studies in Judaism in Late Antiquity |
| SNTSMS | Society for New Testament Studies Monograph Series |
| STANT | Studien zum Alten und Neuen Testament |
| Str-B. | H. Strack and P. Billerbeck, *Kommentar zum Neuen Testament* |
| SUNT | Studien zur Umwelt des Neuen Testaments |
| *TBT* | *The Bible Today* |
| *TDNT* | G. Kittel and G. Friedrich (eds.) *Theological Dictionary of the New Testament* |
| THKNT | Theologischer Handkommentar zum Neuen Testament |
| *TPQ* | *Theologisch-Praktische Quartalschrift* |
| TU | Texte und Untersuchungen |
| *TZ* | *Theologische Zeitschrift* |
| UBS | United Bible Societies |
| *USQR* | *Union Seminary Quarterly Review* |
| *VD* | *Verbum domini* |
| *VSpir* | *Vie spirituelle* |
| *VT* | *Vetus Testamentum* |
| WUNT | Wissenschaftliche Monographien zum Alten und Neuen Testament |
| *ZAW* | *Zeitschrift für die alttestamentliche Wissenschaft* |
| *ZNW* | *Zietschrift für die neutestamentliche Wissenschaft* |
| *ZTK* | *Zeitschrift für Theologie und Kirche* |
| *ZWT* | *Zeitschrift für wissenschaftliche Theologie* |

# INTRODUCTION

## THE PROBLEM

"What Really Happened at the Transfiguration?" This title of a recent article by Jerome Murphy-O'Connor[1] poses once again a question that has never been satisfactorily resolved. The existing studies of the transfiguration are as varied as the accounts themselves. The approaches taken by exegetes range from regarding the transfiguration as a real, historical event to viewing it as a mythic creation of the early church. As G. B. Caird has remarked, "Almost every item in the narrative can be made the starting point of a theory."[2] A current judgment on the situation is given by J. A. Fitzmyer in his commentary on the Gospel of Luke. After giving a brief sketch of the various theories, he then writes, "Given the diversity of the way in which the incident is reported, no real historical judgment can be made about it; to write it all off as mythical is likewise to go beyond the evidence. Just what sort of an incident in the ministry of Jesus—to which it is clearly related—it was is impossible to say."[3]

Is it necessary to resign oneself to this impasse? Or is it possible that it may be overcome by taking a different approach to the tradition history of the three accounts? Almost all scholars begin with the basic assumption that Mark's account of the transfiguration was the primary source of the story and that the versions of Matthew and Luke are subsequent redactions of it. This presupposition has been questioned by M.-É. Boismard, who discerns a source in Luke that is independent of Mark.[4] Jerome Murphy-O'Connor agrees with Boismard and has argued that, when refined, this source contains a historical element that can easily be integrated into the ministry of Jesus.[5] Several other scholars have suggested Luke's dependence on a special source for the transfiguration narrative.[6] To date, this

---

[1]*Bible Review* 3 (1987) 8-21.

[2]G. B. Caird, "The Transfiguration," *ExpTim* 67 (1955-56) 291.

[3]J. A. Fitzmyer, *The Gospel According to Luke I-IX* (AB 28; Garden City, NY: Doubleday, 1981) 796.

[4]M.-É. Boismard, *Synopse des quatre évangiles en français* (Paris: Cerf, 1972) 2. 50-55.

[5]Murphy-O'Connor, "Transfiguration," 9-10.

[6]J. V. Bartlet, "The Sources of St. Luke's Gospel," *Studies in the Synoptic Problem by Members of the University of Oxford* (ed. W. Sanday; Oxford: Clarendon, 1911) 322; W. Dietrich, *Das Petrusbild der lukanischen Schriften* (BWANT 5; Stuttgart: Kohlhammer, 1972) 104-9; B. S. Easton, *The Gospel According to St. Luke* (Edinburgh: Clark, 1926) 142-46; E. E. Ellis, "La composition de Luc 9 et les sources de sa christologie," *Jésus aux Origines de la Christologie* (ed. J. Dupont; BETL 11; Gembloux: Leuven University, 1975) 193-200; R. H. Fuller, *The Foundations of New Testament Christology* (New York: Scribner, 1965) 172; W. Grundmann, *Das Evangelium nach Lukas* (THKNT 3; Berlin: Evangelische Verlagsanstalt, 1974) 191-92; K. H. Rengstorf, *Das Evangelium nach Lukas* (NTD 3; Göttingen: Vandenhoeck & Ruprecht, 1958) 123; T. Schramm,

hypothesis has not been tested by a full-length scholarly investigation.[7] This study of Luke 9:28-36 will test the possibility proposed by Murphy-O'Connor that information about a historical event in the earthly life of Jesus can be discerned from the special source behind Luke's version of the story. The method used is historical-critical, primarily source and redaction criticism. Chapter one is devoted to a survey of the literature on the transfiguration narratives. Chapter two analyzes the transmission of the tradition by examining the internal consistency of Luke 9:28-36, and by making a detailed comparison between the Lucan and Marcan accounts. Chapter three is devoted to a verse-by-verse exegesis of Luke 9:28-36, including a discussion of the context and function of the pericope. In chapter four the results of the study are summarized and its implications are spelled out with regard to synoptic source relationships, Luke's particular redactional methodology, and the evidence for the historicity of the transfiguration event. Concluding remarks summarize the contributions made by Luke 9:28-36 to the understanding of Lucan theology, especially with regard to christology and discipleship.

---

*Der Markus-Stoff bei Lukas: Eine literarkritische und redaktionsgeschichtliche Untersuchung* (SNTSMS 14; Cambridge: Cambridge University, 1971) 136-39.

[7]The book-length studies that have been done on the transfiguration are few and, for the most part, are dated. In chronological order they are: J. Blinzler, *Die neutestamentlichen Berichte über die Verklärung Jesu* (NTAbh 17/4; Münster: Aschendorff, 1937); J. Höller, *Die Verklärung Jesu. Eine Auslegung der neutestamentlichen Berichte* (Freiburg: Herder, 1937); E. Dabrowski, *La transfiguration de Jésus* (Scripta Pontificii Instituti Biblici 85; Rome: Biblical Institute, 1939); G. H. Boobyer, *St. Mark and the Transfiguration Story* (Edinburgh: Clark, 1942); A. M. Ramsey, *The Glory of God and the Transfiguration of Christ* (London/New York: Longmans, Green, 1945); H. Riesenfeld, *Jésus transfiguré. L'arrière-plan du récit évangélique de la transfiguration de Notre-Seigneur* (ASNU 16; Copenhagen: Munksgaard, 1947); H. Baltensweiler, *Die Verklärung Jesu. Historisches Ereignis und synoptische Berichte* (ATANT 33; Zurich: Zwingli, 1959); J. M. Nützel, *Der Verklärungserzählung im Markusevangelium. Eine redaktionsgeschichtliche Untersuchung* (FB 6; Würzburg: Echter, 1973). Most deal with all three accounts, with the exception of Boobyer and Nützel, who concentrate on Mark's version. Two recent doctoral dissertations analyze the Lucan account: P. R. Baldacci, *The Significance of the Transfiguration Narrative in the Gospel of Luke: A Redactional Investigation* (Ph.D. Diss. Marquette University, 1974); R. H. Gause, *The Lukan Transfiguration Account: Luke's Pre-Crucifixion Presentation of the Exalted Lord in the Glory of the Kingdom of God* (Ph.D. Diss. Emory University, 1975). Neither of these two studies investigates the source question.

# CHAPTER ONE

# SURVEY OF PREVIOUS STUDIES

This chapter surveys the literature on the transfiguration according to the various approaches taken by exegetes. These include the historical approach, the resurrection-appearance approach, the mythological approach, the approaches from OT background and Jewish apocalyptic, and the redaction-critical approach. Each of these trends in interpretation will be described and evaluated and its major proponents cited. The treatment of each is not exhaustive, and the reader is referred to individual works for more minute detail and for additional references.[1] The aim of this survey is to set forth the various entry points to the study of the transfiguration narratives according to the kinds of presuppositions that are brought to the texts by exegetes. The approach used in this study will then be seen in the context of those that have preceded.

## I. HISTORICAL APPROACH

From the first recorded commentary on the transfiguration, that of Origen,[2] until the nineteenth century, the predominant approach to the story began with the presupposition of the historical truth of the event as a real, objective occurrence. The transfiguration was understood to be a factual experience of the three disciples that took place shortly after Peter's confession of Jesus' messiahship at Caesarea Philippi, in which Jesus' supernatural glory was manifested to them in his physical transformation.

The proponents of this historical interpretation fall into two categories: (1) those who understand the transfiguration as an objective, external happening; and (2) those who regard it as a subjective, internal experience. Exegetes who view the event as an external happening are again divided into two camps: those who explain it as a supernatural incursion into the natural realm[3] and those who use natural phenomena to explain the origin of the description of the transfiguration.[4]

---

[1]For a critical examination of individual major books and articles that have appeared on the subject between 1942 and 1970, the reader is referred to chapter one of the dissertation by Nützel, *Verklärungserzählung*, 1-86.

[2]*Comm. in Matt.* 12:37; *GCS*, 40. 152.

[3]E.g., Blinzler, Höller, Dabrowski, Baltensweiler.

[4]E.g., H. E. G. Paulus, *Exegetisches Handbuch über die drei ersten Evangelien* (3 vols.; Heidelberg: Winter, 1842) 2. 437; F. Spitta, "Die evangelische Geschichte von der Verklärung Jesu," *ZWT* 53 (1911) 121-23.

## A. OBJECTIVE, EXTERNAL EVENT

### 1. Supernatural Occurrence

Some scholars approach the transfiguration as an objective, externally observable, supernatural event directed primarily to the disciples that served to prove Jesus' divine dignity. Both Jesus' changed appearance and the voice from heaven are understood to be for the benefit of the disciples in order to strengthen their faith in the face of Jesus' approaching passion.[5] Others interpret the event in terms of its meaning for Jesus. For example, H. Baltensweiler conjectures that on the occasion of the feast of Tabernacles,[6] when the messianic hopes of the people were heightened, Jesus took his three most intimate disciples up the mountain with him to confront once again the temptation to be a nationalistic messiah who would resort to violent means for the liberation of Israel from its pagan oppressors. The mysterious occurrence that transpired was a means of fortifying Jesus against this temptation so that he could be obedient to the way of suffering and death. Similar interpretations are given by G. B. Caird[7] and M. Coune.[8] Caird understands the event to be the beginning of Jesus' journey of discovery in the unmapped territory of what obedience to God means, a territory that had to be discovered in his own experience. In Coune's opinion, the transfiguration was for Jesus an intense coming to grips with his messiahship, a critical moment in his ministry like his baptism and temptation.

### 2. Natural Phenomena

The other way of interpreting the transfiguration as an objective, external happening does not appeal to the realm of the supernatural but looks rather to natural phenomena to explain the occurrence. Paulus understands the transfiguration as an experience of the half-asleep disciples when a mountaintop sunrise illuminated the person of Jesus.[9] Spitta posits a night storm atop the mountain, seen as a manifestation of God, where lightning and thunder explain the elements of flashing light and the voice from heaven.[10]

---

[5]E.g., Dabrowski, *Transfiguration*, 157-65.

[6]The Tabernacles setting is deduced from Peter's suggestion to build tents and from the time reference "after six days" (Mark 9:2), which Baltensweiler interprets as indicating Jesus' intention to spend the seventh day of the feast, the most solemn one, in solitude on the mountain.

[7]"Transfiguration," 293.

[8]"L'Évangile de la transfiguration," *Paroisse et liturgie* 52 (1970) 157-70.

[9]*Handbuch*, 2. 437.

[10]"Geschichte," 121-23.

## B. SUBJECTIVE, INTERNAL EXPERIENCE

In another category of the historical approach are a number of scholars who understand the transfiguration as a subjective, visionary, interior experience, either of Jesus, or of Peter, or of all three of the chosen disciples. As an experience of Jesus, P. W. Schmiedel interprets it as permission from heaven that Jesus may now present himself as the Messiah.[11] C. Binet-Sanglé understands the transfiguration as "une attaque d'extase de Jésus."[12] D. Evans regards it as an experience of Jesus that involved "what we now call 'paranormal' changes discernible to 'psychics' and also, more importantly, a total surrender and transparency of a human being in body, passions, mind, and spirit to the divine Spirit."[13] He goes on to say, "For Christians, this transfiguration happens through contemplative identification with Christ" such as Paul describes in 2 Cor 3:18-4:6.[14] Others see the transfiguration as an experience of Peter confirming his confession of faith.[15]

Still others say the vision was experienced by all three of the disciples as a momentary revelation of what lay beyond.[16] Some exegetes interpret the narrative as a combined experience of both Jesus and the disciples, i.e., a vision or mystical experience of Jesus into which his companions are drawn.[17]

## C. EVALUATION OF THE HISTORICAL APPROACH

Whatever distinctions are made by the adherents of the historical interpretation, they do share the following arguments for their position that the

---

[11]P. W. Schmiedel, "Simon Peter," *Encyclopedia Biblica* (4 vols.; ed. T. K. Cheyne; New York: Macmillan, 1903) 4. 4570-71.

[12]C. Binet-Sanglé, *La folie de Jésus* (Paris: Maloine, 1909) 189-94.

[13]D. Evans, "Academic Scepticism, Spiritual Reality and Transfiguration," in *The Glory of Christ in the New Testament. Studies in Christology* (Ed. L. D. Hurst and N. T. Wright. Oxford: Clarendon, 1987) 182-83.

[14]*Ibid.*, 185-86.

[15]E.g., A. von Harnack, "Die Verklärungsgeschichte Jesu, der Bericht des Paulus (1 Kor 15,3ff) und die beiden Christusvisionen des Petrus," *SBAW* (1922) 62-80; E. Meyer, *Ursprung und Anfänge des Christentums* (3 vols.; Stuttgart & Berlin: Cotta'sche, 1921) 1. 152-60.

[16]E.g., A. Plummer, *The Gospel According to St. Luke* (ICC; New York: Scribner, 1903) 250-54; C. E. B. Cranfield, *The Gospel According to St. Mark* (CGTC; Cambridge: University Press, 1966) 294; W. Manson, *The Gospel of Luke* (New York: Harper, 1930) 112-15.

[17]E.g., Caird, "Transfiguration," 291; S. H. Hooke, *The Resurrection of Christ as History and Experience* (London: Darton, Longman & Todd, 1967) 117-27; J. W. C. Wand, *Transfiguration* (London: The Faith Press, 1967) 62.

transfiguration was a historical event during the earthly ministry of Jesus.[18] In all three synoptic accounts, the transfiguration is clearly placed by the evangelists in the context of Jesus' Galilean ministry. In this setting, it has an important function as a revelation of Jesus' divine majesty and as a confirmation of Peter's confession of faith at Caesarea Philippi in view of Jesus' coming passion. The exactitude of details such as time, place, and circumstances argues for the historicity of the event. Furthermore, details such as Jesus' choice of the three disciples Peter, James, and John, the characteristic impulsiveness of Peter, the disciples' misunderstanding, are all in accord with details provided in other narratives that relate events from the earthly ministry of Jesus.

There are several arguments to support the visionary interpretation. The word ὅραμα, "vision," is explicitly used in Matthew's account (17:9). Many of the details, such as whiteness, fright, a cloud, the voice from heaven, sleep followed by return to a normal state, are elsewhere associated with visions. Also, Peter's confession of Jesus as the Messiah provides a context in which the disciples could be disposed to such a vision. In addition, the history of attested mystical experiences in the faith tradition confirms the possibility of such occurrences.[19] Finally, visions are plentiful in both the OT and the NT and the transfiguration could easily be explained against such a backdrop.

The historical approach is not devoid of difficulties. The supernatural interpretation implies that experiences from the realm of the transcendent can break into the natural sphere and be experienced by human beings. While some exegetes would be willing to accept such a premise, others would not. There is also the question that if the disciples had been accorded such an experience during Jesus' earthly ministry, how is Peter's vehement denial of Jesus and the disciples' abandonment of him during his passion to be explained? Also problematic is how to explain the means by which the disciples were able to recognize Moses and Elijah. As for the explanations that appeal to natural phenomena, these involve a great deal of conjecture and imaginative reconstruction. There are no scholars who adhere to this latter line of interpretation today.

Regarding the visionary approach, the greatest obstacle is that the psychological assumptions go beyond the literal accounts of the texts. As for the

---

[18]The question of the historicity of the event is a separate question from that of the placement of the account in the earthly ministry of Jesus in the gospel tradition. Because the synoptic evangelists have situated the story in the context of Jesus' Galilean ministry, a number of scholars continue to advocate that the transfiguration is best interpreted as an incident in the lifetime of Jesus, but go no further than that in explaining it or in making a determination regarding the historicity of the event. See Fitzmyer, *Luke*, 796; V. Taylor, *The Gospel According to Mark* (2d ed.; London: Macmillan, 1966) 388; R. H. Stein, "Is the Transfiguration (Mark 9:2-8) a Misplaced Resurrection Account?" *JBL* 95 (1976) 79-96.

[19]See E. Underhill (*The Mystic Way* [London/New York: Dent, 1913] 114-23), who presents evidence that physical transfiguration has been known to accompany the intense devotional experiences of saints and mystics.

term ὅραμα, in addition to "vision" ὅραμα also connotes something seen in the ordinary way (e.g., Deut 28:34,67; Eccl 6:9). It is true that the details of whiteness, fright, a cloud, the voice from heaven, and sleep can be interpreted in terms of a visionary experience, but this is not the only possible explanation.

Overall, the greatest difficulty with the above explanations is that the exegetes who espouse them approach the text with the presupposition of the historicity of the event and make their reconstructions of it the starting point of their investigations. This method should be reversed: the determination of the historical situation should stand at the end of the study as one of its possible conclusions.

With the advent of rationalism in the nineteenth century came challenges to the historical interpretation. The objective reality of supernatural occurrences was questioned, and other explanations for the provenience of the story of the transfiguration were proposed. Many scholars began to regard the narrative as a fictional development from mythological, apocalyptic, or symbolic themes. The basis for the story was sought by some in OT concepts, while others looked to the influence of foreign mythology. Still others saw the narrative as an elaboration of NT themes.

## II. RESURRECTION-APPEARANCE APPROACH

One hypothesis with a considerable following is that the transfiguration account was originally a story of a resurrection appearance of Jesus that has been retrojected[20] into Jesus' Galilean ministry by the evangelists.[21] The predating of

---

[20]Such retrojection is also proposed in other instances in the gospel tradition. On the likelihood that the miraculous catch recounted in John 21:1-8 is a postresurrection event transferred by Luke to solemnize the calling of the disciples in 5:1-11, see R. E. Brown, *The Gospel According to John XIII-XXI* (AB 29a; Garden City, NY: Doubleday, 1970) 1089-92; Fitzmyer, *Luke*, 560-61; R. Leaney, "Jesus and Peter: The Call and Post-Resurrection Appearance (Luke v.1-11 and xxiv.34)," *ExpTim* 65 (1953-54) 381-82. Cf. C. H. Dodd, "The Appearances of the Risen Christ: an Essay in Form-Criticism of the Gospels," *Studies in the Gospels: Essays in Memory of R. H. Lightfoot* (ed. D. E. Nineham; Oxford: Blackwell, 1957) 22-23; R. Pesch, *Der reiche Fischfang: Lk 5,1-11/Jo 21,1-14:Wundergeschichte—Berufungserzählung—Erscheinungsbericht* (Düsseldorf:Patmos,1969). Another possible example is the pericope about Peter walking on the water in Matt 14:28-33 (cf. Mark 6:45-51; John 6:16-21). See Brown, *John*, 1087-88; Dodd, "Appearances," 23-24. Similarly, the sayings in Matt 16:16b-19; 18:18 may have originally had a postresurrection setting as those in John 20:23. See Brown, *John*, 1040, 1088-89; R. H. Fuller, "The 'Thou Art Peter' Pericope and the Easter Appearances," *McCQ* 20 (1967) 309-15. Cf. C. H. Dodd ("Some Johannine 'Herrnworte' with Parallels in the Synoptic Gospels," *NTS* 2 [1955] 85-86), who explains the similarities between Matt 16:16b-19; 18:18, and John 20:23 as due to each evangelist independently following alternate forms of the tradition. There are no clear examples of a story from the ministry of Jesus being postponed to a resurrection setting. See Fitzmyer, *Luke*, 561; G. Klein, "Die Berufung des Petrus," *ZNW* 58 (1967) 34-35.

the experience reflects the conviction of the disciples that the Christ of the kerygma was the same as the Jesus of the earthly ministry. The arguments for the story originally having been that of a resurrection appearance will be examined according to the outline of R. H. Stein,[22] who analyzes it according to terminological considerations, form-critical considerations, redactional considerations, historical considerations, nonsynoptic parallels, and *a priori* assumptions.

## A. TERMINOLOGICAL CONSIDERATIONS

First, some of the terminology contained in the transfiguration accounts is said to be better explained if the original story were that of a resurrection appearance. These terms include: (a) ὤφθη, which is regarded by Weeden[23] as almost a technical term for resurrection appearances; (b) νεφέλη, which is a vehicle for ascension (Acts 1:9; Rev 11:12) and is appropriate to a resurrection context; (c) ὄρος ὑψηλὸν, which is identified with the mountain in Matt 28:16; (d) δόξα, which is frequently associated with the resurrected Lord,[24] as well as with the glorification of clothes, which in apocalyptic literature is characteristic of the exalted state of a heavenly being (e.g., *1 Enoch* 62:15-16; *2 Enoch* 22:8; Rev 4:4; 7:9); (e) the temporal designation μετὰ ἡμέρας ἓξ (Mark 9:2; Matt 17:1)/ὡσεὶ ἡμέραι ὀκτὼ (Luke 9:28), in light of the fact that the few explicit datings found in the synoptic gospels are usually related to the passion and resurrection.[25]

Some objections to these terminological arguments are as follows:

---

[21]It is generally acknowledged that this hypothesis was first formulated by J. Wellhausen, *Das Evangelium Marci* (Berlin: Reimer, 1909) 71. For a fairly complete list of those who follow him, see Stein, "Transfiguration," 79 n. 2.

[22]"Transfiguration," 80-90. See also R. Bultmann, *Die Geschichte der synoptischen Tradition* (3d ed.; Göttingen: Vandenhoeck & Ruprecht, 1957) 278-81; C. E. Carlston, "Transfiguration and Resurrection," *JBL* 80 (1961) 233-40; C. S. Mann, *Mark* (AB 27; Garden City, NY: Doubleday, 1986) 356; T. J. Weeden, *Mark—Traditions in Conflict* (Philadelphia: Fortress, 1971) 119-20.

[23]*Traditions*, 119.

[24]E.g., Acts 7:55; 9:3; 22:6,9,11; 26:13; 1 Cor 15:8,40; 1 Pet 1:11,21; Heb 2:9; 1 Tim 3:16.

[25]Temporal designations occur in the passion-resurrection predictions: Mark 8:31; 9:31; 10:34 and parr.; in connection with Jesus' last days in Jerusalem and the passion: Mark 11:12,19,20; 14:1,12,17; 15:1,25,33,34,42 and parr.; in the resurrection appearances: Mark 16:2,9; Matt 27:63; 28:1; Luke 24:1; John 20:1,6; and in Paul's kerygmatic "on the third day," 1 Cor 15:4. W. Schmithals ("Der Markusschluss, die Verklärungsgeschichte und die Aussendung der Zwölf," *ZTK* 69 [1972] 379-411) builds his whole theory from the mention of six days and the inconceivability of there being no resurrection appearances in Mark's Gospel. He proposes that in Mark's source the transfiguration followed directly after 16:8, the discovery of the empty tomb, and was dated six days after that event. The relocation of the transfiguration story by Mark was carried out in the interests of his messianic secret theory. Two other terminological parallels pointed out by Mann (*Mark*, 356) are: ὧδε εἶναι Mark 9:5, which parallels οὐκ ἔστιν ὧδε in Mark 16:6; and οὐ γὰρ ᾔδει τί ἀποκριθῇ, ἔκφοβοι γὰρ ἐγένοντο (Mark 9:6), which parallels οὐδενὶ οὐδὲν εἶπαν, ἐφοβοῦντο γάρ in Mark 16:8.

(a) The word ὤφθη is not used in the transfiguration accounts to describe Jesus' appearance, but rather that of Moses and Elijah. Furthermore, ὤφθη can hardly be regarded as a technical term for resurrection appearances, since it is used as such only once in the synoptic gospels (Luke 24:34).[26] In all other instances it refers to a figure other than Jesus (e.g., an angel in Luke 1:11; Moses and Elijah in the transfiguration accounts). Other forms of the verb ὁράω occur in varied uses. The verb ὁράω is associated more often with the parousia than with the resurrection.[27]

(b) Clouds are never part of a resurrection-appearance story. To connect clouds with the resurrection presumes taking the resurrection and ascension as a unity. Furthermore, the cloud does not function in the transfiguration accounts as a vehicle for ascension. It does not come upon Jesus alone, and it does not transport him either to or from heaven. Rather, it is Moses and Elijah who have vanished after the cloud's disappearance, while Jesus remains behind. The cloud can just as readily be connected with the parousia: then, it is said, the Son of Man will be seen coming on the clouds.[28] The cloud can also be explained as a symbol of the presence of God (e.g., Exod 16:10; 19:9; 24:15-18; 40:34),[29] or as an apocalyptic stage prop.

(c) The reference to a high mountain does not necessarily evoke a resurrection context. The only resurrection appearance that takes place on a mountain is that of Matt 28:16, and such a mountain is very much a redactional theme in Matthew.[30] There are also many other places in the NT where mountains figure that have no connection to the resurrection (e.g., Mark 3:13-19; Matt 5:1-2; 14:23). Some of these instances make the mountain a place of epiphany or divine encounter, but these encounters are not with the resurrected Christ.

(d) The term δόξα is used only in Luke's account (9:32) and need not refer to Christ's resurrected glory, although this is the most common application of the

---

[26]In Acts it is found in 13:31 and 26:16 in Paul's preaching about the resurrection.

[27]Stein ("Transfiguration," 80), in reply to those who would say that ὤφθη in the transfiguration account originally referred to Jesus but was changed in the Marcan redaction, argues that the term occurs too late in the pericope to refer to Jesus who is there all along in the story and has already been transfigured. Furthermore, if Mark employed ὤφθη in the transfiguration account placed in Jesus' earthly ministry, it could no longer be said that ὤφθη is a *terminus technicus* for the resurrection in the mind of Mark.

[28]E.g., Mark 13:26; 14:62; Matt 24:30; 26:64; 1 Thes 4:17; Rev 1:17.

[29]So Fitzmyer, *Luke*, 802; M. Horstmann, *Studien zur markinischen Christologie: Mk 8:27-9:13 als Zugang zum Christusbild des zweiten Evangeliums* (NTAbh 6; Münster: Aschendorff, 1969) 99; Baltensweiler, *Verklärung*, 85 n. 87; Riesenfeld, *Jésus transfiguré*, 130-45.

[30]See T. L. Donaldson, *Jesus on the Mountain: A Study in Matthean Theology* (JSNTSup 8; Sheffield: JSOT, 1985).

term.[31]  In the synoptic gospels, δόξα is also associated with the parousia (e.g., Mark 8:38; 10:37; 13:26 and parr.; Matt 19:28; 25:31).  Furthermore, there are instances in the NT where δόξα is associated with the earthly Jesus (e.g., Luke 2:9; John 1:14; 2 Pet 1:16-18) and is not a prefigurement of the resurrection.

(e) The presence of the temporal designation does not necessarily indicate a connection with the resurrection.  There are several other examples of explicit time references given in the synoptic gospels that are quite removed from the resurrection narratives (e.g., Mark 1:32,35; 11:12,20).  Moreover, nowhere else is there a reference to "six days" with regard to a resurrection appearance.  The temporal designations with resurrection associations are rather "the third day" (Luke 24:21,46; 1 Cor 15:4), "on the first day" (Matt 28:1; Mark 16:2,9; Luke 24:1), and "during forty days" (Acts 1:3).

In sum, although terminological links to resurrection-appearance stories can be shown in each of the above examples, none of these terms demands a resurrection context for intelligibility.  Furthermore, there are terms and phrases in the account that are quite incongruent in a resurrection-appearance story.[32]  One incongruity is the heavenly voice with the directive, ἀκούετε αὐτοῦ.  No resurrection account employs a heavenly voice or gives the command to listen to Jesus.[33]

## B. FORM-CRITICAL CONSIDERATIONS

Some scholars see similarities in the form of the transfiguration and resurrection appearance stories: (a) the occurrence of the event on the sabbath;[34] (b) mention of the divine sonship of Jesus, which in many NT passages (e.g., Rom 1:4; Acts 13:33) is associated with the resurrection; (c) the description of Jesus' appearance at the transfiguration, as paralleled by the description of the dress and the glory of the angels in the resurrection stories; (d) the fact that the miracle is performed on Jesus rather than by Jesus; (e) the motif of fear, as in Mark 16:8; Matt 28:10; Luke 24:5,37.

Stein shows that these similarities do not support the conclusion that the

---

[31]See G. Kittel, "δόξα," *TDNT* 2 (1964) 248.

[32]One incongruity identified by Stein ("Transfiguration," 90-91) is Peter's address to Jesus as ῥαββί in Mark 9:5. According to him, one would expect κύριε in a resurrection context. B. T. Viviano, however, ("Rabbouni and Mark 9:5," *RB* 97 [1990] 207-18) has shown that Mark's ῥαββί carries a pre-rabbinic, pre-Jamnian meaning "lord."

[33]Carlston ("Transfiguration," 238-39), however, argues that a voice, φωνή is an element in the postresurrection experience of Paul in Acts 9:4-6, and that the directive ἀκούετε αὐτοῦ has a parallel in the mandate give in Matt 28:18-20.

[34]Thrall ("Elijah and Moses in Mark's Account of the Transfiguration," *NTS* 16 [1969-70] 311) argues that Mark's μετὰ ἡμέρας ἕξ means "on the seventh day," that is, the sabbath, and that Mark 15:42 and 16:1-2 show that Mark understands the resurrection to have occurred on the sabbath.

transfiguration was a resurrection-appearance story.[35]

(a) With regard to the occurrence of the event on a sabbath, even if μετὰ ἡμέρας ἓξ is interpreted as "on the seventh day," i.e., on the sabbath, that still does not necessarily make the transfiguration a resurrection appearance. Although the resurrection may have been presented as occurring on the sabbath, especially in the Marcan account, as maintained by Thrall, not so the appearances. Rather, most are said to have taken place after the sabbath (Mark 16:1; Matt 28:1), on the first day of the week (Matt 28:1; Mark 16:2,9; Luke 24:1; John 20:1). Furthermore, what is to be made of Thrall's understanding when Luke's version makes the time frame ὡσεὶ ἡμέραι ὀκτώ?

(b) The reference to Jesus' divine sonship does not irrefutably indicate association with the resurrection. Many other such references are made throughout the gospels (e.g., Mark 3:11; 5:7; 12:6; 13:32; 14:61-62; 15:39; Matt 2:15; 4:3,6; 14:33; 16:16; 27:40,43; Luke 1:35; 4:41), showing the early church's association of divine sonship with the earthly Jesus.

(c) Regarding the similarity of dress, the comparison is drawn between the clothing of the angels at the resurrection and that of Jesus at the transfiguration, not between Jesus' apparel at the resurrection as compared to his clothing at the transfiguration. No mention of Jesus' clothing is made in any resurrection-appearance story.

(d) The transfiguration is not the only gospel story about a miracle worked on Jesus rather than by him. The baptism accounts relate just such a story, and in fact contain many more similarities to the story of the transfiguration than do the accounts of resurrection appearances.[36]

(e) The motif of fear is found in stories other than those of resurrection appearances. It occurs in angelophanies (e.g., Luke 1:13,30; 2:9,10), call stories (e.g., Luke 5:10), and miracle stories (e.g., Luke 8:25,35,50).

C. H. Dodd's analysis has shown that the transfiguration story contrasts on almost every point with the typical stories of resurrection appearances:[37] (a) in a resurrection appearance, the disciples are seen to be orphaned before their reunion with Jesus; in the transfiguration, they are with Jesus the whole time; (b) in the former, a word of Jesus (a greeting, reproach, command) always has a significant place; in the latter, Jesus is silent throughout; (c) in stories of resurrection appearances, no voice from heaven is heard, but there is in the transfiguration; (d) in resurrection appearances, Jesus always appears alone; in the transfiguration, it is not Jesus who appears, but rather Moses and Elijah; (e) there is no reference to Jesus' being clothed in visible glory in resurrection-appearance stories, but there is in the transfiguration.

In addition to these reasons, Stein adds that the presence of Peter, James,

---

[35]Stein, "Transfiguration," 83-84, 91-94.

[36]See M. Coune, "Baptême, Transfiguration et Passion," NRT 92 (1970) 165-79.

[37]Dodd, "Appearances," 9-35.

and John in the story is an element that argues for its placement in the earthly ministry of Jesus.[38]  In every other instance in which the three figure (Mark 1:16-20,29; 5:37; 13:3; 14:33 and parr.), the story is related to Jesus' earthly ministry. These three disciples are never singled out in a resurrection-appearance story.[39]

## C. REDACTIONAL CONSIDERATIONS

A third means of showing that the transfiguration was originally a resurrection-appearance story comes from redactional considerations.  Some scholars attempt to show that the present placement of the story is due to Marcan redaction and that in the pre-Marcan tradition it was not originally connected to its present context.  Bultmann argues that Mark 9:1 was originally connected with 9:11-13 and that vv 2-10 are a later insertion.[40]  Stein objects that even if it could be proved that Mark 9:2-10 was a later insertion, that still does not prove that the original context of the story was the resurrection.[41]  Also, those who see Mark as a conservative editor, i.e., one who tends to hold together large complexes as he receives them,[42] object to this argument as contrary to Mark's editorial habits.

Another argument for an original resurrection account is that in its present location the transfiguration story clearly serves as a confirmation of Peter's confession of faith and a ratification of Jesus' prediction of his passion and resurrection. The conclusion is then reached that, because the placement of the account fits Mark's purpose so well, it must be due to Marcan rearrangement of an original resurrection account.[43]  This conclusion is unwarranted. The present position of the transfiguration account does, indeed, serve Mark's purpose well, but that does not prove that the narrative was taken by Mark from a resurrection

---

[38]"Transfiguration," 92-93.

[39]See also J. E. Alsup, *The Post-Resurrection Appearance Stories of the Gospel Tradition. A History-of-Tradition Analysis* (Calwer theologische Monographien 5; London: SPCK, 1975) 141-43; P. Perkins, *Resurrection. New Testament Witness and Contemporary Reflection* (Garden City: Doubleday, 1984) 95-99.

[40]*Geschichte*, 131-32. Also Horstmann, *Studien*, 72.

[41]"Transfiguration," 84.

[42]E.g., E. Best, "Mark's Preservation of the Tradition," *L'Évangile selon Marc* (ed. M. Sabbe; BETL 34; Gembloux: Duculot, 1974) 21-34; R. Pesch, *Das Markusevangelium* (HTKNT; 2 vols.; Freiburg: Herder, 1976); E. Trocmé, *The Formation of the Gospel According to Mark* (London: SPCK, 1975) 68-71. For the contrary position, i.e., that a great deal of Mark's Gospel is due to his own composition, see, for example, W. Kelber, *The Oral and the Written Gospel* (Philadelphia: Fortress, 1983); *The Passion in Mark* (Philadelphia: Fortress, 1976); D. B. Peabody, *Mark as Composer* (New Gospel Studies 1; Macon, GA: Mercer University, 1987); N. Perrin, "The Christology of Mark: A Study in Metholodogy," *JR* 51 (1971) 173-87; Weeden, *Traditions*, 1-19.

[43]Carlston, "Transfiguration," 240.

context.

## D. HISTORICAL CONSIDERATIONS

A fourth line of argumentation for the transfiguration having originally been a resurrection-appearance story comes from historical considerations. It is proposed that the cowardly behavior of the disciples in the passion narrative is more easily explained if the transfiguration was not an event experienced by them during Jesus' Galilean ministry. In reply, one may ask whether such an experience as the transfiguration would necessarily transform definitively the behavior of the disciples. Other signs and wonders that they witnessed did not have this effect on them. Rather, their transformation took place only with their experiences of the risen Jesus.

## E. NONSYNOPTIC PARALLELS

A fifth argument for the transfiguration having been a resurrection appearance story is that the *Apocalypse of Peter* and 2 Pet 1:16-18 reflect such an understanding. K. G. Goetz maintains that the *Apocalypse of Peter* is clearly a resurrection-ascension account, especially in the Ethiopic version, and that it is more original than the synoptic accounts.[44] However, most scholars agree that the *Apocalypse of Peter* is to be dated to the second century, between 125 and 150 C.E.[45] This late date makes it probable that, if there is a dependence, it is the *Apocalypse of Peter* that is dependent on the synoptic tradition. This also appears to be true when one examines the schema of the story in *Apoc. Pet.* 15-17. The outline is the same as in the synoptic tradition,[46] but the narrative is more cohesive in the *Apocalypse of Peter*. In the latter, the details of the story are more fully elaborated and are expanded upon in an apocalyptic fashion. These can be taken as signs of the secondary nature of the narrative.[47]

---

[44]K. G. Goetz, *Petrus* (Leipzig: Hinrichs, 1927) 81-82.

[45]R. E. Brown and R. F. Collins, "Canonicity," *NJBC*, art. 66 §68 p.1048; E. Hennecke, *New Testament Apocrypha* (2 vols.; ed. W. Schneemelcher and R. McL. Wilson; Philadelphia: Westminster, 1965) 2. 663-83.

[46]Interestingly, it contains the details of prayer and "two men" that are found in Luke's account.

[47]Boobyer, *Transfiguration*, 13-14. However, elaboration and increasing detail are not always signs of later redaction. Sometimes redactors synthesize the material found in their sources, as is the case in a number of Matthean pericopes, e.g., Matt 8:28-34; 9:18-26; 14:3-12, where Matthew has considerably shortened the Marcan material. See further E. P. Sanders, *The Tendencies of the Synoptic Tradition* (Cambridge: University, 1969). He demonstrates that there is a tendency toward increasing length and greater detail in the post-canonical tradition, but that there are no hard and fast laws in the development of the synoptic tradition with regard to length, detail, and Semitisms. The synoptic tradition developed in both directions and the editorial preferences of individual transmitters of the tradition must be taken into consideration.

Finally, there is no mention of the resurrection in the *Apocalypse of Peter*, a fact that also weakens the argument that its writer knew of the transfiguration as a resurrection account. The work as a whole is concerned with the afterlife, and the meaning that the transfiguration takes on in this context seems to be a disclosure of the nature of heavenly existence. What the material contained in the *Apocalypse of Peter* contributes is an understanding of how a later author used the tradition underlying the synoptic accounts.

As for 2 Pet 1:16-18, the basic argument used to advocate its interpretation as a resurrection account is that the phrase τιμὴν καὶ δόξαν (v 17) can refer only to the resurrection and exaltation.[48]   But these terms are by no means used exclusively for the resurrection, as has been pointed out above in the section on terminological considerations. There is no clear evidence that 2 Peter relies on a separate, independent tradition[49] and its date is considerably later than that of Mark.[50]

One further observation is that those who are challenging Petrine authority in this letter are supporters of Paul and his teaching. If the transfiguration were a resurrection account, it could not be used to claim the superiority of Peter, since Paul, too, could boast of having seen the risen Lord. The author's purpose is best served if the transfiguration is understood to be an event during the earthly ministry of Jesus, in which Paul did not share.[51]   In sum, it is not certain that the authors of either the *Apocalypse of Peter* or 2 Pet 1:16-18 understood the transfiguration

---

[48]Those who interpret 2 Pet 1:16-18 as referring to the resurrection include G. Bertram, "Die Himmelfahrt Jesu von Kreuz und der Glaube an seine Auferstehung," *Festgabe für Adolf Deissmann* (Tübingen: Mohr, 1927) 189-90; Bultmann, *Geschichte*, 278 n. 1; J. M. Robinson, "On the *Gattung* of Mark (and John)," *Jesus and Man's Hope* (2 vols. Pittsburgh: Pittsburgh Theological Seminary, 1970) 1. 117; Schmithals, "Markusschluss," 395-97; Weeden, *Traditions*, 120-21.

[49]E. Best ("The Marcan Redaction of the Transfiguration," *International Congress on Biblical Studies* [Ed. E. A. Livingstone; SE 7; TU 126; Berlin: Akademie, 1982] 42) considers 2 Pet 1:16-18 to be independent of the synoptic tradition. However, the slight differences in wording that Best cites as evidence for a separate tradition are also explainable as redactional variations of the same tradition.

[50]Most scholars agree that the author of 2 Peter was not the apostle Peter and that the letter is to be dated sometime in the second century. W. G. Kümmel (*Introduction to the New Testament* [Nashville: Abingdon, 1973] 430-34) dates it to the second quarter of the second century. See also E. M. Sidebottom, *James, Jude, and 2 Peter* (Century Bible; London: Nelson, 1967) 98-99; D. Senior, *1 & 2 Peter* (New Testament Message 20; Wilmington, DE: Glazier, 1980) 99. For a different opinion, see C. Bigg (*The Epistles of St. Peter and St. Jude* [ICC; Edinburgh; Clark, 1902] 242) who asserts that the epistle is to be dated before the second century and that the author is St. Peter, but that he employed a different amanuensis for this letter. B. Reicke (*The Epistles of James, Peter, and Jude* [AB 37; Garden City, NY: Doubleday, 1964] 144) also dates this letter before the second century. He places it about 90 C.E.

[51]Stein, "Transfiguration," 89. See further J. Neyrey, "The Apologetic Use of the Transfiguration in 2 Peter 1:16-21," *CBQ* 42 (1980) 504-19, who argues that 2 Pet 1:16-21 is to be understood as a prophecy of the parousia and not as a resurrection account.

as a resurrection-appearance. Nor is it likely that either work witnesses to an independent, more authentic tradition than that found in the synoptics.

## F. *A PRIORI* ASSUMPTIONS

A final argument for the resurrection-appearance approach is that a supernatural event of the sort described in the stories of the transfiguration does not harmonize with what we know about the earthly ministry of Jesus and the laws of nature and is better explained as originating in the context of the resurrection. However, this argument is not relevant to the discussion, since the historicity of the account is not at issue. In the mind of the evangelist, or for that matter, of any bearer of early Christian tradition, such an event is as easily placed within the framework of the ministry of Jesus (as indeed it is placed by all three synoptic gospel writers) as in a resurrection context.

A few final observations made by Stein make it difficult to regard the transfiguration narrative as a resurrection appearance story.[52]   First, Peter's suggestion to build three tents is inexplicable in a resurrection context, where the risen Jesus would not be seen on the same level as Moses and Elijah.[53] A second objection is that the transience of the glory of Christ in the transfiguration story would be strange in a resurrection context, for in the latter the transformation or glory of Jesus is permanent. Finally, in resurrection stories the emphasis is not on the transformation of Jesus, but rather on the identification of the resurrected one with Jesus of Nazareth.[54]    In conclusion, the connections between the transfiguration and the resurrection appearances are best explained as the redactional work of the evangelists and are not due to the transfiguration tradition having originally been cast in the form of a resurrection-appearance story.[55]

## III. MYTHOLOGICAL APPROACH

### A. CHRIST MYTHOLOGY

Another major approach to the transfiguration narrative begins with the supposition of its mythical character. D. F. Strauss defines *evangelical mythus* as "a narrative relating directly or indirectly to Jesus, which may be considered not as the expression of a fact, but as the product of an idea of his earliest followers: such a narrative being mythical in proportion as it exhibits this character. The

---

[52]"Transfiguration," 92-95.

[53]Bultmann's answer to this objection (*Geschichte*, 280) is that in the pre-Marcan tradition, v 7 originally followed v 4.

[54]X. Léon-Dufour, "La Transfiguration de Jésus," *Études d'évangile* (Parole de Dieu 2; Paris: Éditions du Seuil, 1965) 106.

[55]See further Perkins, *Resurrection*, 95-99.

*mythus* in this sense of the term meets us, in the gospel as elsewhere, sometimes in its pure form, constituting the substance of the narrative, and sometimes as an accidental adjunct to the actual history."[56]

Strauss posits two sources for myths in the gospel: (1) the messianic ideas and expectations existing in the Jewish mind before Jesus, and independently of him; and (2) the particular impression that was left by the personal character, actions, and fate of Jesus, and that served to modify the messianic idea of his people.    These two sources contributed simultaneously, though in different proportions, to form each myth.

The account of the transfiguration, according to Strauss, is a myth derived almost entirely from the first source.  The only amplification taken from the second is the conversation among Jesus, Moses, and Elijah about Jesus' impending death.[57]   Strauss understands the purpose of the narrative as twofold: first, to exhibit in the life of Jesus an enhanced repetition of the glorification of Moses, and second, to bring Jesus as the Messiah into contact with his two forerunners, representing Jesus as the perfector of the kingdom of God and the fulfillment of the law and the prophets.[58]

M. Dibelius defines myths as "stories which in some fashion tell of many-sided doings of the gods."[59]   According to his definition, the story of Jesus itself is not of mythological origin, but a mythology of Christ did gain a place within the description of the life of Jesus.   Dibelius finds in Paul's letters clear indications of a Christ-mythology that "told the story of the Son of God who abandoned his cosmically intermediate place; in obedience to the Will of God he suffered a human fate, even to death on the Cross; he was finally raised by the power of God from the deepest humiliation to the status of 'Lord' to whom all the world owed honour till He should come to conquer His enemies and to rule His Kingdom."[60]

According to Dibelius, the only narratives in the gospels that describe a mythological event are those of the baptism, temptation, and transfiguration.[61] The traits he identifies as mythological in these narratives include the opening of the heavens, the apparition of heavenly or mythological figures, and the perception of heavenly voices.  In Dibelius's estimation, it is in the transfiguration narrative, where Jesus is seen for a moment for what he really is, the Son of God, that the Christ-myth is best reflected.

---

[56]*The Life of Jesus Critically Examined* (Philadelphia: Fortress, 1972) 86.

[57]*Ibid.*, 86-87.

[58]*Ibid.*, 535-46.

[59]*From Tradition to Gospel* (New York: Scribner, 1934) 266.

[60]*Ibid.*, 268.

[61]For similarities between the baptism and transfiguration accounts, see Coune, "Baptême," 165-79. For parallels to the temptation account, see Baltensweiler, *Verklärung*, 57-59.

More currently, I. H. Marshall agrees with Dibelius in categorizing the transfiguration as myth since, as he says, the three main items comprising the event—the mysterious metamorphosis of Jesus, the apparition of the heavenly visitors, and the voice from the cloud—are all supernatural and have biblical parallels.[62]  Marshall poses the further question whether the transfiguration has to do with a supernatural event described in biblical language or is simply an expression of the nature of Jesus employing mythical motifs cast into the form of a narrative.  He opts for the former, proposing an actual event as the trigger for the narrative, but says nothing further about the nature of that event, since he deems it one that defies historical investigation.

Although the three traits that Dibelius identifies as characteristic of mythological narratives are present in the transfiguration story, a difficulty with categorizing the story in this way is that Jesus was not a mythological person and is not presented as such in the gospels.  The same is true of Peter, John, and James.  Even the two figures who appear from heaven (Moses and Elijah in the Marcan tradition) were historical persons.

## B. FOREIGN MYTHOLOGY

Taking the mythological approach farther afield, beyond the arena of biblical tradition, some scholars have turned to foreign mythology for the interpretive key to the transfiguration.[63]  A background from Hellenistic mystery religions has been proposed.  The term $\mu\epsilon\tau\epsilon\mu\rho\phi\omega\theta\eta$ (Mark 9:2; Matt 17:2) is taken as an indication of the influence of ideas popular in the Hellenistic world.  There are two separate concepts involved in speaking of metamorphosis.  First is the widespread idea in the Greco-Roman world that deities could transform themselves and appear in visible form to human beings.[64]  Then there is the thought that human beings could achieve a change from earthly to supraterrestrial appearance.  In Hellenistic mystery religions, metamorphosis is a process of deification or regeneration, which is the goal of each initiate to a cult.  So, for example, the Isis initiation rite[65]

---

[62]I. H. Marshall, *Commentary on Luke* (New International Greek Testament Commentary 3; Grand Rapids: Eerdmans, 1978) 380-89.

[63]E.g., W. Bousset, *Kyrios Christos; Geschichte des Christusglaubens von den Anfängen des Christentums bis Irenaeus* (FRLANT 21; Göttingen: Vandenhoeck & Ruprecht, 1913) 109, 168; E. Lohmeyer, "Die Verklärung Jesu nach dem Markus-Evangelium," *ZNW* 21 (1922) 185-215.

[64]See C. K. Barrett, *The New Testament Background: Selected Documents* (New York: Harper & Row, 1961) 91-104; O. Gruppe, "Verwandlung," *Griechische Mythologie und Religionsgeschichte* (2 vols.; Munich: Beck, 1906) 2. 1920-21; M. P. Nilsson, *A History of Greek Religion* (Oxford: Clarendon, 1925) 27, 142-46.

[65]As described in Apuleius's *Metamorphoses* 11. 23-24. See also H. Koester, *Introduction to the New Testament*, vol. 1, *History, Culture, and Religion of the Hellenisitic Age* (Philadelphia: Fortress, 1982) 188-91; R. Reitzenstein, *Hellenistic Mystery Religions: Their Basic Ideas and Significance* (PTMS 15; Pittsburgh: Pickwick, 1978) 333-37.

describes a series of stages by which one is physically and spiritually transformed into a godlike being.

An objection to this background being operative in regard to the transfiguration is that the presence of similar terminology or parallel ideas does not indicate dependence. Furthermore, the use of the term μεταμόρφωσις is not the same in the NT as in the Hellenistic world. There is no correlation between the transfiguration of Jesus and the idea of deities transforming themselves into human form. If the transfiguration is a foretaste of the transformation of the just, this change is understood very differently in the NT than in Hellenistic mystery religions.[66] Finally, there are those who maintain that a change in Jesus is not at all what is involved at the transfiguration, but understand it rather as a momentary revelation of Jesus' true nature shining through the veil of his fleshly appearance.[67]

Another Hellenistic concept, that of θεῖος ἀνήρ,[68] one who displays superhuman characteristics, is regarded by some to be at work in the creation of the transfiguration story. Combined with this is the notion of ἐπιφάνεια, the idea of a divine being becoming visible to certain human beings. This idea eventually came to be used of human beings for whom divine powers were claimed. H. Conzelmann, W. Kümmel, and S. Schulz connect this concept with the transfiguration.[69] Weeden's thesis of the transfiguration as a misplaced resurrection story also incorporates the notion of θεῖος ἀνήρ.[70] He holds that Mark's purpose in relocating the story within the public ministry of Jesus was to undermine the proponents of a θεῖος ἀνήρ christology.

A difficulty with this line of interpretation is the fluidity of the expression θεῖος ἀνήρ, that is, it carried a variety of meanings in pre-Christian times.[71] Furthermore, the motif does not become discernible in Hellenistic literature until

---

[66]See J. Behm, "μεταμορφόω," TDNT 4 (1967) 758-59.

[67]E.g., J. B. Bernardin, "The Transfiguration," JBL 52 (1933) 181-89; T. A. Burkill, Mysterious Revelation (Ithaca: Cornell University Press, 1963) 145-64.

[68]For treatments of the θεῖος ἀνήρ concept in relation to christology, see H. D. Betz, "Jesus as Divine Man," Jesus and the Historian (Philadelphia: Fortress, 1968); L. Bieler, ΘΕΙΟΣ ANHP: Das Bild des 'Göttlichen Menschen' in Spätantike und Frühchristentum (Darmstadt: Wissenschaftliche Buchgesellschaft, 1967); C. R. Holladay, ΘΕΙΟΣ ANHP in Hellenistic-Judaism: A Critique of the Use of This Category in New Testament Christology (SBLDS 40; Missoula: Scholars, 1977); D. L. Tiede, Charismatic Figure as Miracle Worker (Missoula: Scholars, 1972).

[69]H. Conzelmann, An Outline of the Theology of the New Testament (New York: Harper & Row, 1969) 128; W. Kümmel, The Theology of the New Testament (Nashville: Abingdon, 1973) 121-23; S. Schulz, Die Stunde der Botschaft. Einführung in die Theologie der vier Evangelisten (Hamburg: Furche, 1967) 57.

[70]Traditions, 121-24.

[71]Tiede, Charismatic Figure, 253-55, 289.

the second century C.E.,[72] nor does the term ἐπιφάνεια acquire a religious significance in Hellenistic usage until then.[73]  Again, the discernment of parallel ideas does not indicate dependence.  Some scholars reject entirely any idea of influence on the transfiguration story from Hellenistic myths, maintaining that the interpretive background is wholly provided by Jewish literature.[74]

A compromise between the indigenous and foreign avenues of interpretation was proposed by E. Lohmeyer, who detected the combination of both Hellenistic and Jewish ideas at work in the narrative.[75]  He saw Mark's account as the product of the combination of two sources: vv 2,4-10 reflected a legend based on Jewish eschatological speculations, whereas v 3 was a later addition, reflecting ideas from Hellenistic mystery religions.  Lohmeyer originally argued from internal criteria that v 3 was not integral to the rest of the story but later revised his stance in his commentary on Mark,[76] noting that ideas similar to that expressed in Mark 9:3 are found in Jewish apocalyptic.  His later position, then, is that the whole story is to be regarded as a unity and of Jewish provenience.

## IV. JEWISH BACKGROUND

### A. OT CONCEPTS

#### 1. Exodus-Wilderness Imagery

Taking the Jewish background of the story as their starting point, a number of scholars appeal to OT concepts to explain the details of the account.[77]  The most obvious OT imagery evoked is that of the Sinai theophany and the exodus-wilderness events as described in Exodus 24 and 34.  Almost every element in the transfiguration story has a parallel there.  Going up on the mountain parallels Exod 24:1,12-13.  The phrase "after six days" reflects Exod 24:16, where six days

---

[72]E. Schweizer, *Jesus* (Richmond: John Knox, 1971) 127 n. 10.  See Holladay, ΘΕΙΟΣ ΑΝΗΡ, 18-22, and throughout for evidence and further discussion.

[73]R. Bultmann and D. Lührmann, "ἐπιφάνεια," *TDNT* 9 (1974) 7-10.

[74]E.g., Baltensweiler, *Verklärung*, 63; Boobyer, *Mark*, 2-4; W. Gerber, "Die Metamorphose Jesu, Mark 9.2f. par.," *TZ* 23 (1967) 385-95; H. C. Kee, "The Transfiguration in Mark: Epiphany or Apocalyptic Vision?" *Understanding the Sacred Text* (ed. J. Reumann; Valley Forge, PA: Judson, 1972) 137-52; Riesenfeld, *Transfiguré*, 108-110.  Gerber also sees parallels in Jewish mysticism, but some of his examples date from the third century C.E. or later.  At most, they show that the form of the transfiguration narrative is not incompatible with Jewish religious expectation.

[75]"Verklärung," 185-215.

[76]E. Lohmeyer, *Das Evangelium des Markus* (MeyerK 2; Göttingen: Vandenhoeck & Ruprecht, 1938) 173-81.

[77]E.g., U. Mauser, *Christ in the Wilderness* (London: SCM, 1963) 11-18; J. A. Ziesler, "The Transfiguration Story and the Markan Soteriology," *ExpTim* 81 (1969-70) 263-68.

designates a time of preparation for the reception of the revelation. The purpose
of prayer given in Luke 9:28 echoes the motive given in Exod 24:1 for ascending
the mountain, that of worship. In the transfiguration story, Jesus is accompanied
by three others, just as Moses was in Exod 24:1,9. The elements of the cloud and
glory correspond to those found in Exod 24:15-17. The voice of God from a cloud
correlates with Exod 24:16. In fact, the combination of cloud and voice is unique
to these two narratives. The detail of entering the cloud has a parallel in Exod
24:18. The radiance of Jesus' face parallels the description of the face of Moses
transformed by the vision of God's glory in Exod 34:29-30,35. The fear of the
disciples is like the fear of Aaron and the people of Israel in Exod 34:30. Peter's
proposal to build tents is seen as a reference both to the wilderness sojourn and to
the tent of meeting in which Moses encountered YHWH (Exod 27:21). Finally, it
is not only the appearance of Moses in the transfiguration story that evokes the
Sinai-wilderness experience, but Elijah can also be understood as a man of the
wilderness (e.g., 1 Kgs 17:3-6; 18:4; 19:4-9; 2 Kgs 1:8-9; 2:16). The thrust of the
transfiguration narrative interpreted against this background is to show Jesus as a
new Moses, superior to him and replacing the old dispensation.

The problems with this interpretation are summarized by E. Best.[78] First,
both Mauser and Ziesler base their studies of Moses-Jesus typology on Mark's
version. But there is no clear Moses typology and no "new exodus" theme in
Mark's Gospel as a whole. These themes are much clearer in Luke or Matthew
than in Mark. Second, this interpretation does not account equally for the presence
of Elijah as it does for that of Moses. And lastly, this approach fails to consider
the elements of Marcan, Matthean, or Lucan redaction and to set the transfiguration
account in its total context.

## 2. The Living God

Another OT concept that has been proposed as the operative idea behind the
transfiguration is that of "the living God." W. H. Williams traces examples in the
OT (e.g., Num 14:21-22; Deut 4:32-34; 5:24-26), where this concept has special
relevance to moments of crisis and opportunity, and sees the transfiguration as just
such a moment.[79] His OT examples focus especially on the saving acts of "the
living God" witnessed by Israel in the Sinai-exodus-wilderness events. He
concludes that the transfiguration expresses this same OT concept of the "living
God" in the form of an event where the locus of the "living God" is seen to be
Jesus, the "living Word."

The difficulty with this approach is that it imposes on the pericope the
outlines and limits of a single OT theological concept. The concept "living God"

---

[78]Best, "Redaction," 41-53.

[79]W. H. Williams, "The Transfiguration—A New Approach?" *International Congress on New
Testament Studies* (ed. E. A. Livingstone; SE 6; TU 112; Berlin: Akademie, 1973) 635-50.

may provide some insight for the Matthean version of the transfiguration, which comes on the heels of Peter's declaration of Jesus as "the Christ, the Son of the living God" (16:16), but the phrase "living God" is not found in the Marcan or Lucan versions of the Petrine confession.

### 3. The Glory of God

The OT concept of the glory of God provides the framework for A. M. Ramsey's study.[80] From this approach, the glory of Jesus at the transfiguration is understood against the background of the *kĕbôd YHWH* in the OT as well as the messianic glory and the glory of the righteous as found in Jewish apocalyptic literature. The transfiguration is interpreted as a prefigurement of the glory of the exalted Jesus that would become visible to the church at his parousia. Again, a problem with basing an interpretation entirely on one OT concept is the failure to consider the accounts in terms of their context in the individual gospels and the redactional activity of each evangelist.

### B. JEWISH APOCALYPTIC

Jewish apocalyptic[81] provides another starting point for intepretation. M. Sabbe regards the account of the transfiguration as an apocalyptic revelation of the Son of Man and his eschatological enthronement as awaited in Jewish apocalyptic. He first paints in broad strokes the elements of the genre that can be seen in the transfiguration story.[82] These are the following: heavenly mysteries revealed in visions that primarily concern the Son of Man and his eschatological enthronement; the apparition of one clothed in light and glory; a voice that speaks and frightens the visionary, who faints and falls face down on the ground; a hand that touches and comforts. Examples of such elements are found in Daniel 7:2-8:27; 10:4-21; *1 Enoch* 14:8-24; 71:1-17; 4 Ezra 10:25-33; Ezek 1:4,13-14,22-23,26-28; 2:1-2.

Next Sabbe outlines the parallelism between the transfiguration story, especially Matthew's version, and Daniel 10. He shows that the illumination of Jesus' face in Matt 17:2 corresponds to the man's coming out of the light in Dan 10:5 with his face having the appearance of lightning and his eyes like flaming torches (Dan 10:6). The brilliant radiance of Jesus' clothes in Mark 9:3 and Luke 9:29 recalls the description of the man's arms and legs like the brilliance of gleaming bronze in Dan 10:6. The voice from the cloud in Matt 17:5 and parr. corresponds to the description of the voice in Dan 10:6. In Matt 17:6 the disciples

---

[80]Ramsey, *Glory*.

[81]On the development of Jewish apocalyptic and its presence in the last books of the OT see J. J. Collins, "Old Testament Apocalypticism and Eschatology," *NJBC* art. 19, pp. 298-304.

[82]M. Sabbe, "La Redaction du récit de la transfiguration," *La venue du Messie* (RechBib 6; Bruges: Desclée, 1962) 65-100.

hear (the voice) and fall on their faces, as in Dan 10:9, where the seer hears a
voice and falls on his face.  The fear described in Mark 9:6 and Luke 9:34 is like
the great fear in Dan 10:7.  Jesus' touch and instruction to the disciples to arise and
to have no fear in Matt 17:7 have their counterpart in Dan 10:10, where the
visionary reports that a hand touched him and raised him up, and then tells him to
have no fear (Dan 10:12).  The expression "lifting their eyes, they saw no one but
Jesus" of Matt 17:8 corresponds to Dan 10:5, "I lifted my eyes and I saw."
Finally, the term ὅραμα used by Matthew in 17:9 is the same as in Dan 10:1,
which Sabbe regards as a technical term for an apocalyptic vision.

Sabbe goes on to point out several other apocalyptic elements that have
echoes in the transfiguration account.  The theme of secrecy in Mark 9:9 parr.
corresponds to that in Dan 12:4,9.  Mysterious dialogues such as those found in
Dan 8:13; Zech 1:8-17 have their counterpart in Luke 9:31.  The figures of Elijah
and Moses can be related to divine assistants that play a revelatory role in
epiphanies, as in 1 Kgs 22:19; Isaiah 7; Dan 7:10; Zechariah 4; Rev 4:4-8.  Or,
more generally, they can be likened to the angels who constitute God's entourage,
as in Deut 33:2-3 and Zech 14:5.  Or they may be more closely aligned with the
company of angels and saints that escorts the Son of Man at his parousia, as in 4
Ezra 7:28; 13:52 or *1 Enoch* 46:2,3; 47:2.

The geographical scheme also has an apocalyptic connection.  In the genre
of apocalyptic, divine revelations are staged in magnificent settings such as the edge
of a great river (Ezek 1:1; Dan 10:4; *1 Enoch* 13:7) or an imposing mountain *T.
Lev.* 2:5; Ezek 40:2).  Similarly, the transfiguration, linked to Caesarea Philippi in
the previous episode, is seen by Sabbe to have taken place in northern Galilee,
probably atop Mount Hermon, not far from the region where the Jordan river
begins.

The element of the glorification of Jesus, Sabbe maintains, can be explained
in terms of the expected transformation of the just, as in *2 Apoc. Bar.* 51:10 and
in the NT (1 Cor 15:51; 2 Cor 3:18).  The motif of divine pleasure (Matt 17:5) and
esteem for the elect visionaries is found in Dan 9:23; 10:11,19.  The sleep motif
in Luke 9:32 could have its inspiration in apocalyptic, as found in *1 Enoch* 13:7-10;
14:2; *T. Lev.* 2:5; 5:7.  In addition to all these apocalyptic overtones, Sabbe also
recognizes the aforementioned motifs from the Sinai theophany.  Thus for him, an
account that is essentially an eschatological revelation of the enthronement of the
Son of Man has assimilated Sinai allusions.

Léon-Dufour and Kee also interpret the transfiguration as an apocalyptic
vision.  Léon-Dufour understands it to be a historical event reported in an
apocalyptic literary genre,[83] whereas Kee states, "The scene itself is not historical,
even if one can imagine some historical kernel or experience lying in the dim
background."[84] Further apocalyptic parallels are identified by them.  The radiance

---

[83]"Transfiguration," 83-122.

[84]"Transfiguration," 143.

pertains to those who come into God's presence as described in Dan 12:3 and *2 Apoc. Bar.* 51:1-3. The white clothing corresponds to that of the righteous at the eschaton as in Rev 7:13-14. Elijah is the messenger of the end time,[85] and Moses is the announcer of Jesus as the eschatological prophet, as seen from the allusion to Deut 18:15. The title ὁ υἱὸς τοῦ θεοῦ is understood against the background of Jewish kingship, and points forward to the eschatological enthronement announced to Jesus at his baptism. The tents are evocative of the eschatological coming of God to dwell once again with the chosen people. The cloud is an apocalyptic stage prop that surrounds the glory in the end times (2 Macc 2:8), as it did at the tent of meeting (Exod 40:34-35) and at the dedication of Solomon's temple (1 Kgs 8:10-12; Ezek 10:3-4).

One particular aspect of apocalyptic expectation, that of messianic enthronement, is taken up by H. Riesenfeld.[86] Building on S. Mowinckel's hypothesis of a celebration of messianic enthronement in the cult,[87] he sees the transfiguration as taking place during the feast of Tabernacles, during which this enthronement would be celebrated. Riesenfeld sees messianic connotations in each of the motifs of the transfiguration account. The mountain is the throne of God and the place to demonstrate the glory of the Messiah. The cloud is a sign announcing the coming of the Messiah. The proclamation of Jesus as the Son of God signifies that he is enthroned as king, especially given the association between the figure of the messiah-king and the interpretation of Ps 2:7. Moses and Elijah are two acolytes of the Messiah, as well as his prototypes. The tents refer to the Jewish conception of the Messiah dwelling in a tent. The declaration of Peter that it was good for the disciples to be on the mountain-top reflects the joy that accompanies the arrival of the Messiah or the joy that is born in the cult when the Christ is considered present. Thus Riesenfeld concludes that Jesus' transfiguration is to be understood as his messianic enthronement. More recently, D. Stanley also interprets the transfiguration in terms of the feast of Tabernacles, adding the observation that the predominant characteristic of light in all three accounts of the transfiguration corresponds to the nightly illumination of the temple during the feast.[88]

## C. EVALUATION

A question that arises regarding the interpretations based exclusively on OT concepts or on Jewish apocalyptic parallels is whether these concepts gave rise to the narrative of the transfiguration (i.e., that the story may be a total fabrication

---

[85]See Str-B, 28e Excursus: "Der Prophet Elias nach seiner Entrückung aus dem Diesseits," 4. 764-98; J. Jeremias, "Ἠλ(ε)ίας," *TDNT* 2 (1964) 928-41.

[86]Riesenfeld, *Transfiguré.*

[87]*The Psalms in Israel's Worship* (2 vols.; New York: Abingdon, 1967).

[88]*The Apostolic Church in the New Testament* (Westminster: Newman, 1967) 134-35.

from them) or whether there was a historical event behind it, whose retelling was colored by these familiar themes.

A problem with Sabbe's study, as shown by J. M. Nützel,[89] is that the parallels between the transfiguration and the vision in Daniel may be valid for Matthew's version, but are hardly present in the accounts of Mark or Luke. Furthermore, Nützel questions Sabbe's use of the LXX for some of the citations from Daniel and the version of Theodotion for others. Finally, Sabbe's postulation of Matthew's version as the original has many difficulties.

A serious difficulty with Riesenfeld's approach is that it misses a major point of the episode in which Jesus is identified as more than a messiah. He is called "son of God" and "chosen one," titles that have connotations other than messianic.[90] In addition, Riesenfeld's case is greatly dependent on the validity of the still-debated hypothesis of an enthronement festival[91] that he sees as underlying much of the NT idea of messiahship. Further, Riesenfeld's whole theory depends on a connection of the transfiguration with the feast of Tabernacles. But this is not the only possible interpretation of Peter's suggestion to build tents. Finally, Riesenfeld himself admits that several of the elements in the transfiguration account, especially the figures of Moses and Elijah and the voice from the cloud, cannot be explained adequately from the background he proposes.

## V. REDACTION-CRITICAL APPROACH

### A. MARCAN REDACTION

A turning point in the approaches to the transfiguration was reached with Boobyer's study of Mark's account. His was the first attempt at a redaction-critical approach, recognizing that there are two separate questions that must be asked in trying to interpret the gospel material: (1) How did the evangelist understand the narrative and to what end has he incorporated it into his gospel? and (2) What was the original nature of the occurrence described?[92] Like the majority of present-day scholars, Boobyer reviewed the main hypotheses about the original nature of the occurrence but declined to take up the task of trying to reach a sure answer to the second question. Instead, he focused on the first question: the meaning of the story for Mark. On the whole, redaction-critical methodology has held sway over the approaches to the transfiguration narrative from the time of Boobyer on. For the most part, exegetes focus primarily on Mark's version, operating from the presupposition that this is the most original of the three synoptic accounts. The results of investigations of the Marcan story are varied.

---

[89] *Verklärungserzälung*, 27-29.

[90] Fitzmyer, *Luke*, 793.

[91] See R. de Vaux, *Ancient Israel, Its Life and Institutions* (New York: McGraw-Hill, 1965) 495-502.

[92] Boobyer, *St. Mark*, viii.

## 1. Proleptic Parousia in Mark

The conclusion of Boobyer's study was that "for Mark, the transfiguration was a divine confirmation of the Messianic status of Jesus in the form of a visionary forecast of the parousia of Jesus."[93] To arrive at such an interpretation, Boobyer examines the portrayals of Clement of Alexandria, the *Apocalypse of Peter* and 2 Pet 1:16-18, which all treat the transfiguration as a prefigurement of the parousia. Then he analyzes the text in terms of the structure and outlook of the Gospel of Mark as a whole, then in terms of the immediate context of 8:38; 9:1; and 9:11-13. Finally, he shows how the details of the story—the mountain, the radiant glory, the cloud, the voice from the cloud, the presence of Moses and Elijah, the reference to tents—can all be understood in reference to the parousia.

Horstmann, in her redactional study of Mark 9:2-8, reaches the same conclusion as Boobyer: that in Mark the transfiguration is a preview of the parousia, a provisional fulfillment of the promise of 9:1.[94] She maintains that one of the elements that Mark employs to serve this purpose is an emphasis on Elijah. Horstmann holds that in the pre-Marcan tradition, Moses was the more important figure, but that Mark makes Elijah more prominent in his redaction in order to stress Jesus' eschatological qualification. The close connection with vv 11-13 also serves this end.

Best raises several questions about the interpretation of the transfiguration as a prediction of the parousia.[95] He grants that this understanding might have been relevant to Mark's readers in a time of persecution, but queries what point the command ἀκούετε αὐτου might have in this interpretation.[96] He also questions whether Mark 9:2-8 has a special relation to 9:1 or whether the connection is rather between 9:1 and 8:38. That is, in Best's opinion, 9:1 is the conclusion to 8:34-38, not the introduction to 9:2-8.[97] Moreover, Williams asks the question: "Can we really rest content with the purely anticipatory?" He points out that the element of anticipation was most likely present in the mind of the evangelist, but this does not permit us to waive the historical question. "Proleptic presence is real presence," he maintains.[98]

---

[93]*Ibid.*, 29.

[94]*Studien*, 72-103.

[95]"Redaction," 52.

[96]Horstman (*Studien*, 88-90) explains the object of this command as being the passion predictions, the instruction to the disciples to be silent about what they had seen on the mountain, and the saying in Mark 10:45. The command stresses Jesus' word and higher authority.

[97]Similarly, Nützel (*Verklärungserzählung*, 39-43) signals a weak point in Horstmann's interpretation. If her assumptions of a chronological connection between Mark 9:2-10 and 9:11-13 and a special Marcan interest in Elijah are not accepted, then the mainstays of her thesis are undermined.

[98]Williams, "Transfiguration," 637.

## 2. Separating Tradition From Redaction

Several scholars, in their attempts to separate tradition from redaction in Mark, discern distinct strands of pre-Marcan sources. H.-P. Müller sees in the narrative two separate complexes: vv 2c-6,8 that reflect a messiah-christology; and vv 2ab,7,(9) that contain a Son of Man christology. The two strands, he believes, were united at a time when these two christological ideas were blended. The ensuing transfiguration story is a creation of the Jerusalem community.[99]

C. Masson examines the Marcan account with special attention to its context and a close reading of the story line.[100] He claims that only vv 2c,3,7 refer strictly to the transfiguration itself and proposes that vv 2ab,4,5,6a,8 contain a coherent story that Mark received from the tradition. From his examination of the word order of v 4 (Elijah's name preceding that of Moses) as well as the absence of any other mention of Moses in the Gospel of Mark, Masson concludes that the original account contained only Elijah and that Moses, being a better-known figure to Mark's readers, was introduced into the story by the evangelist. Masson pushes his theory even further by insisting that Mark's source originally described a transfiguration of Elijah, which Mark converts into that of Jesus.

Best focuses his analysis on the Marcan editorial additions, which he discerns from internal evidence. In his opinion, 9:2-8 was originally connected to 8:27-30 in the tradition as it lay before Mark, and its purpose was christological: to confirm the confession made by Peter of Jesus' true identity. According to Best, all of Mark's additions relate to the theme of discipleship. Thus in the transfiguration story, a new facet of the meaning of discipleship is brought out. Whereas previously in Mark discipleship is interpreted as following, now it takes on the dimension of obedience.

Another redactional study of Mark's version yields yet again other conclusions. B. D. Chilton's analysis of the vocabulary and syntax of Mark 9:2-8 results in the identification of the following elements as due to Mark's editorial hand:[101] the connecting καὶ and καὶ ἐγένετο each time they appear: παραλαμβάνει ὁ Ἰησοῦς; ἔμπροσθεν αὐτῶν; λίαν; οὐ δύναται; οὕτως; αὐτοῖς; Ἠλίας σὺν Μωϋσεῖ; ἦσαν; τῷ Ἰησοῦ; καὶ ἀποκριθεὶς ὁ Πέτρος λέγει τῷ Ἰησοῦ; ῥαββί; καλόν ἐστιν ἡμᾶς ὧδε εἶναι; οὐ γὰρ ᾔδει τί ἀποκριθῇ; γὰρ; ἐγένοντο; φωνὴ ἐκ τῆς νεφέλης; ἐξάπινα περιβλεψάμενοι οὐκέτι οὐδένα εἶδον; τὸν Ἰησοῦν μόνον μεθ' ἑαυτῶν. Chilton concludes from his reconstruction of the tradition that the transfiguration was a visionary representation (akin to those in the Book of Revelation) of the Sinai motif of Exodus 24, and that in its present form the narrative cannot be reduced to historical events. He believes the traditional shape

---

[99]H.-P. Müller, "Die Verklärung Jesu: Eine motivgeschichtliche Studie," *ZNW* 51 (1960) 56-64.

[100]C. Masson, "La Transfiguration de Jésus," *RTP* 14 (1964) 1-14.

[101]B. D. Chilton, "The Transfiguration: Dominical Assurance and Apostolic Vision," *NTS* 27 (1981) 115-24.

of the narrative came from the disciples Peter, James, and John, and that it developed to emphasize the continuity of the power of God in connection with the dominical saying of 9:1.

The most recent full-length study of the Marcan redaction is that of Nützel. His painstaking analysis of each word and phrase of Mark 9:2-10 attempts to separate tradition from redaction and results in his identification of the following elements as Marcan: the phrases $\kappa\alpha\tau$ ' $\iota\delta\iota\alpha\nu$ $\mu\delta\nu\sigma\upsilon\varsigma$ and $\mu\epsilon\tau\dot{\alpha}$ $\dot{\eta}\mu\dot{\epsilon}\rho\alpha\varsigma$ $\dot{\epsilon}\xi$ (v 2); the mention of Moses (v 4); Peter's reaction to the vision (v 5); the explanatory comment (v 6); the voice from the cloud (v 7); and references to the resurrection (vv 9-10). Nützel classifies the pre-Marcan story as christological midrash, whose aim was to proclaim the fulfillment of messianic expectations in Jesus. In the Marcan redaction, the purpose of the story becomes that of revealing Jesus' divine sonship, especially as it will become publicly manifest in his death and resurrection.

Some objections may be raised against these studies. First, the methodology used to detect redactional additions is flawed. Vocabulary and style cannot be primary criteria. Only when different literary levels have been determined on other grounds can the vocabulary and style of each level be tabulated. Second, some of these works fail to show how the Marcan redactor understood the narrative as a whole after he united the separate pieces of tradition. In particular, the credibility of Masson's theory is questionable, because Masson does not demonstrate how Marcan editing produced a transfiguration of Jesus from an account that was originally one of Elijah.[102]

## B. MATTHEAN REDACTION

No full-length study of the transfiguration focuses exclusively on the Matthean account. Only a few recent articles on isolated elements of the Matthean narrative have appeared. In his article on Matt 17:1-13, S. Pedersen focuses on the voice from heaven as the central feature of the story. The main thrust, according to him, is to show that Jesus is the eschatological bearer of revelation.[103] Two short text-critical articles by J. O'Callaghan have recently appeared on Matt 17:4 and 17:7,[104] and two articles examine the figures of Moses and Elijah in the Matthean transfiguration.[105] P. Dabeck sees in Matthew's account a depiction of Jesus as the new Moses, the representative and revealer of God. Similarly, J. Moiser's conclusions procede from the observation that Moses and Elijah were both

---

[102]Best, "Redaction," 48 n. 42.

[103]S. Pedersen, "Die Proklamation Jesu als des eschatologischen Offenbarungsträgers (Mt 17.1-13)," *NovT* 17 (1975) 241-64.

[104]J. O'Callaghan, "Discusión crítica en Mt 17,4," *Bib* 65 (1984) 91-93; "Mt 17,7: revisión crítica," *Bib* 66 (1985) 422-23.

[105]P. Dabeck, "Siehe es erschienen Moses und Elias (Matt 17.3)," *Bib* 23 (1942) 175-89; J. Moiser, "Moses and Elijah," *ExpTim* 96 (1984-85) 216-17.

prophets who were privileged to hear God on Mt. Sinai. The thrust of the Matthean transfiguration, according to him, is that just as Moses and Elijah now listen to Jesus on the mountain and bear him testimony, so too must the disciples do.

## C. LUCAN REDACTION

As is the case with Matthew's account, so also with Luke's: little attention has been given to this version of the transfiguration. Two unpublished doctoral dissertations have recently focused on Luke 9:28-36. P. R. Baldacci examined the Lucan narrative from a redaction-critical perspective.[106] Baldacci's intent was not to investigate the nature of pre-synoptic tradition behind the transfiguration, nor to discover the layers of redaction. Rather, he investigated the transfiguration as it now stands in Luke's Gospel, with particular attention to the redactional elements. The significance of these redactional elements was determined from the context of Luke 9:1-50 and the wider context of Luke-Acts. From these, Baldacci concluded that Luke's special concerns are the question of Jesus' identity (in messianic terms), the future fate of the suffering son of man, discipleship norms, and the ultimate necessity of a right response to Jesus and his words.

The study of R. H. Gause[107] proceeds from a comparison of Luke's account with Mark's, and concludes that Luke has based his version on Mark's and, in addition, has used an L tradition. From there Gause focuses on the special Lucan themes of the kingdom of God, prayer, glory, and "exodus" to show that the transfiguration scene is a depiction of the kingdom of God in consummation, gathered around the exalted Messiah. Gause asserts that the Lucan ascension stories in Luke 24:50-52 and Acts 1:3-11 provide the best formal correspondence to the Lucan transfiguration. He points out parallels in vocabulary: mountain ($\check{o}\rho o\varsigma$), white garments ($\grave{\iota}\mu\alpha\tau\iota\sigma\mu\grave{o}\varsigma$ $\lambda\epsilon\upsilon\kappa\acute{o}\varsigma$, $\grave{\epsilon}\sigma\theta\acute{\eta}\sigma\epsilon\sigma\iota$ $\lambda\epsilon\upsilon\kappa\alpha\hat{\iota}\varsigma$), two men ($\kappa\alpha\grave{\iota}$ $\grave{\iota}\delta o\grave{\upsilon}$ $\check{\alpha}\nu\delta\rho\epsilon\varsigma$ $\delta\acute{\upsilon}o$), and cloud ($\nu\epsilon\phi\acute{\epsilon}\lambda\eta$).

Gause also sees common themes: the disciples are given an eschatological preaching mission (9:1; Acts 1:8); distinction between the roles of Jesus and John the Baptist (Luke 9:18-20; Acts 1:5); the centrality of Jerusalem (Luke 9:31,51; Acts 1:4,12); Jesus' eating with his disciples (Luke 9:10-17; Acts 1:4); Jesus' death spoken of in relation to his exaltation (Luke 9:22,31,51; Acts 1:2,3); a promise of the coming of the kingdom (Luke 9:27; Acts 1:11); and the primarily eschatological focus of both narratives.

Ultimately, Gause regards the accounts of the transfiguration and ascension as "cultic narratives," instruments of worship used to reenact the experience and to

---

[106]P. R. Baldacci, *The Significance of the Transfiguration Narrative in the Gospel of Luke: A Redactional Investigation* (Ph.D. Diss; Milwaukee: Marquette University, 1974).

[107]*The Lukan Transfiguration Account: Luke's Pre-Crucifixion Presentation of the Exalted Lord in the Glory of the Kingdom of God* (Ph.D. Diss.; Atlanta: Emory University, 1975).

affirm faith.  He believes the Lucan transfiguration provided the early Christian community with a knowledge of the consummated kindgom of God and a proleptical experience of it.  An objection to Gause's analysis is that the common themes he sees do not come from Luke's transfiguration account itself, but from the surrounding material in chapter 9.  Although Gause is correct in seeing coincidences in vocabulary, he fails to show that there is a correspondence in the form of the narratives.[108]

In a similar vein, J. G. Davies examines Luke 9:1-36 vis-à-vis Acts 1:1-12[109] and concludes that Luke 9:28-36 is a prefigurement of the ascension. The unique Lucan alterations in vv 28-36 are shown to serve this end.  Luke's change of ἀναφέρει (Mark 9:2) to ἀνέβη (Luke 9:28) is evocative of ascension;[110] the phrase καὶ ἰδοὺ ἄνδρες δύο (9:30) is repeated in Acts 1:10; the term ἔξοδος (9:31) embraces the whole complex of passion, death, resurrection, and ascension; and the δόξα referred to in 9:31 is considered by Luke to be what Jesus enters on the occasion of his ascension.  The few other articles that are written on the Lucan transfiguration focus, for the most part, on the meaning of ἔξοδος in 9:31.[111]

*VI. CONCLUSION*

From the preceding survey it is obvious that the approaches to the transfiguration story are manifold and that there has been no systematic progression in the treatments of the narratives.  Recent investigations for the most part, have been isolated probes into single details or aspects of the problems connected with the tradition, with no universal point of entry.  The basic approach has shifted since the advent of redaction criticism from the question of how to understand the transfiguration event to the query of how to understand the narrative in Mark's Gospel as an interpretation of his sources, and how to understand the versions of Matthew and Luke as interpretations of Mark.  Still there are no totally satisfactory answers to these questions.

One wonders if it is possible that there is a different starting point that can yield more satisfactory results both in terms of the tradition history of the narrative and in determining what kind of event, if any, in the life of the historical Jesus gave rise to it.  Almost all of the existing studies begin with the presupposition that

---

[108]Gause himself admits that neither story manifests a particular literary form (*Transfiguration*, 55).

[109]J. G. Davies, "The Prefiguration of the Ascension in the Third Gospel," *JTS* 6 (1955) 229-33.

[110]Davies explains that although Luke doesn't use ἀνέβη in his descriptions of Jesus' ascension, it is found in Acts 2:34 in reference to David's not having ascended into the heavens.

[111]J. Mánek, "The New Exodus of the Books of Luke," *NovT* 2 (1957) 8-23; A. Feuillet, "'L'exode' de Jésus et le déroulement du mystère rédempteur d'après S. Luc et S. Jean," *RevThom* 77 (1977) 181-206; S. Ringe, "Luke 9:28-36: The Beginning of an Exodus," *The Bible and Feminist Hermeneutics* (Semeia 28; ed. Mary Ann Tolbert; Chico, CA: Scholars, 1983) 83-99; S. R. Garrett, "Exodus from Bondage: Luke 9:31 and Acts 12:1-24," *CBQ* 52 (1990) 656-80.

the Marcan version is primary and that the Matthean and Lucan accounts are subsequent redactions of Mark's.  But if the Lucan version were taken as the starting point, and another source besides the Marcan tradition were discerned, as proposed by Boismard and Murphy-O'Connor, perhaps more satisfactory solutions would result.

The following chapters of this study engage in just such an approach. Chapter two examines the transmission of the tradition, first outlining the similarities and differences among the synoptic accounts and then analyzing the internal consistency of Luke 9:28-36.  An hypothesis that Luke used a special source discernible in 9:28-33a,36b will be presented.  This will be tested in a detailed analysis of the Lucan account vis-à-vis Mark's and a form-critical study of the L material.  The agreements of Luke and Matthew against Mark will also be treated.

# CHAPTER TWO

# TRANSMISSION OF THE TRADITION

## I. INTRODUCTION

In this chapter the transmission of the tradition of the transfiguration as found in the synoptic gospels (Matt 17:1-9; Mark 9:2-10; Luke 9:28-36) will be examined. Prescinding from presuppositions of priority and source relationships among the three, we will first examine their similarities. Then the unique features of the Lucan version and its internal inconsistencies will be outlined, leading to a hypothesis that a special Lucan tradition can be discerned. Next the variations between the accounts of Mark and Luke will be scrutinized, with a view toward answering the question of whether the differences can be explained adequately as Lucan redaction of the Marcan tradition. A form-critical analysis of the proposed L material will then be made, followed by a hypothesis regarding the relation of the L material to Mark 9:2-8. Finally, the agreements of Luke and Matthew against Mark will be studied.

### A. SIMILARITIES IN THE SYNOPTIC ACCOUNTS

At first appearance, the Lucan version of the story of the transfiguration is similar to the renditions of Matthew and Mark. One observes coincidences with regard to (1) context, (2) narrative sequence, and (3) verbal agreements.

#### 1. Context

In all three accounts the context of the transfiguration story is the same. Each of the synoptic evangelists situates the story in the same place in his account of Jesus' Galilean ministry. The pericope of the transfiguration follows directly upon Peter's confession of Jesus as the Messiah and Jesus' subsequent first prediction of his passion. Following the story of the transfiguration in all three gospels is an account of the healing of a boy by Jesus at the request of the boy's father. In Matthew and Mark there is also an intervening pericope on the coming of Elijah that is located between the transfiguration story and that of the healing of the boy.

#### 2. Narrative Sequence

The following elements of the story are told in this same sequence in all three accounts:

(1) Jesus takes Peter, James, and John with him
(2) and they go up a mountain.
(3) There some perceivable change occurs in the person of Jesus
(4) and his clothing becomes white.

(5) Moses and Elijah appear
(6) and speak with Jesus.
(7) Peter then speaks to Jesus,
(8) remarking on how good it is to be there
(9) and suggesting that he/they make three tents:
one for Jesus, one for Moses, and one for Elijah.
(10) Then a cloud overshadows them
(11) and a voice comes from the cloud
(12) that identifies Jesus as the Son of God
(13) and gives the command, "Listen to him."
(14) At the end Jesus is alone with the disciples.
(15) In the sequel (Mark 9:9; Matt 17:9; Luke 9:36b),
the disciples are silent about what they have seen.

## 3. Verbal Similarities

The three accounts share a number of verbal similarities:

(1) Each begins with a temporal designation in terms of days, with a precise numeral: ἡμέρας ἓξ in Matthew and Mark; ἡμέραι ὀκτὼ in Luke.

(2) These verbs are used in common:

    (a) παραλαμβάνω
        (παραλαμβάνει in Matthew and Mark; παραλαβὼν in Luke);
    (b) συλλαλέω
        (συλλαλοῦντες in Matthew and Mark; συνελάλουν in Luke);
    (c) ὁράω in the aorist passive
        (ὤφθη in Matthew and Mark; ὀφθέντες in Luke);
    (d) ποιέω in the aorist subjunctive
        (ποιήσωμεν in Mark and Luke; ποιήσω in Matthew);
    (e) ἐπισκιάζω
        (ἐπεσκίασεν in Matthew; ἐπισκιάζουσα in Mark;
        ἐπεσκίαζεν in Luke);
    (f) ἀκούω in the present imperative (ἀκούετε in all three).

(3) Nouns used in common are: ὄρος, σκηνή, νεφέλη, and φωνή.

(4) Adjectives used in common are: λευκός, and μόνος.

(5) The remark of Peter to Jesus is phrased by all three evangelists in exactly the same words: καλόν ἐστιν ἡμᾶς ὧδε εἶναι.

(6) The first part of the message of the voice from the cloud is identical in all three accounts: οὗτός ἐστιν ὁ υἱός μου and concludes with the imperative ἀκούετε.

At first glance one is tempted by these similarities to conclude that all three evangelists are telling their own version of the same story and that a common tradition underlies them all. However, a closer examination reveals that there are also substantial differences among the three versions, particularly in Luke's account as compared with the other two.

## B. THE UNIQUENESS OF THE LUCAN ACCOUNT

There are a number of unique features in the Lucan rendition. Luke alone provides the content of the conversation of Moses and Elijah with Jesus. The detail about the sleepiness of the disciples is unique to Luke. Key words and concepts such as ἔξοδος, δόξα, πληροῦν, and Jesus' prayer are contained in Luke's account but are absent from the other two. Conversely, the vocabulary of metamorphosis, used by Mark and Matthew, is absent from Luke's version. To these major differences can be added many smaller divergences in vocabulary and narrative sequence.

Since the majority of scholars presuppose Marcan priority and Luke's dependence on Marcan tradition, the ensuing analysis will examine Luke 9:28-36 vis-à-vis Mark 9:2-8. The differences between the two will be outlined and a verse-by-verse comparison will be made. Before embarking on this comparison, however, an analysis of the internal consistency of Luke's narrative is required.

## II. INTERNAL CONSISTENCY OF LUKE'S NARRATIVE

### A. INTRODUCTION

Leaving aside presuppositions of interdependence between Luke and Mark, the focus of this section is on Luke's narrative alone. The questions to be dealt with are: What does the Lucan story of the transfiguration tell? Is the story internally consistent?

As it now stands in Luke's Gospel, the story is recounted as an event that took place shortly after the incident in which Peter identified Jesus as ὁ χριστὸς τοῦ θεοῦ (Luke 9:18-20). Following that is further instruction by Jesus to the disciples about his coming passion (Luke 9:21-22) and the consequences of discipleship (Luke 9:23-27). The transfiguration is then related in this way by Luke:[1]

> (28) It happened that about eight days after these words, taking Peter and John and James, he went up the mountain to pray. (29) And while he was praying, the appearance of his face became different and his clothes became flashing white. (30) And lo!, two men were talking to him, who were Moses and Elijah, (31) appearing in glory. They were speaking about his "exodus," which he was to fulfill in Jerusalem. (32) Now Peter and those who were with him were

---

[1]The translation attempts, as far as possible, to preserve the awkwardness that is present in places in the Greek text so that the inconsistencies remain apparent.

weighed down with sleep. But awaking, they saw his glory and the two men standing with him. (33) And it happened that when they parted from him, Peter said to Jesus, "Master, it is good that we are here; let us make three tents: one for you and one for Moses and one for Elijah," not knowing what he was saying. (34) While he was saying this, a cloud came and overshadowed them. They became afraid as they entered into the cloud. (35) And a voice came from the cloud saying, "This is my chosen Son; listen to him." (36) And when the voice had spoken Jesus was found alone.

## 1. Focus

There are several inconsistencies and tensions in the narrative. One that is immediately apparent is a confusion in the focus of the story. In Luke's version it is a puzzle as to whether the story is about an occurrence that was directed toward Jesus, or toward the disciples, or both. In the first half of the narrative, vv 28-33a, the accent is on Jesus. Jesus (understood to be the subject of v 28 from the preceding pericope), taking along Peter, John, and James, goes up the mountain to pray. While he is praying (ἐν τῷ προσεύχεσθαι αὐτὸν) the appearance of his face (τὸ εἶδος τοῦ προσώπου αὐτοῦ) changes, as well as that of his clothes (ὁ ἱματισμὸς αὐτοῦ). The two men speak with him (συνελάλουν αὐτῷ) about his "exodus" (τὴν ἔξοδον αὐτοῦ). All the personal pronouns (αὐτόν, αὐτοῦ, αὐτῷ) emphasize Jesus. Even when Peter and his companions are reintroduced in v 32, Jesus still occupies center stage. They see his glory (τὴν δόξαν αὐτοῦ) and the two men standing with him (συνεστῶτας αὐτῷ), who then depart from him (ἀπ' αὐτοῦ).

At v 33b the focus shifts to the disciples. Having started out as ancillary characters who formed part of the backdrop for the story, the disciples move to center stage in vv 33b-35. Peter remarks how good it is for them to be there (now the pronoun is ἡμᾶς) and proposes that they set up three tents (the disciples are the subject of the verb ποιήσωμεν). When the cloud comes, it overshadows them (αὐτούς). They become fearful (ἐφοβήθησαν) as they (αὐτούς) enter it.[2] When the voice is heard, although the subject of the message is Jesus (οὗτος ἐστιν ὁ υἱός μου ὁ ἐκλελεγμένος), this revelation is directed to the disciples. The same is true of the command (αὐτοῦ ἀκούετε). The pronoun αὐτοῦ refers to Jesus, but the disciples remain in the spotlight as the recipients of the command. In the last half of v 36, however, the disciples recede from view as the focus returns to the person of Jesus, εὑρέθη Ἰησοῦς μόνος.

This vacillation between Jesus and the disciples as the focus of attention does

---

[2]The determination of the referents of the two ambiguous pronouns αὐτούς in v 34 is a notorious difficulty in the exegesis of this passage. The question of whether αὐτούς refers in both instances to the disciples, or to Jesus, Moses, and Elijah, or to all six will be taken up in the exegesis in chapter three. The point being made at present is that the pronouns no longer refer to Jesus alone. Some MSS eliminate the difficulty by substituting ἐκείνους for the second αὐτούς (P⁴⁵ A D R W Θ Ψ f¹·¹³ M syʰ sa), thus conveying that only Jesus, Moses, and Elijah entered the cloud. The oldest MS of Luke, P⁷⁵, omits the second αὐτούς so that it is understood that the disciples entered the cloud. But the *lectio difficilior* is to be preferred, as it is attested in the best MSS (א B ( ſ C) L 1241 *pc*).

not occur in Mark. In the latter, the disciples are integral to the story from the beginning. In Mark 9:2 ἀναφέρει αὐτοὺς includes the disciples at the outset, in contrast to Luke's ἀνέβη (v 28), which has in view only Jesus. Similarly, Mark's κατ' ἰδίαν μόνους refers to the disciples, a detail missing from Luke. Mark gives the impression that the ascent of the mountain is for the sake of the disciples. What is conveyed by Luke, on the other hand, is that the going up the mountain to pray is for Jesus' own sake, not for that of the disciples. There is nothing in Luke's description of the change in Jesus in v 29 that indicates any involvement on the part of the disciples, whereas Mark 9:2 specifies that the metamorphosis took place before them, ἔμπροσθεν αὐτῶν. Mark explicitly includes the disciples (αὐτοῖς) in v 4 as those to whom Elijah and Moses appeared. Luke's οἱ ὀφθέντες ἐν δόξῃ (v 31) leaves it unspecified as to whom the two appeared. Finally, there is no dramatic shift of focus in Mark's final verse as there is in Luke's. The disciples are still the subject of Mark's οὐκέτι οὐδένα εἶδον ἀλλὰ τὸν Ἰησοῦν μόνον μεθ' ἑαυτῶν, in contrast to Luke's εὑρέθη Ἰησοῦς μόνος.

A further confusion in Luke's story is who perceived whose glory? In v 31 Luke says that they (Moses and Elijah) appeared in glory, οἳ ὀφθέντες ἐν δόξῃ. But v 32 says that when the disciples awoke they saw his (Jesus is the implied antecedent of the possessive pronoun) glory, εἶδον τὴν δόξαν αὐτοῦ. In v 31a it is not specified to whom Moses and Elijah appeared in glory. Up to v 31 the focus of the story is Jesus. Is v 31a to be interpreted as Moses and Elijah appearing in glory only to Jesus? Why is it said in v 32 that the disciples saw the two men standing with him (Jesus), with no reference to the disciples' perceiving their glory as well?

## 2. Two Men

Another inconsistency in Luke's narrative is the odd vacillation in the references to the two that appeared. In vv 30a and 32 they are called "two men," (ἄνδρες δύο in v 30; δύο ἄνδρας in v 32) but in v 30b and v 33 they are designated Moses and Elijah. Once identified as Moses and Elijah, it is strange that they are again referred to as δύο ἄνδρας in v 32.

## 3. Sleeping and Waking

Another element that is puzzling is the sleepiness and awakening of the disciples, ἦσαν βεβαρημένοι ὕπνῳ, διαγρηγορήσαντες δε, in v 32b. Why should the disciples have been so tired? What awakened them? How is this detail that is unique to Luke relevant to the story?

## B. AN HYPOTHESIS

All these tensions and inconsistencies make for a rather disjointed story. They present a number of difficulties for determining precisely what Luke intended to convey. The usual starting point for attempting to understand the Lucan account is the theory that Luke's story is simply a redaction of Mark's and that all the differences between the two versions can be explained by Lucan composition and redaction. But Luke usually improves on Mark's style and smooths out awkward phrases or narrative jumps that he finds in his source. The fact that Luke's account of the transfiguration is more disjointed and less clearly expressed than Mark's leads one to look for another explanation for the tradition-history of Luke's narrative.

An hypothesis that would explain the incongruencies in Luke is that the evangelist had before him two separate pieces of tradition that he wove together to form his story of the transfiguration. The similarites with Mark's account suggest that one of these sources was Marcan. The greatest correspondence with Mark lies in the second half of Luke's story, beginning with v 33b. This is precisely the place where the section that is peculiar to Luke (vv 31-33a) ends. Verse 33 betrays a redactional seam where Luke has joined another piece of tradition to the Marcan tradition. The dissimilarities with Mark's account in Luke 9:28-33a,36 and the internal inconsistencies in the whole pericope can best be explained by Luke's use of a unique, non-Marcan source. It will become clear that Luke's treatment of the Marcan tradition of the transfiguration was very different from Matthew's, whose editorial changes can all be explained as Matthean composition or redaction of Mark.[3]

## 1. Focus

The shift in focus from Jesus to the disciples that occurs in the middle of Luke 9:33 and the swing back again to Jesus in v 36 can best be explained by the hypothesis that Luke welded together two separate pieces of tradition at these points. In one tradition (L) Jesus is the center of attention and in the other (Marcan) the focus is on the disciples. The proposition that v 36b, which focuses on Jesus, was originally connected to v 33a is quite plausible. The sentence would have read: καὶ ἐγένετο ἐν τῷ διαχωρίζεσθαι αὐτοὺς ἀπ' αὐτοῦ εὑρέθη Ἰησοῦς μόνος. Not only is this a logical progression of thought but it also explains why v 36a diverges as it does from Mark's v 8 in the section where Mark and Luke otherwise correspond very closely. By constructing a temporal clause for v 36a, Luke links the Marcan material very naturally with v 36b, which had originally been connected to the temporal clause ἐν τῷ διαχωρίζεσθαι αὐτοὺς ἀπ' αὐτοῦ of v 33a.

## 2. Two Men

The hypothesis of a special Lucan source in which the two men were anonymous is a more satisfactory explanation than the current consensus that ἄνδρες δύο is attributable to Lucan redaction.

---

[3]See for example, Boismard, *Synopse*, 2. 250; R. H. Gundry, *Matthew: A Commentary on his Literary and Theological Art* (Grand Rapids: Eerdmans, 1982) 342-46; A. H. McNeile, *The Gospel According to St. Matthew* (London: Macmillan, 1952) 248-52; J. P. Meier, *Matthew* (NTM 3; Wilmington, DE: Glazier, 1980) 188-92; E. Schweizer, *The Good News According to Matthew* (Atlanta: John Knox, 1975) 348-50.

### a. Current Consensus

The phrase ἄνδρες δύο in v 30 is regarded by most commentators as a secondary addition by Luke. Few, however, offer an explanation as to why Luke would add this phrase. Those who do, see it as Luke's intent to make a connection with the two men at the empty tomb in Luke 24:4 and at the ascension in Acts 1:10.[4] Another explanation is that ἄνδρες δύο is an apologetic expression by which Luke softens the use of foreign words and names retained from his sources.[5]

### b. Objections

Close examination shows that these explanations are not convincing. Those who propose that ἄνδρες δύο of 9:30 is Luke's redactional link with 24:4 and Acts 1:10 often make the assumption that the phrase is attributable to Luke's hand in all three instances. In the case of Acts, the question of sources is more enigmatic, since we are not in possession of any of the traditions Luke used for his second volume.[6] M.-É. Boismard and A. Lamouille have recently proposed three sources: one of Petrine traditions, one from Johannine circles, and a travel journal, that have undergone three stages of redaction. They attribute the ἄνδρες δύο of 1:10 to the pre-Lucan source of Petrine traditions.[7]

In the case of Luke 24:4 there is a great likelihood that the phrase ἄνδρες δύο came from tradition and not from Lucan redaction. One indication of this is that John 20:12 also speaks of two figures at the empty tomb. It is probable that both evangelists drew on tradition for this detail.[8] In Luke 24:5, both men ask the question τί ζητεῖτε τὸν ζῶντα μετὰ τῶν νεκρῶν. Lagrange takes this unusual

---

[4]E.g., F. Danker, *Jesus and the New Age. A Commentary on St. Luke's Gospel* (Philadelphia: Fortress, 1988) 199-200; R. J. Dillon, *From Eye-Witnesses to Ministers of the Word. Tradition and Composition in Luke 24* (AnBib 82; Rome: Biblical Institute, 1978) 22-25; A. R. C. Leaney, *The Gospel According to St. Luke* (Black's New Testament Commentaries. London: Black, 1958) 167.

[5]H. J. Cadbury, *The Style and Literary Method of Luke.* (HTS 6; Cambridge: Harvard University, 1920) 154-56. Cadbury claims that Luke dislikes foreign words and names and that he often omits, translates, or softens them by adding explanatory phrases. He cites Luke 4:31: Καφαρναοὺμ πόλιν τῆς Γαλιλαίας and 23:51: Ἀριμαθαίας πόλεως τῶν Ἰουδαίων as instances similar to Luke 9:30. The Marcan parallels have the names of the places and persons without the explanatory phrase.

[6]On the whole source-question in Acts, see E. Haenchen, *The Acts of the Apostles* (Philadelphia: Westminster, 1971) 81-90; J. Dupont, *The Sources of Acts. The Present Position* (London: Darton, Longman & Todd, 1964).

[7]*Les Actes des Deux Apôtres* (3 Vols. EBib 12,13,14; Paris: Gabalda, 1990) 1. 27, 93.

[8]Because of elements such as this in Luke 24:1-12 that bear resemblance to those found in Johannine tradition, J.-M. Guillaume (*Luc interprète des anciennes traditions sur la résurrection de Jésus* [EBib; Paris: Gabalda, 1979] 15-30) argues for Luke's use of a source independent of Mark. So also Perkins, *Resurrection*, 151-57. Perkins also regards the description of how the angels are dressed as another hint of pre-Lucan tradition (*Resurrection*, 153), in that Luke does not use ἀστραπτούσῃ elsewhere in connection with angelic figures.

expression as an indication of traditional material.[9]  He also notes that it is not
Luke's habit to create double characters out of a single Marcan figure (i.e., ἄνδρες
δύο from νεανίσκος in Mark 16:5).  This type of change occurs in Matthew's
Gospel, but not in Luke's.[10]  Also, in his infancy narratives Luke has regarded a
single angel as sufficient to deliver the messages.[11]  If he has not increased their
number to two in those cases, one wonders why he would have felt it necessary to
do so in 24:4.[12]

The suggestion that the two men have been added in Luke 24:4 as legal
witnesses, as required by Deut 19:15,[13] can also be discounted.  The two figures
in Luke 24:4 do not function as witnesses.[14]  Rather, they are interpreting
angels—Luke 24:23 identifies them as ἀγγέλων—as are the angels that appear in
Luke 2:8-15 and Acts 1:10.

Whatever determination is made about 24:4, however, still does not provide
a solution to the source question for ἄνδρες δύο in 9:30,32.  If the phrase is from
L in 24:4, then it may be that in 9:30,32 it is also from a peculiarly Lucan source.
But if it is from Luke's hand in 24:4 (and also Acts 1:10), this does not necessitate
the conclusion that the phrase was also composed by Luke for 9:30,32.  The
opposite is possible: that, having retained ἄνδρες δύο from his special tradition for
the transfiguration account, Luke then reintroduced two similar figures in his
narratives of the empty tomb and the ascension to deliberately connect the three.
The phrase ἰδοὺ ἄνδρες δύο becomes, thus, the verbal link in the three stories in
which heavenly messengers articulate the mystery of the Messiah's passion,
resurrection, and ascension.  Taken by itself, the connection of 9:30,32 with 24:4

---

[9]M.-J. Lagrange, *Évangile selon Saint Luc* (EBib; 2d ed.; Paris: Gabalda, 1921) 598-99.

[10]E.g., in Matt 8:28-34 there are two demoniacs, but in Mark 5:1-20 and Luke 8:26-39 there is only
one; in Matt 9:27-31 and 20:29-34 there are two blind men, whereas in Mark 10:46-52 and in Luke
18:35-43 there is only one.

[11]When human messengers are involved, Luke does make them two: in Luke 7:18, he has John send
two of his disciples; in Luke 24:13, the two on the road to Emmaus serve as messengers of the good
news to the community in Jerusalem; in Acts 9:38, two disciples are sent to entreat Peter to come
to Joppa.

[12]See E. E. Ellis, *The Gospel of Luke* (NCB; London: Nelson, 1966) 272; Marshall, *Luke*, 885;
Schramm, *Markus-Stoff*, 62; V. Taylor, *The Passion Narrative of St. Luke* (SNTSMS 19;
Cambridge: University, 1972) 103-9; who also support the view that ἄνδρες δύο was a phrase
contained in Luke's tradition for 24:4 and was not a redactional addition by the evangelist.  On the
grounds of lack of agreement with Mark throughout Luke 24:2-9, A. M. Perry (*The Sources of
Luke's Passion-Narrative* [Chicago: University of Chicago, 1919] 50) ascribes the whole pericope
to another source.  For the position that ἄνδρες δύο in Luke 24:4 is an element of Lucan redaction,
see Dillon, *Eye-Witnesses*, 20-26. R. H. Fuller (*The Formation of the Resurrection Narratives* [New
York: MacMillan, 1971] 95) takes a middle position: that Luke has edited an independent tradition
while keeping Mark in his purview.  For a survey of the literature on the subject, see G. Schneider,
"Das Problem einer vorlukanischen Passionserzahlung," *BZ* 16 (1972) 222-44.

[13]J. Jeremias, *Das Evangelium nach Lukas* (Chemnitz/Leipzig: Müller, 1930) 263.

[14]Dillon, (*Eye-Witnesses*, 22 n. 63) shows that interpreting ἄνδρες δύο as two witnesses in 24:4 runs
counter to the intention of Luke's narrative as a whole, which does not make the empty tomb the
basis of a convinced Easter witness.

and Acts 1:10 does not allow for a sure determination of the source(s) for ἄνδρες δύο.

The explanation that Luke added ἄνδρες δύο as a stylistic tendency to soften foreign names does not hold up when Luke's additions of ἀνήρ to Marcan tradition elsewhere are examined. When Luke adds ἀνήρ to the introduction of a character that is given a proper name, he constructs an almost constant formula. The pattern often begins with καὶ ἰδού, followed by ἀνήρ (or γυνή, or ἄνθρωπος), and a form of ὄνομα (usually ὀνόματι or τὸ ὄνομα) plus the proper name.[15] This pattern for the introduction of characters that are given proper names is such a constant in Lucan writings that the absence of it in Luke 9:30 is a strong indication that something other than simple Lucan redaction is operative here. If the phrase ἄνδρες δύο were added by Luke, it would be expected that with it he would have created his usual formula.

A further characteristic of Luke's style that is violated in Luke 9:28-36 is that once a character has been named, s/he is not again referred to with the indefinite designation ἀνήρ, γυνή, or ἄνθρωπος. in the same pericope. Rather, the proper name continues to be used throughout. Only when Lucan characters remain anonymous do they continue to be referred to as ἀνήρ, γυνή, or ἄνθρωπος.[16]

### c. Luke's Addition of Moses and Elijah

The difficulties encountered in explaining ἄνδρες δύο as a Lucan addition, particularly the stylistic abnormalities, suggest a different solution: that the phrase οἵτινες ἦσαν Μωϋσῆς καὶ Ἠλίας is the secondary addition, and not ἄνδρες δύο. It is much more likely that the two men were anonymous in the special Lucan tradition behind vv 28-33a. It was only when Luke joined this to the Marcan tradition that he attempted to identify the two with Mark's figures.[17] That οἵτινες ἦσαν Μωϋσῆς καὶ Ἠλίας came from Luke's editorial hand is quite in accord with his redactional tendencies. In Luke, relative clauses, especially with ὅστις, are most often the work of the evangelist. They appear in Lucan redaction of Mark,[18] in Luke's version of Q material,[19] and in material that is specific to Luke.[20]

This hypothesis also explains the confusion in the story over who perceived whose glory. The insertion of οἵτινες ἦσαν Μωϋσῆς καὶ Ἠλίας before the relative clause οἳ ὀφθέντες ἐν δόξῃ (v 31a) created the tension in the narrative between Moses' and Elijah's glory in v 31a and that of Jesus in v 32. If Luke had

---

[15]E.g., Luke 1:5,27; 2:25; 5:27; 8:41; 10:38; 16:20; 19:2; 23:50; 24:18; Acts 5:1,34; 8:9; 9:10,33,36; 10:1; 11:28; 12:13; 13:6; 16:1,14; 17:34; 18:2,7,24; 19:24; 20:9; 21:10; 27:1; 28:7.

[16]E.g., Luke 5:18,20; 7:37,39,44,50; 8:27,38,43,47; 13:11,12.

[17]As Murphy-O'Connor has noted ("Transfiguration," 15), if Luke were working from Marcan tradition that named Elijah and Moses, an editorial addition of ἄνδρες δύο would be a needless emphasis on the fact that Moses and Elijah were males.

[18]E.g., Luke 8:26,43; 12:1; 23:19,55.

[19]E.g., Luke 14:15,27; 15:7.

[20]E.g., Luke 1:20; 2:4,10; 7:37,39; 8:3; 10:42.

been simply redacting Mark's tradition, it is difficult to explain why he would have obscured what Mark had presented more clearly. Although Mark does not use the terminology of δόξα, he does make it explicit that it was to the disciples and Jesus that Elijah and Moses appeared, ὤφθη αὐτοῖς Ἠλίας σὺν Μωϋσωι (v 4). Luke 9:30-31a is much less straightforward due to Luke's fusing of two disparate traditions.

### 3. Sleeping and Waking

The strangeness of the reference to the disciples' sleeping and waking betrays another redactional seam in the narrative. Sleeping and waking are inexplicable details in the context of the transfiguration story. Neither the account of Mark nor that of Matthew contains these components. These can, however, be understood as elements transferred from the Gethsemane story. In Christian tradition, from at least as early as Mark's Gospel, the two stories were associated, forming a striking diptych. The transfiguration expressed the height of the revelation of Jesus' divine glory; the agony revealed the depth of his humiliation as a human being.[21] The conscious uniting of the two scenes can be demonstrated by the numerous parallels between Mark 9:3-8 and Mark 14:26,32-42.

Verbal similarities in the two accounts include: παραλαμβάνει, τὸν Πέτρον, [καὶ] τὸν Ἰάκωβον, καὶ [τὸν] Ἰωάννην in Mark 9:2 and 14:33; εἰς τὸ ὄρος in Mark 9:2 and 14:26; οὐ γὰρ ᾔδει τί ἀποκριθῇ in Mark 9:6 and καὶ οὐκ ᾔδεισαν τὶ ἀποκριθῶσιν αὐτῷ in 14:40. The element of Jesus' special filial relationship with God is stressed in both accounts, as is seen in Jesus' address, ἀββα ὁ πατήρ in Mark 14:36 and in the message of the voice in Mark 9:7, οὗτος ἐστιν ὁ υἱός μου ὁ ἀγαπητός. Peter plays a prominent role in both stories, while the other two disciples recede to the background. In both accounts, the disciples remain uncomprehending of the ultimate significance of what they witness. These similarities are too many to be purely coincidental. It is clear that Mark has consciously patterned the two narratives in like manner to stress the relationship between the christological revelations contained in each.

Likewise, John 12:27-35 juxtaposes the two traditions of the transfiguration and the agony in the garden. Although John does not recount either story as such in his Gospel,[22] his interweaving in 12:27-35 of elements from the two as contained in the synoptic tradition shows that he too was aware of their association. In John 12:27 there are echoes of the synoptic Gethsemane scenes. On the lips of Jesus is: νῦν ἡ ψυχή μου τετάρακται, strikingly similar to Mark 14:34: περίλυπός ἐστιν ἡ ψυχή μου. Jesus' refusal to ask to be saved from his "hour," καὶ τί εἴπω; Πάτερ, σῶσόν με ἐκ τῆς ὥρας ταύτης, in John 12:27 parallels Mark 14:36, in which Jesus resists the desire to ask to be saved from his impending passion, and prays Αββα ὁ πατήρ...οὐ τί ἐγὼ θέλω ἀλλὰ τί σύ. In both cases, the prayer is

---

[21]Murphy-O'Connor, "Transfiguration," 15; A. Kenny, "The Transfiguration and the Agony in the Garden," *CBQ* 19 (1957) 444-52.

[22]See R. E. Brown, "Incidents That are Units in the Synoptic Gospels but Dispersed in St. John," *CBQ* 23 (1961) 143-48.

directed to God as πατήρ. There are also verbal similarities between John's references to "the hour," ἡ ὥρα (12:27), and to darkness, σκοτία (12:35), and Luke's scene of the agony (22:53), where Jesus pronounces αὕτη ἐστὶν ὑμῶν ἡ ὥρα καὶ ἡ ἐξουσία τοῦ σκότους.

In John 12:28 reminsicences of the synoptic accounts of the transfiguration come to the fore. The voice from heaven, φωνὴ ἐκ τοῦ οὐρανοῦ, is similar to the voice from the cloud, φωνὴ ἐκ τῆς νεφέλης, in Mark 9:7 and parr. The remark in John 12:29 that it was an angel that spoke with Jesus matches the two heavenly figures conversing with Jesus in the transfiguration accounts (Mark 9:4 and parr.). The reference to Jesus' death in John 12:33 corresponds to the discussion of Jesus' ἔξοδος in Luke 9:31. Also, both John 12:27-28 and the synoptic accounts of the transfiguration are situated in their gospel contexts after a scetion that stresses the death of Jesus. In sum, it is evident that John was also aware of the association of the stories of the transfiguration and the agony and has preserved that connection in 12:27-35.

Because of the close association of the two stories of the transfiguration and the agony in Christian tradition, details could easily pass from one to the other in the transmission of the tradition.[23] Thus, a detail that was originally part of the story of the agony in the garden, i.e., the sleep of the disciples, has come to be attached to the Lucan story of the transfiguration. By incorporating this detail in his final form of the narrative, Luke strengthens the connection between his transfiguration account and that of the agony. The links between these two are weaker in Luke than in Mark because other theological concerns are operative in Luke 22:39-46.[24] In Luke's version of the agony, he does not include the details of Peter, James, and John accompanying Jesus (in contrast to Mark 14:33 and Matt 26:37), nor does he mention the heaviness of their eyes as do Mark and Matthew.[25] These details are preserved, instead, in Luke's transfiguration narrative.[26]

As for the way the phrase functions in its present position in the Lucan transfiguration narrative, ἦσαν βεβαρημένοι ὕπνῳ· διαγρηγορήσαντες δε continues to keep the disciples peripheral to the story, thus working together with the non-Marcan tradition that focuses on Jesus. Furthermore, it explains the disciples' lack of perception and comprehension of what transpired at the transfiguration.

---

[23]See A. Legault, "An Application of the Form-Critique Method to the Anointings in Galilee (Lk 7,36-50) and Bethany (Mt 26,6-13; Mk 14,3-9; Jn 12,1-8)," *CBQ* 16 (1954) 131-45 and R. E. Brown, *The Gospel According to John I-XII* (AB29A; Garden City, NY: Doubleday, 1966) 449-52 for illustrations of how details can transfer from one story to another.

[24]Kenny ("Transfiguration," 452) demonstrates that Luke's interest in developing the motif of prayer and the parallels with Luke 11:1-4 in 22:39-46 cause him to weaken the parallels with the transfiguration account.

[25]Mark 14:40: ἦσαν γὰρ αὐτῶν οἱ ὀφθαλμοὶ καταβαρυνόμενοι; Matt 26:43: ἦσαν γὰρ αὐτῶν οἱ ὀφθαλμοὶ βεβαρημένοι.

[26]Although Luke does not speak of eyes in 9:32, ἦσαν βεβαρημένοι ὕπνῳ is evocative of Mark's ἦσαν γὰρ αὐτῶν οἱ ὀφθαλμοὶ καταβαρυνόμενοι(14:40) and διαγρηγορήσαντες is reminiscent of Mark's triple use of γρηγορέω in 14:34,37,38.

They missed the import of the conversation between Jesus and the two figures because they were asleep. All they saw was a change in Jesus and the two men with him, but they lost out on the meaning of the exchange between those three during their sleep. The best way to understand the phrase ἦσαν βεβαρημένοι ὕπνῳ· διαγρηγορήσαντες δε is that it was inserted by Luke into the final form of the transfiguration story in order to preserve the traditional link with the narrative of the agony in the garden, and to explain the disciples' lack of understanding of the transfiguration.

## C. CONCLUSION

In sum, the account of the transfiguration as we now have it in Luke 9:28-36 is a composite of two originally separate pieces of tradition that Luke has redacted to fit his own style and theological purposes. To one piece of tradition (Lucan) belong vv 28-33a,36b; to the other (Marcan) belong vv 33b-35.[27] The number of similarities between Luke's special source and Mark 9:2-4 prompted Luke to join the two traditions. Both relate a story that begins with Jesus and his three closest disciples going up a mountain. Both recount a change that occurred in Jesus and a conversation he had with two other figures. But in the weaving together of these two traditions Luke has not entirely succeeded in making his narrative internally consistent.

Several tensions in the story reveal his redactional seams. The Lucan tradition recounts an incident that focused on Jesus; the Marcan version relates an event that was directed to the disciples. The Lucan tradition tells of a conversation between Jesus and two heavenly envoys. When Luke adopts Mark's identification of them, adding οἵτινες ἦσαν Μωϋσῆς καὶ Ἡλίας, the phrase ἄνδρες δύο is rendered non-sensical. The unusual detail about the disciples' sleeping and waking is an element transferred by Luke from the tradition of the agony and inserted into his transfiguration account to forge the link between the two.

---

[27]R. Martin ("Semitic Traditions in Some Synoptic Accounts," *SBL Seminar Papers* 26 [ed. K. Richards; Atlanta: Scholars, 1987] 295-335; and *Syntax Criticism of the Synoptic Gospels* [New York: Mellen, 1987]) draws the same conclusions based on his observation that there is a difference in the number of Semitisms in the two halves of the narrative. Martin has demonstrated from a comparison of documents known to be written originally in Greek with those that are known to be a translation into Greek from a Semitic document that there is a measurable frequency of the occurrence of certain syntactical features when a Semitic source is being used. From the data he collects, Martin shows that in those sections of the transfiguration narrative where Luke makes the least use of Mark (vv 28-33a,36), the frequency of translation Greek features is significantly higher than in the verses where Luke closely follows Mark (vv 33b-35). Martin's conclusion from the study of this and other pericopes in Luke, is that when the third evangelist depends on Mark, he improves Mark's Greek and, thus, is less Semitic than Mark. But, where Luke differs radically from Mark, he is more Semitic than Mark and more Semitic than normal Lucan style. This indicates dependence on a separate, Semitic tradition. He believes that such is the case for Luke 9:28-33a,36. One caution with regard to Martin's work is whether he sufficiently allows for conscious imitation of Septuagintal Greek by NT writers, particularly by Luke.

A provisional text of what was contained in this non-Marcan piece of tradition can be proposed from our analysis to this point:

(28) ἐγένετο δὲ μετὰ τοὺς λόγους τούτους ὡσεὶ ἡμέραι ὀκτὼ [καὶ] παραλαβὼν Πέτρον καὶ Ἰωάννην καὶ Ἰάκωβον ἀνέβη εἰς τὸ ὄρος προσεύξασθαι. (29) καὶ ἐγένετο ἐν τῷ προσεύχεσθαι αὐτὸν τὸ εἶδος τοῦ προσώπου αὐτοῦ ἕτερον καὶ ὁ ἱματισμὸς αὐτοῦ λευκὸς ἐξαστράπτων. (30) καὶ ἰδοὺ ἄνδρες δύο συνελάλουν αὐτῷ, (31) οἳ ὀφθέντες ἐν δόξῃ ἔλεγον τὴν ἔξοδον αὐτοῦ ἣν ἤμελλεν πληροῦν ἐν Ἰερουσαλήμ. (32) ὁ δὲ Πέτρος καὶ οἱ σὺν αὐτῷ εἶδον τὴν δόξαν αὐτοῦ καὶ τοὺς δύο ἄνδρας τοὺς συνεστῶτας αὐτῷ. (33) καὶ ἐγένετο ἐν τῷ διαχωρίζεσθαι αὐτοὺς ἀπ᾽ αὐτοῦ (36) εὑρέθη Ἰησοῦς μόνος.

This is a complete story in itself, with a beginning, middle, and end; one that could quite plausibly have existed as an independent unit of tradition. Whether or not it was telling the same story as the Marcan tradition, or was referring to the same incident in the life of Jesus (if, indeed, the traditions were based on a historical incident), remains to be seen.

The next step is to test this hypothesis in a verse-by-verse comparison of Luke's and Mark's accounts to see if that kind of analysis will confirm the conclusions reached above.

## III. LUKE VIS-A-VIS MARK

The similarities between Luke 9:28-36 and Mark 9:2-8 with regard to context, narrative sequence, and wording have already been outlined at the beginning of this chapter. There is only one similarity that the Lucan and Marcan versions share that is not common to all three synoptic accounts, namely, the reference to Peter's not knowing what he was saying (Luke 9:33, μὴ εἰδὼς ὃ λέγει/Mark 9:6, οὐ γὰρ ᾔδει τί ἀποκριθῇ).

The differences between Luke's account and Mark's are of three kinds: (1) material contained in Mark's account and absent from Luke's; (2) material found in Luke's account and absent from Mark's; (3) variations of material held in common by Luke and Mark. Following is a synopsis of the two accounts and an outline of their differences.[28]   The differences will be indicated as follows: material contained in Mark and absent from Luke will appear in brackets; material contained in Luke and absent from Mark will be underlined; variations of material held in common will appear with double underlining.

---

[28]The text given is that of the 26th edition of Nestle-Aland.   There are no major text-critical problems in the passage.   Where minor variants occur they will be noted in the footnotes of the discussions on individual verses.

| Luke 9:28-36 | Mark 9:2-8 |
|---|---|

(28) <u>ἐγένετο δὲ</u>
μετὰ <u>τοὺς λόγους τούτους</u>
<u>ὡσεὶ ἡμέραι ὀκτὼ</u>
[καὶ] <u>παραλαβὼν</u>
Πέτρον καὶ Ἰωάννην
καὶ Ἰάκωβον
<u>ἀνέβη</u>
εἰς <u>τὸ</u> ὄρος
προσεύξασθαι.

(2) <u>καὶ</u>
μετὰ
<u>ἡμέρας ἓξ</u>
<u>παραλαμβάνει</u> [ὁ Ἰησοῦς]
[τὸν] Πέτρον καὶ [τὸν] Ἰάκωβον
καὶ [τὸν] Ἰωάννην
[καὶ] <u>ἀναφέρει</u> [αὐτοὺς]
εἰς ὄρος [ὑψηλὸν]
[κατ᾽ ἰδίαν μόνους.]

(29) <u>καὶ ἐγένετο</u>
ἐν τῷ προσεύχεσθαι αὐτὸν
<u>τὸ εἶδος τοῦ προσώπου</u>
αὐτοῦ ἕτερον
καὶ <u>ὁ ἱματισμὸς</u> αὐτοῦ
<u>λευκὸς ἐξαστράπτων.</u>

<u>καὶ</u>

<u>μετεμορφώθη</u>
[ἔμπροσθεν αὐτῶν,]
(3) καὶ <u>τὰ ἱμάτια</u> αὐτοῦ
[ἐγένετο στίλβοντα] <u>λευκὰ λίαν,</u>
[οἷα γναφεὺς ἐπὶ τῆς γῆς]
[οὐ δύναται οὕτως λευκᾶναι.]

(30) <u>καὶ ἰδοὺ</u>
ἄνδρες δύο <u>συνελάλουν αὐτῷ</u>
οἵτινες ἦσαν
Μωϋσῆς καὶ Ἠλίας,

(4) <u>καὶ ὤφθη αὐτοῖς</u>
Ἠλίας σὺν Μωϋσεῖ,
καὶ <u>ἦσαν συλλαλοῦντες</u>
<u>τῷ Ἰησοῦ.</u>

(31) οἳ ὀφθέντες ἐν δόξῃ
ἔλεγον τὴν ἔξοδον αὐτοῦ,
ἣν ἤμελλεν πληροῦν
ἐν Ἰερουσαλήμ.

(32) ὁ δὲ Πέτρος καὶ οἱ σὺν αὐτῷ
ἦσαν βεβαρημένοι ὕπνῳ,
διαγρηγορήσαντες δὲ εἶδον
τὴν δόξαν αὐτοῦ
καὶ τοὺς δύο ἄνδρας
τοὺς συνεστῶτας αὐτῷ.

(33) <u>καὶ ἐγένετο</u>
ἐν τῷ διαχωρίζεσθαι αὐτοὺς
ἀπ᾽ αὐτοῦ
<u>εἶπεν ὁ Πέτρος</u>
<u>πρὸς τὸν Ἰησοῦν,</u>
<u>ἐπιστάτα,</u> καλόν ἐστιν
ἡμᾶς ὧδε εἶναι,
καὶ ποιήσωμεν <u>σκηνὰς τρεῖς,</u>
<u>μίαν</u> σοὶ καὶ <u>μίαν Μωϋσεῖ</u>
<u>καὶ μίαν Ἠλίᾳ,</u>
<u>μὴ εἰδὼς ὃ λέγει</u>

(5) [καὶ] <u>ἀποκριθεὶς</u> ὁ Πέτρος
<u>λέγει τῷ Ἰησοῦ,</u>
<u>ῥαββί,</u> καλόν ἐστιν
ἡμᾶς ὧδε εἶναι,
καὶ ποιήσωμεν <u>τρεῖς σκηνάς,</u>
<u>σοὶ μίαν καὶ Μωϋσεῖ μίαν</u>
<u>καὶ Ἠλίᾳ μίαν.</u>

(6) <u>οὐ γὰρ ᾔδει τί ἀποκριθῇ,</u>
<u>ἔκφοβοι γὰρ ἐγένοντο.</u>

(34) ταῦτα δὲ αὐτοῦ λέγοντος          (7) καὶ
     ἐγένετο νεφέλη                        ἐγένετο νεφέλη
     καὶ ἐπεσκίαζεν αὐτούς;                ἐπισκιάζουσα αὐτοῖς,
     ἐφοβήθησαν δὲ
     ἐν τῷ εἰσελθεῖν αὐτοὺς
     εἰς τὴν νεφέλην.
(35) καὶ φωνὴ ἐγένετο                      καὶ ἐγένετο φωνὴ
     ἐκ τῆς νεφέλης λέγουσα,               ἐκ τῆς νεφέλης,
     οὗτός ἐστιν ὁ υἱός μου                οὗτός ἐστιν ὁ υἱός μου
     ὁ ἐκλελεγμένος,                       ὁ ἀγαπητός,
     αὐτοῦ ἀκούετε.                        ἀκούετε αὐτοῦ.
(36) καὶ ἐν τῷ γενέσθαι              (8) [καὶ ἐξάπινα]
     τὴν φωνὴν                            [περιβλεψάμενοι]
     εὑρέθη Ἰησοῦς μόνος.                 [οὐκέτι οὐδένα εἶδον]
                                          [ἀλλὰ τὸν] Ἰησοῦν μόνον
                                          [μεθ᾿ ἑαυτῶν.]

The preceding synopsis reveals a great many differences between the accounts of Luke and Mark. In fact, the differences far outweigh the similarities. In contrast to those who would explain each of these variations as Luke's redaction of the Marcan source, we believe the more satisfactory solution is that Luke used two separate sources, as proposed above. The following analysis of the divergences in each verse between the Lucan and Marcan accounts aims to determine if the deviations in Luke 9:28-33a,36b are better accounted for by Luke's reliance on a separate source. If this hypothesis is correct only the differences in Luke 9:33b-35 can be attributed to Luke's redaction of Mark.

## Luke 9:28

The opening of Luke's narrative differs considerably from that of Mark. The formula ἐγένετο δὲ + καὶ + a finite verb in the indicative is a construction used very frequently by Luke in his introductions to new pericopae.[29] It appears twelve times in the Gospel of Luke and twice in Acts[30] and is best understood as a Septuagintism,[31] since it closely represents the Hebrew construction wayhî . . .

---

[29]Cadbury, Style, 106; Plummer, Luke, 45. Some MSS omit καὶ (P⁴⁵ᵛⁱᵈ ℵ * B H pc itᵖ), and because of this, Nestle-Aland 26th ed. places it in brackets. However, it is well attested (ℵ² A C D L R W Θ Ξ Ψ f¹·¹³ M lat syʰ boᴹˢ) and its retention is the preferred reading.

[30]Luke 5:1,12,17; 8:1,22; 9:28,51; 14:1; 17:11; 19:15; 24:4,15; Acts 5:7; 9:19-20.

[31]Although the more frequent construction in the LXX is καὶ ἐγένετο/ἐγένετο δὲ + a finite verb without an intervening καὶ, the same construction with καὶ is also found in the LXX (e.g., Gen 4:8; 1 Sam 24:17; 2 Kgs 19:1; 22:11) and can be regarded as a Septuagintism. See Zerwick, Biblical Greek; §388, 389; Fitzmyer, Luke, 119; and K. Beyer, Semitische Syntax im Neuen Testament. Band 1, Satzlehre Teil 1 (SUNT 1; 2d ed.; Göttingen: Vandenhoeck & Ruprecht, 1968) 31. The frequency in every kind of material in the Gospel of Luke (infancy narrative, Q material, L material, Lucan composition and redaction) leads one to believe that the Septuagintisms come from the evangelist's own hand. See Fitzmyer, Luke, 107-24; H. F. D. Sparks, "The Semitisms of St.

. wĕ-. Mark opens his account with the particle καὶ. This use of καὶ at the beginning of a narration is a typically Marcan trait.[32] Mark never employs the formula ἐγένετο δὲ + καὶ + a finite verb. Luke uses it to introduce material from every one of his sources:[33] material that he has redacted from Mark, Q, and L.[34] This widespread use of the formula within the Third Gospel indicates that it is a piece of Lucan composition.[35] Thus in Luke 9:28 and Mark 9:2 each evangelist uses his own typical opening. The presence of the introductory formula ἐγένετο δὲ + καὶ + a finite verb in Luke 9:28 is probably due to Luke's editorial hand and yields no conclusions regarding Luke's source for the beginning of the narrative.

The temporal designations at the opening of both Luke's and Mark's narratives begin with the preposition μετά followed by the accusative and contain a reference to a specific number of days. These two elements are the only two agreements between Luke's introduction and Mark's. Luke frequently uses μετά + the accusative in transitional verses, especially his stereotypical μετὰ ταῦτα.[36] In no other case where Mark uses μετά + the accusative in a transition[37] does Luke retain it in his parallel. The conclusion can be drawn that for Luke 9:28 as well, the provenience of the construction with μετά is non-Marcan. The transitional phrase with μετά + the accusative was probably composed by Luke.

The phrase τοὺς λόγους τούτους never occurs in Mark's Gospel. In Luke's Gospel, in addition to Luke 9:28, it is found in Luke 9:44, where the phrase has been inserted into Marcan material. It also occurs in Acts 2:22; 5:5,24. As in Luke 9:44, τοὺς λόγους τούτους in Luke 9:28 may be attributed to Lucan composition or it may have been found by Luke in the non-Marcan source. Because of the way τοὺς λόγους τούτους functions in the narrative, it is somewhat more likely that the phrase was constructed by Luke. It connects the transfiguration

---

Luke's Gospel," *JTS* 44 (1943) 129-38; E. Schweizer, "Eine hebraisierende Sonderquelle des Lukas?" *TZ* 6 (1951) 161-85. However, it is also entirely possible that the sources used by Luke contained Septuagintisms as well. On the question of using Semitisms as a test for antiquity see M. Black, *An Aramaic Approach to the Gospels and Acts* (3d ed.; Oxford: Clarendon, 1967). But see also Sanders, *Tendencies*, 190-255, who shows that Semitic syntax and grammar do not prove a tradition to be early. See Schramm, *Markus-Stoff*, on the use of Semitisms as a criteria for identifying sources. Cf. F. Neirynck, "La materière marcienne dans l'évangile de Luc," *L'Évangile de Luc. Problèmes littéraires et théologiques* (Gembloux: Duculot, 1973) 157-201. In themselves, Septuagintisms in Luke are not sure indications of Lucan redaction.

[32] Zerwick, *Biblical Greek*, §454; BDF §442; M. Reiser, *Syntax und Stil des Markusevangeliums im Licht der hellenistischen Volksliteratur* (WUNT 11; Tübingen: Mohr, 1984) 101-103.

[33] Most scholars posit three sources used by Luke in the composition of his Gospel: Mark, Q (a hypothetical source shared with Matthew, containing mostly sayings of Jesus), and L, written or oral traditions specific to Luke. See Fitzmyer, *Luke*, 65-97. See also Fitzmyer, "Priority," 3-40, where he includes a discussion of other solutions as well.

[34] From Mark: Luke 5:12,17; 8:22; 9:51; 24:4; from Q: Luke 19:15; from L: Luke 5:1; 8:1; 14:1; 17:11; 24:15.

[35] So Fitzmyer, *Luke*, 695, 826, 1149, 1231.

[36] Luke 5:27; 10:1; 12:4; 17:8; 18:4; Acts 7:7; 13:20; 15:16; 18:1.

[37] Mark 1:14; 8:31; 9:31; 10:34; 13:24; 14:1,28,70.

story both with the preceding sayings in Luke 9:21-27, where a similar phrase, τοὺς ἐμοὺς λόγους is found (v 26), and with the instruction that follows in Luke 9:43-45, which contains the other instance of τοὺς λόγους τούτους in Luke's Gospel (9:44). The phrase μετὰ τοὺς λόγους τούτους may also reflect a Septuagintal influence, which is typical of Luke.[38]

The temporal designation ἡμέραι ὀκτὼ is very difficult to explain as a Lucan modification of Mark's ἡμέρας ἕξ. To begin with, the meaning of Mark's time indicator is not clear. Was it an actual historical remembrance[39] or did Mark construct it with symbolic intent? If ἡμέρας ἕξ is symbolic, there is no consensus among scholars on what the symbolism is.[40] To explain Luke's ἡμέραι ὀκτὼ as an editorial change of Mark's ἡμέρας ἕξ is equally difficult. The proposition that Luke changed Mark's expression because he did not grasp the symbolism of ἡμέρας ἕξ is understandable in light of the multiple interpretations of that time designation. But the further claim that Luke formulated ἡμέραι ὀκτὼ to serve his own purposes is not convincing. Luke's phrase does not improve Mark's chronology and its symbolism is no clearer than Mark's.[41] Several unsuccessful attempts have been made to give a theological motivation for Luke's supposed change to ἡμέραι ὀκτὼ. These will be examined below in chapter three.

The difficulty of trying to explain Luke's ἡμέραι ὀκτὼ as an editorial change with a symbolic meaning is resolved if this detail is regarded as one that Luke retained from his non-Marcan source. The only other time Luke uses an eight-day time reference in his Gospel is in 2:21, in connection with Jesus' circumcision. No other Lucan transitional formula contains ἡμέραι ὀκτὼ. There are a number of Lucan transitions that are constructed with μετά + ἡμέρας.[42] Each of these occurs in material specific to Luke and is probably from his own hand. However, in each instance, there is no intervening phrase between μετά and ἡμέρας, which always occurs in the accusative.

The best explanation for the unusual ἡμέραι ὀκτὼ in the nominative is that it was found by Luke in his special source and now serves to situate the transfiguration narrative meaningfully in its context. In the atypical construction that results from the amalgamation of Luke's introductory formula + ἡμέραι ὀκτὼ, the nominative functions parenthetically.[43] The assertion that ἡμέραι ὀκτὼ came to Luke from a special source is further supported if the phrase is meant to denote a week's time. Luke's usual way of designating a week is with ἡμέρας/ἡμέραι

---

[38]The phrase μετὰ τοὺς λόγους τούτους is found in the LXX in Esth 1:1; 2:1; 2 Chr 32:1. Similarly, μετὰ τὰ ʽρήματα ταῦτα is found in the LXX in Gen 22:1; 39:7; 40:1.

[39]Caird, "Transfiguration," 291.

[40]There are at least a dozen different interpretations. The one given most often is that the six days echoes Exod 24:16, in accord with other Sinai-Moses allusions in the story.

[41]Some exegetes who presume Lucan dependency on Mark do not even attempt to explain the motivation for Luke's supposed change. For example, Fitzmyer (Luke, 797) simply states, "For some reason Luke has changed Mark's dating."

[42]Luke 1:24; 2:46; 15:13; Acts 1:5; 15:36; 20:6; 21:15; 24:1,24; 25:1; 28:13,17.

[43]BDF §144.

ἑπτά.[44] The formulation ἡμέραι ὀκτώ does not agree with Luke's habits elsewhere and points to provenience from another source.

As for ὡσεί, this adverb is used very frequently by Luke to qualify a number.[45] The only other instance of such a usage in the NT is Matt 14:21, which is suspected of having been assimilated to Luke 9:14.[46] Five of the times that the construction ὡσεί + a number appears in Luke's Gospel, the passages are part of the triple tradition, but Luke is the only one to use ὡσεί.[47] In addition, this expression occurs once in material peculiar to Luke and five times in Acts.[48] It is also possible that the construction is another Lucan Septuagintism, after the pattern of 1 Sam 25:38.[49] This evidence indicates that elsewhere in his writings ὡσεί comes from Luke's hand, and that this is also the case in Luke 9:28.[50]

Summarizing the conclusions reached for Luke's introduction to his transfiguration narrative, it has been shown that most of the opening expression is attributable to Lucan composition. Typically Lucan are: ἐγένετο δὲ + καί + a finite verb; μετά with the accusative τοὺς λόγους τούτους; the adverb ὡσεί. The identification of elements of Lucan redaction yields no information, however, about the source that Luke was redacting. The one clear indication of a non-Marcan source is the expression ἡμέραι ὀκτώ. That Luke freely composes introductions and transitional verses is typical.[51] The fact that Mark 9:2 also opens with a temporal designation constructed with μετά + a specific number of days was one of the coincidental agreements that prompted Luke's joining of the story from his special source to the Marcan rendition of the transfiguration.

The second part of Luke 9:28 has these similarities with Mark 9:2: in both, the verb παραλαμβάνω is used, and the same three disciples are named as companions of Jesus. The differences include: the tense of the verb παραλαμβάνω, the absence of Jesus' name in Luke's account, the absence of the definite article τόν before the names of all three disciples, and the order of the names John and James.

Luke's use of the participle παραλαβών has been explained as his redaction of Mark's παραλαμβάνει, i.e., a typical instance of Luke's avoidance of Mark's historical present in which Luke replaces the Marcan form with a participle.[52]

---

[44]Acts 21:4,27; 28:14.

[45]Luke 3:23; 9:14(2x); 9:28; 22:59; 23:44.

[46]Cadbury, *Style*, 129.

[47]Luke 9:14(2x),28; 22:59; 23:44.

[48]Luke 3:23; Acts 1:15; 2:41; 10:3; 19:7,34.

[49]1 Sam 25:38 (LXX): ὡσεὶ δέκα ἡμέραι; similarly, Gen 24:55 (LXX): μεθ'. . . ἡμέρας ὡσεὶ δέκα.

[50]So Schramm, *Markus-Stoff*, 139. Marshall (*Luke*, 382) also attributes ὡσεί to Luke's hand but, holding for Lucan dependency on Mark, he suggests that Luke's addition of ὡσεί may indicate that he is conscious of giving an approximation of Mark's figure.

[51]Cadbury, *Style*, 105.

[52]E.g., Luke 8:41; 19:33; 23:34. See F. Neirynck, *The Minor Agreements of Matthew and Luke Against Mark With a Cumulative List* (BETL 37; Leuven: Leuven University, 1974) 209-10 for a

Also, Luke's supposed change has been understood in light of another typically Lucan redactional habit. When Luke finds pairs of finite verbs connected by καί in his Marcan source (in this instance, παραλαμβάνει . . . καὶ ἀναφέρει), he often substitutes a participle for one of them, usually the first. Cadbury[53] lists Luke 9:28 as just such an example. However, the verb παραλαβών can also be explained as coming from Luke's non-Marcan source. Of the five other times that παραλαμβάνω occurs in Luke's Gospel, three times it comes from the Q source,[54] once it is retained from Mark,[55] and once it is a Lucan addition to Marcan material.[56] Four times Luke omits the verb παραλαμβάνω from his redaction of a Marcan pericope.[57] The verb παραλαμβάνω is found six times in Acts,[58] always in the second aorist participle.

The preceding data are inconclusive regarding the source for παραλαβών. It is possible that if Luke were redacting Marcan material that contained παραλαμβάνει, he would have retained it, as he does in his redaction of Q in 11:26. However, it can also be argued that παραλαβών was contained in Luke's special source and that Luke retained it in 9:28 as he does in 18:31 where he keeps the second aorist participle from the Marcan source. In favor of παραλαβών having been found in Luke's special source is the way it functions in this part of the story that has Jesus as the focus of attention. The participial form[59] serves to include the disciples in the narrative parenthetically, while giving more emphasis to the verb ἀνέβη, stressing Jesus' action of going up the mountain. This stress on Jesus is characteristic of the non-Marcan source.

The absence of ὁ Ἰησοῦς from Luke's version is difficult to account for as a Lucan omission from the Marcan tradition. Luke's general practice is to retain the name of Jesus whenever he finds it in the Marcan source. The phrase ὁ Ἰησοῦς is sometimes omitted by Luke when he narrates a string of Jesus' sayings[60] or alters an introductory verse of Mark's that contained Jesus' name.[61] A number of times Luke adds the name of Jesus in a passage where it was absent

---

complete list.

[53]*Style*, 134-35.

[54]In 11:26, Luke has παραλαμβάνει, as does Matthew (12:45). In 17:34,35, Luke has παραλημφθήσεται, whereas Matthew (24:40,41) has παραλαμβάνεται.

[55]Both Mark (10:32) and Luke (18:31) have παραλαβών.

[56]In 9:10, Luke adds καὶ παραλαβὼν αὐτούς to the Marcan tradition.

[57]Luke 5:44; 8:22; 11:38; 22:39.

[58]Acts 15:39; 16:33; 21:24,26,32; 23:18.

[59]Whenever Jesus is the subject of παραλαμβάνω in Luke's Gospel (Luke 9:10,28; 18:31), the second aorist participle παραλαβών is used. Also, disciples are always the object of the verb: αὐτούς in 9:10 (referring back to οἱ ἀπόστολοι); Πέτρον καὶ Ἰωάννην καὶ Ἰάκωβον in Luke 9:28; τοὺς δώδεκα in Luke 18:31. Mark, on the other hand, prefers the finite form of the verb. See Mark 4:36; 5:40; 7:4; 9:2; 14:33. Only once (10:32) does Mark use the participle.

[60]E.g., Luke 4:24; 18:27,29, where Jesus is the implied subject of εἶπεν.

[61]E.g., Luke 6:17; 9:10.

from the Marcan tradition.[62] Luke's characteristic habit is to specify the subject of a verb by adding a name or a pronoun even if the subject is fairly obvious.[63] There is no satisfactory explanation in terms of Lucan redaction of Mark for the absence of ὁ Ἰησοῦς from Luke 9:28. The best solution is simply that ὁ Ἰησοῦς was not in Luke's special source. To deliberately eliminate the name of Jesus would go against Luke's redactional habits.

The absence of the definite article τόν before the names Πέτρον, Ἰωάννην, and Ἰάκωβον has usually been explained as Luke's conformity with the customary usage in NT Greek.[64] This may well be true. However, when the data regarding Luke's use of the definite article in connection with these three names are collected, some interesting patterns emerge. With the name Peter, Luke usually does use the definite article when the name occurs in the nominative. This is so whether his source for the pericope is Mark, Q, or L.[65] There are two instances in which the Marcan source does not have the definite article and Luke adds ὁ to Πέτρος (Luke 22:58,60).[66] Mark has the same tendency to use ὁ before Πέτρος in the nominative.[67] However, when the name Peter is in the accusative, Luke omits the definite article.[68] The same is not true of Mark, who uses τόν before Πέτρον four times.[69] As for the names John and James, in no instance in Luke's Gospel does the evangelist precede them with the definite article, regardless of the case or the source.[70]

The preceding data illustrate the necessity of nuancing the assertion that it is Lucan practice to eliminate the definite article before proper names. In the examination confined to the names Peter, John, and James, the tendencies observed are that Luke omits the definite article when the names are in the accusative but regularly includes it when the name Peter appears in the nominative case. The absence of definite articles before the proper names in Luke 9:28 fits Luke's stylistic tendencies. This detail contributes nothing significant about the source Luke had at his disposal for 9:28.

Five times in Luke's Gospel that the trio Peter, John, and James are named. In two instances (Luke 5:10; 6:14) Luke has the same order of the names as Mark:

---

[62]Luke 5:12; 6:3,9,11; 8:41; 9:41.

[63]Cadbury, *Style*, 150, lists twenty-six such examples.

[64]BDF §260.

[65]E.g., from Mark: Luke 9:33; 18:28; 22:54,55,61; from Q: Luke 12:41; from L: Luke 9:32; 24:12.

[66]The one exception is Luke 9:20 where Luke omits the definite article whereas Mark 8:29 has it. In Acts the usage varies. Twice ὁ Πέτρος is found: Acts 1:13; 4:19; twice Πέτρος occurs without the article: Acts 3:1,4.

[67]Mark 8:29,32; 9:5; 10:28; 11:21; 14:29,54,72. The one exception is Mark 13:3.

[68]Luke 8:51; 9:28; 22:8; Acts 3:3; 8:14. Acts 3:11 is the only exception.

[69]Mark 5:37; 9:2; 14:33,67. The only exception is Mark 3:16.

[70]In L material: Luke 5:10; 9:54; in Luke's redaction of Marcan material: Luke 6:14; 8:51; 9:49. The same is true in Acts 3:3, 8:14; 12:2. The only exception is Acts 3:11.

Peter, James, and John. It is probable that in these examples Luke simply adopted this order from the Marcan tradition.[71] This same order is also found in Luke 9:54, a pericope peculiar to Luke. In Luke 9:28, as in Luke 8:51, the order differs from Mark's in that John's name precedes James'. This same sequence is also found in Acts 1:13, and there are eight times in Acts when Peter and John are named together.[72] The order of the disciples' names, Peter, John, and James, appears to be deliberately constructed by Luke. However, once again, this observation provides no evidence as to what Luke found in his source. The trio of disciples appears in Marcan material as well as in that which is uniquely Lucan. Sometimes Luke retains the order of his source (Luke 5:10; 6:14) and sometimes he alters it (Luke 8:51; Acts 1:13).[73]

In the last third of v 28 there are many more divergences between Luke's version and Mark's. The only commonality between the two is the noun ὄρος with the preposition εἰς. The differences are: two distinct verbs are used (ἀνέβη in Luke's account; ἀναφέρει in Mark's); αὐτούς is absent from Luke's rendition; the definite article τό precedes ὄρος in Luke's account but not in Mark's; the adjective ὑψηλόν describes the mountain in Mark's version but is absent from Luke's; the purpose for ascending the mountain is given as προσεύξασθαι by Luke, whereas Mark simply says Jesus took them apart by themselves, κατ' ἰδίαν μόνους.

The difference in the verbs used by Mark and Luke has been explained as a deliberate Lucan avoidance of the verb φέρω and its compounds when the meaning "to lead" or "to bring" is conveyed. Cadbury[74] lists Luke 9:28 among five other examples[75] in which Luke substitutes another verb for the Marcan φέρω when it is used in this sense. There are difficulties with this explanation. There are instances in which Luke does use the verb φέρω with the connotation "to lead" or "to bring." Once he retains it from Mark (Luke 5:18), once it appears in a passage unique to Luke (15:23), and once it is found in an introduction probably of Lucan composition (Luke 24:1). It also occurs in Acts[76] with this connotation. So the claim that Luke always avoids φέρω when it has the connotation "to lead" or "to bring" is not valid.

If it is granted, however, that there is a tendency by Luke to replace Marcan φέρω, it must be noted that in the other five instances in which Luke makes a substitution for φέρω, the verb he employs is a form of ἄγω.[77] It would be

---

[71]Plummer (*Luke*, 237) asserts that the order of the names preserved in the Marcan tradition reflects the order of the age of the apostles.

[72]Acts 1:13; 3:1,3,4,11; 4:13,19; 8:14.

[73]Luke probably had the same source for the list of disciples in Acts 1:13 as for Luke 6:14.

[74]*Style*, 174.

[75]Luke 4:40; 9:41; 19:30,35; 23:1.

[76]Acts 4:34,37; 5:2,16; 14:13.

[77]See further J. A. Fitzmyer, "The Use of *Agein* and *Pherein* in the Synoptic Gospels," *Festschrift to Honor F. W. Gingrich* (ed. E. H. Barth, R. E. Cocroft; Leiden: Brill, 1972) 147-60. Fitzmyer shows that all three evangelists reflect the fact that φέρειν was encroaching upon ἄγειν in Hellenistic times, but that Matthew and Luke more often follow the older use of ἄγειν. This accord in the use

expected that if Luke were using the Marcan tradition as his source for Luke 9:28, then a form of the verb ἄγω would have been substituted for Mark's ἀναφέρει. A better explanation for ἀνέβη in Luke 9:28 is that Luke was not using Mark as his source at this point and he found ἀνέβη in his special source.

The evidence for the provenience of ἀνβαίνω elsewhere in Luke is mixed. Of the nine instances where Luke uses the verb in his Gospel, five of them[78] occur in passages peculiar to Luke. The verb is also found twenty times in Acts. Four times where ἀνβαίνω appears in Mark, Luke substitutes a different verb,[79] and once he retains it from Mark.[80] Twice the verb appears in Lucan redaction of Marcan passages.[81] Of special note is that the Marcan ἀναβαίνει εἰς τὸ ὄρος (Mark 3:13), which is almost identical to Luke 9:28, is changed by Luke to ἐξελθεῖν εἰς τὸ ὄρος (Luke 6:12). If Luke so altered that expression, it is unlikely that he constructed a similar one for Luke 9:28. The presence of ἀνέβη εἰς τὸ ὄρος in Luke 9:28 is due, rather, to its having been found by Luke in his non-Marcan source.

The presence of the article τό before ὄρος in Luke 9:28 says nothing significant about Lucan tradition and redaction. The articular construction is simply the usual NT usage.[82] In Luke's Gospel, the definite article always accompanies ὄρος with the exception of Luke 3:5, which is a direct quotation of Isa 40:4 (LXX).[83] The phrase εἰς τὸ ὄρος can be ascribed to Luke's special source. There are two other instances of the phrase εἰς τὸ ὄρος in Luke's Gospel (Luke 21:37; 22:39), in which the source is not Mark, i.e., they are due either to a special Lucan source or to Lucan composition.

The absence of the adjective ὑψηλός from Luke 9:28 has been explained in terms of Luke's tendency to tone down or eliminate descriptive words from Mark.[84] However, ὑψηλός is found in Luke 16:15, an L passage, and in Acts 13:17.[85] So it is not the case that Luke always avoids this adjective. One may note, however, that Luke's use of ὑψηλός in both instances is different from Mark's. In Luke, ὑψηλός is used metaphorically, not as a concrete, colorful

---

of ἄγειν by Matthew and Luke is supposed to constitute one of their minor agreements against Mark. However, Fitzmyer demonstrates that there is no case in which Matthew and Luke concur against Mark in substituting ἄγειν for φέρειν. Furthermore, he points out that the synonymous use of the two verbs occurs as early as Homer and does not lend support to those who argue for a later date for the Gospel of Mark.

[78]Luke 2:4,42; 18:10; 19:4; 24:38.

[79]Luke 6:12; 8:6,8; 13:19.

[80]Luke 18:31.

[81]Luke 5:19; 19:28.

[82]Zerwick, *Biblical Greek*, §167.

[83]The same is true of all other times that ὄρος appears in Mark's Gospel. The absence of the definite article in Mark 9:2 is unusual.

[84]Cadbury, *Style*, 118.

[85]Elsewhere in the synoptics, ὑψηλός is found only in Mark 9:2 and Matt 4:8; 17:1. In each of these cases it modifies ὄρος.

adjective, as in Mark. Granted that such Marcan descriptions are sometimes omitted by Luke, this does not preclude the use of a non-Marcan source for Luke 9:28, one which did not contain ὑψηλόν.

The inclusion of προσεύξασθαι in Luke's narrative has been explained as a deliberate Lucan addition to the Marcan tradition to highlight Luke's special interest in prayer.[86] Instances of insertions of a reference to prayer into Marcan material by Luke are found in Luke 3:21; 5:16,33. However, there are also eight times in which mention of prayer occurs in material peculiar to Luke.[87] And there are four instances in which the Lucan version of Q material contains a reference to prayer.[88] One notes that if Luke emphasizes Jesus' prayer it is because his sources informed him of this practice of Jesus. In the case of Luke 9:28, the reference to Jesus' prayer is an integral part of the narration of the story and the greatest likelihood is that Luke found it in his special source.

The absence of the phrase κατ' ἰδίαν μόνους from Luke's narrative is best explained not as an elimination of the phrase from the Marcan source, but rather that for 9:28 Luke was using a non-Marcan source that did not contain the phrase. There is one instance in which Luke eliminates κατ' ἰδίαν from his Marcan source (Luke 21:7). However, he also retains it from Mark in Luke 9:10 and it appears once in a verse of Lucan composition introducing a saying from Q (Luke 10:23). It is also found in Acts 23:19.[89] These examples show that it is not a particular Lucan habit to avoid the expression κατ' ἰδίαν; it simply was not in his source. When Luke joined the Marcan tradition to his special source, he did not include κατ' ἰδίαν μόνους because it would be contrary to the evangelist's normal usage.

In all the instances in both Mark's and Luke's Gospels where κατ' ἰδίαν appears, the expression has to do with Jesus' taking the disciples[90] aside separately, or with their speaking with him in private. There is no example where κατ' ἰδίαν is used of Jesus' own search for seclusion. In the first half of Luke's story, the focus is on Jesus' going up the mountain to pray and what happened to him while he was praying. The disciples are only included in the story parenthetically. The thrust of the story is not that Jesus led the disciples off alone for a purpose that specifically involved them, as in Mark's version.

As for the adjective μόνος, its presence would not have been strange in Luke 9:28 as a similar example in Luke 9:18 shows.[91] In the latter instance, Luke has added the phrase κατὰ μόνας in his reformulation of a Marcan reference to Jesus'

---

[86]E.g., Fitzmyer, *Luke*, 798; Marshall, *Luke*, 383.

[87]Luke 1:10,13; 2:37; 18:1,10,11; 21:36; 22:32.

[88]Luke 6:28; 10:2; 11:1,2. The Matthean parallels to Luke 10:2 and 11:2 have the references to prayer as well. Five times (Luke 9:18; 20:47; 22:40,41,46) Luke's mention of prayer comes from the Marcan source.

[89]Mark's Gospel has the phrase four other times (Mark 4:34; 6:31; 7:33; 9:28) in material that has no Lucan parallel.

[90]In one instance (Mark 7:33) it is a potential follower that Jesus takes apart from the crowd to heal.

[91]Luke 9:18: καὶ ἐγένετο ἐν τῷ εἶναι αὐτὸν προσευχόμενον κατὰ μόνας.

prayer.[92]    Had Luke been working from the Marcan narrative that contained the adjective μόνος with the preposition κατά, it is likely he would have retained it. The best proposition is that the phrase κατ' ἰδίαν μόνους was simply not in Luke's special source for v 28.

In sum, the conclusions reached for Luke 9:28 are: the introductory ἐγένετο δὲ + καί + a finite verb is attributable to Lucan composition, as well as μετὰ τοὺς λόγους τούτους and ὡσεί. The presence of these elements says nothing about the source that Luke was redacting. That there was a source unique to Luke for v 28 and that it was non-Marcan is most clearly seen from the expression ἡμέραι ὀκτώ. Also most likely to have been contained in this special source are: παραλαβών, Πέτρον καὶ Ἰάκωβον καὶ Ἰωάννην, which Luke reordered, ἀνέβη εἰς τὸ ὄρος, and προσεύξασθαι. The coincidences with the Marcan tradition of the transfiguration in the temporal designation, the verb παραλαμβάνω, the naming of the same three disciples, and the location εἰς (τὸ) ὄρος contributed to Luke's bringing together the two traditions to create his own version of the transfiguration.

## Luke 9:29

The only agreement between Luke 9:29 and Mark 9:2b-3 is that they both speak of Jesus' clothing becoming white. The hypothesis proposed in this study explains the great divergence between the two accounts by Luke's use of a special source for this part of his narrative. This hypothesis will be confirmed in the ensuing examination of Luke 9:29 vis-à-vis Mark 9:2b-3.

The construction καὶ ἐγένετο (or ἐγένετο δὲ) followed by the dative of the articular infinitive with ἐν + the subject pronoun in the accusative is found very frequently in Luke's Gospel. It occurs in L material[93] and in introductions to Marcan material composed by Luke.[94] The construction does not occur in Mark's Gospel; it is typically Lucan. Thus the formulation of καὶ ἐγένετο ἐν τῷ προσεύχεσθαι αὐτὸν for v 29 can be attributed to Luke. He constructed the phrase to link two pieces of the story contained in his special source: that Jesus went to the mountain to pray, εἰς τὸ ὄρος προσεύξασθαι, (v 28) and that there the appearance of his face changed, τὸ εἶδος τοῦ προσώπου αὐτοῦ ἕτερον (v 29). Luke inserted the clause καὶ ἐγένετο ἐν τῷ προσεύχεσθαι αὐτὸν to make clear the connection between the prayer and the change that is only implicit in his source. This insertion also reflects Luke's stylistic artistry: the two temporal clauses, καὶ ἐγένετο ἐν τῷ προσεύχεσθαι αὐτὸν in v 29 and καὶ ἐγένετο ἐν τῷ διαχωρίζεσθαι αὐτοὺς in v 33a frame the essential action of the original story in the non-Marcan source.

The use of καὶ ἐγένετο + ἐν τῷ + the infinitive is to be recognized as one

---

[92]This observation is based on the supposition that 9:18 picks up the reference to Jesus' prayer from Mark 6:46, since Luke 9:18 is the point at which Luke resumes the Marcan sequence after his "Great Omission" of Mark 6:45-8:26.

[93]Luke 1:8; 2:6; 11:27; 17:14; 24:15,30,51.

[94]Luke 9:18; 11:1; 18:35.

of the many Septuagintisms in Luke's Gospel.[95] In the LXX, this formula translates the Hebrew construction *wayhî* . . . *wĕ*- . . . + *bĕ*- + infinitive,[96] but omits the καὶ that would translate *wĕ*-. As an element most probably attributable to Luke, this construction tells nothing about the source Luke had at hand.

The expression τὸ εἶδος τοῦ προσώπου αὐτοῦ ἕτερον is widely considered to be a conscious avoidance by Luke of Mark's μετεμορφώθη because of the pagan associations that term would have for a gentile audience such as Luke's.[97] An objection to this explanation is the question of whether Mark would not have had that same concern for his gentile audience and also have avoided the term.[98] Paul, too, uses the verb μεταμορφόομαι in letters to predominantly gentile communities in Rome and in Corinth (Rom 12:2; 2 Cor 3:18).

Another objection to interpreting τὸ εἶδος τοῦ προσώπου αὐτοῦ ἕτερον as a redaction by Luke of Mark's μετεμορφώθη is the question of why Luke would reduce a change in the whole form of Jesus to a simple change in facial expression. There is nothing in Mark's account to prompt such a change by Luke. A shift in the opposite direction would be more understandable, that is, to extrapolate from the face to the whole person, in light of such expressions as τὸ πρόσωπον ἐστήρισεν τοῦ πορεύεσθαι εἰς Ἰερουσαλήμ (Luke 9:51) and τὸ πρόσωπον αὐτοῦ ἦν πορευόμενον εἰς Ἰερουσαλήμ (Luke 9:53), where the noun πρόσωπον connotes the whole person, or personal presence. This is also the meaning of πρόσωπον in the expressions μετὰ τοῦ προσώπου σου in Acts 2:28 (= Ps 15:11), ὁρᾶν τὸ πρόσωπον in Acts 20:25, κατὰ πρόσωπον in Luke 2:31; Acts 3:13; 25:16, and θεορεῖν τὸ πρόσωπον in Acts 20:38.[99]

The best explanation for the provenience of the expression τὸ εἶδος τοῦ προσώπου αὐτοῦ ἕτερον in Luke 9:29 is that it was found by Luke in his non-Marcan source; it was not composed by Luke as an equivalent to Mark's μετεμορφώθη. In support of this explanation is the fact that although Luke uses ἕτερος very frequently,[100] in no other instance does he use it in the sense of "another" or "different from what precedes" as in Luke 9:29. Also, the expression τὸ εἶδος τοῦ προσώπου αὐτοῦ ἕτερον is unusual. The noun εἶδος appears in only

---

[95]Fitzmyer, *Luke*, 119-20; Zerwick, *Biblical Greek*, §387.

[96]E.g., Gen 4:8; 19:29; 2 Kgs 2:9. The dative of the articular infinitive with ἐν, especially in a temporal sense, but not always connected with καὶ ἐγένετο, is found abundantly in the LXX.

[97]For a list of those who hold this view, see F. Neirynck, "Minor Agreements Matthew-Luke in the Transfiguration Story," *Orientierung an Jesus. Zur Theology der Synoptiker. Für Josef Schmid* (Ed. P. Hoffmann; Freiburg: Herder, 1973) 259 n. 32.

[98]See Cranfield, *Mark*, 8-9, for reasons why Mark's audience is thought to be predominantly gentile.

[99]In 2 Sam 17:11 (LXX) πρόσωπον denotes the whole person: τὸ πρόσωπόν σου πορευόμενον ἐν μέσῳ αὐτῶν. The word is used in this same sense in Philo: τί δεῖ τὰς τῶν προσώπων ἀμυθήτους ἰδέας καταλέγεσθαι (*Poster. C.*, 110); τὰ πράγματα καὶ τὰ πρόσωπα (*Poster. C.*, 111); ἐπὶ τιμῇ προσώπων (*Spec. Leg.* 1. 245); and Josephus: προλαβὼν Ἡρώδης μετὰ τῶν οἰκειοτάτων προσώπων, "with the persons most intimate with him," i.e., his closest relatives (*J.W.*, 1. 263). Other NT examples where πρόσωπον denotes personal presence include: Gal 1:22, 1 Thess 2:17; 3:10; Col 2:1. See further E. Lohse, "πρόσωπον," *TDNT* 6 (1968) 769.

[100]Thirty-five times in his Gospel and eighteen times in Acts.

one other place in the synoptic gospels: Luke 3:22. The expression τὸ εἶδος τοῦ προσώπου occurs nowhere else in scripture and is best regarded as an expression that was part of Luke's special tradition.

There are many instances in which πρόσωπον occurs in Luke-Acts. In almost every case it is used in an idiomatic expression of Septuagintal origin. Often πρόσωπον is part of an adverbial expression such as κατὰ πρόσωπον,[101] πρὸ προσώπου,[102] and ἀπὸ προσώπου.[103] The phrases πρόσωπον λαμβάνειν,[104] πρόσωπον στηρίζειν[105] and πρόσωπον πορεύεσθαι[106] are also based on idiomatic Septuagintal phrases. Also found frequently in the LXX is the expression τὸ πρόσωπον τῆς γῆς.[107] Another phrase from the LXX that Luke uses is πίπτειν ἐπὶ πρόσωπον, describing a gesture of reverence.[108] Similar to this is κλίνειν τὸ πρόσωπον εἰς τὴν γῆν.[109] In these last two expressions, πρόσωπον retains its literal connotation, as the gestures of reverence they describe involve an actual inclination of the face. Luke 9:29 is the only example in Luke's Gospel[110] in which the use of πρόσωπον cannot be traced to an idiomatic expression patterned on the LXX. The unusualness of the whole expression τὸ εἶδος τοῦ προσώπου αὐτοῦ ἕτερον points to its provenience from Luke's special source.

It has been suggested that the absence of the phrase ἔμπροσθεν αὐτῶν from Luke 9:29 is due to a deliberate omission by Luke of the phrase from the Marcan source. The fact that Luke three times substitutes ἐνώπιον for ἔμπροσθεν in his Gospel[111] is cited as a Lucan tendency to avoid the preposition ἔμπροσθεν.[112] However, this explanation fails to take into account the ten times that Luke does employ ἔμπροσθεν. There are instances in which he retains it from his source[113] and times when it is attributable to his own composition in redacting Marcan material.[114] In three instances[115] it is found in uniquely Lucan material. These

---

[101]E.g., Luke 2:31; Acts 3:13; 25:16. See LXX Gen 23:17; 25:18; Exod 26:9.

[102]E.g., Luke 7:27; 9:52; 10:1; Acts 13:24. See LXX Exod 23:20; 33:2; Num 14:42.

[103]E.g., Acts 3:20; 5:41; 7:45. See LXX Gen 3:18; 4:16; Exod 2:15.

[104]Luke 20:21. See LXX Lev 19:15; Ps 82:2; Lam 4:16.

[105]Luke 9:51. Seee LXX Ezek 6:2; 13:17; Jer 3:12; 21:10.

[106]Luke 9:53. Lee LXX 2 Sam 17:11.

[107]Luke 12:56; 21:35; Acts 17:26. See LXX Gen 4:14; 6:7; 8:13.

[108]Luke 5:12; 17:16. See LXX Gen 17:3,17; Num 14:5.

[109]Luke 24:5.

[110]One instance is found in Acts in the description of Stephen's face (6:15).

[111]Once in Marcan material, Luke 5:25, and twice in Q material, Luke 13:8,9.

[112]Cadbury, Style, 203.

[113]From Q: Luke 10:21; 12:8 (2x); from Mal 3:1: Luke 7:27.

[114]Luke 5:19; 19:28.

[115]Luke 14:2; 19:4; 21:36.

data do not support the assertion that Luke avoids prepositional phrases with ἔμπροσθεν. There is no other instance in which Luke simply omits a prepositional phrase with ἔμπροσθεν, and such a redactional change by him in 9:29 would be very unusual. The best explanation for the absence of ἔμπροσθεν αὐτῶν from Luke's narrative in 9:29 is that it was not in his special source. The phrase ἔμπροσθεν αὐτῶν places the focus on the disciples in the Marcan tradition. Unlike the Marcan version, Luke's source for the first half of the narrative focuses on Jesus.

The phrase ὁ ἱματισμὸς αὐτοῦ λευκὸς ἐξαστράπτων is the only real agreement in Luke's v 29 with Mark 9:2b-3. Given the extent of the differences between Luke and Mark in vv 28-33a and the evidence for a separate Lucan source for this section, one suspects that the detail about Jesus' clothing has been inserted secondarily in v 29 when the two traditions were joined. An analysis of the vocabulary shows that ὁ ἱματισμὸς αὐτοῦ λευκὸς ἐξαστράπτων is explainable as Luke's version of τὰ ἱμάτια αὐτοῦ ἐγένετο στίλβοντα λευκὰ λίαν (Mark 9:3). But the point at which this detail was incorporated into Luke's account was not until the two sources were conflated.

A further indication of a redactional seam in this verse is that if the expression τὸ εἶδος τοῦ προσώπου αὐτοῦ ἕτερον is understood as a description of a natural change of facial expression, then the phrase following it, καὶ ὁ ἱματισμὸς αὐτοῦ λευκὸς ἐξαστράπτων, is very strange. In Mark's account, τὰ ἱμάτια αὐτοῦ ἐγένετο στίλβοντα λευκὰ λίαν belongs to the same supernatural plane as μετεμορφώθη and is quite understandable in its context. In Luke, the two expressions, τὸ εἶδος τοῦ προσώπου αὐτοῦ ἕτερον and καὶ ὁ ἱματισμὸς αὐτοῦ λευκὸς ἐξαστράπτων, are not necessarily compatible. That the latter phrase was not originally part of Luke's special source will become clearer when an overall picture of what was contained therein is achieved.

The term Luke uses for Jesus' clothing is ὁ ἱματισμός rather than Mark's τὰ ἱμάτια. There are two other instances of Luke's use of ἱματισμός: Luke 7:25 (Lucan redaction of Q material) and Acts 20:33. It is clear from Luke 7:25, where both ἱματίοις and ἱματισμός appear, that Luke regards the two nouns as interchangeable. Luke uses ἱμάτιον more frequently than ἱματισμός.[116] In 9:29 Luke has replaced Mark's ἱμάτια with ἱματισμός perhaps as an improvement in elegance or exactness of expression.[117]

It is characteristic of Luke that he abbreviates Marcan tradition by omitting circumstantial or anecdotal details, such as οἷα γναφεὺς ἐπὶ τῆς γῆς οὐ δύναται οὕτως λευκᾶναι.[118] That Luke should also alter Mark's ἐγένετο στίλβοντα λευκὰ

---

[116]Five times Luke retains ἱμάτιον from Marcan tradition: Luke 5:36; 8:44; 19:35,36; 23:34; once he adds it to Marcan material: Luke 8:27; twice it is found in Luke's redaction of Q material: Luke 6:29; 7:25; once it occurs in specifically Lucan material: Luke 22:36; and eight times it is found in Acts: 7:58; 9:39; 12:8; 14:14; 16:22; 18:6; 22:20,23.

[117]Cadbury, *Style*, 187.

[118]Cadbury, *Style*, 130, has a list of examples where Luke omits various details from Marcan material.

λίαν to λευκὸς ἐξαστράπτων is not unusual.[119]    The rare use of the verb στίλβω[120] is listed by Cadbury among the verbs censured by Atticists and avoided by Luke.[121]  The adverb λίαν occurs only once in Luke (23:8), in L material, and was probably found in Luke's source for the passage.  Elsewhere Luke omits λίαν wherever it occurs in his source.[122]

The participle ἐξαστράπτων, used by Luke in v 29 to modify λευκός, is the only occurrence of the compound verb ἐξαστράπτω in the NT.  However, the related verb ἀστράπτω and the noun ἀστραπή occur several times in Luke's Gospel.  The noun ἀστραπή is found once in material peculiar to Luke (10:18) and twice in Lucan redactions of Q material.[123]  The verb ἀστράπτω occurs twice as a participial adjective,[124] and the compound verb περιαστράπτω is found twice in Acts (9:3; 22:6).  So the participle ἐξαστράπτων in Luke 9:29 is recognizable as a touch from Luke's pen, possibly with the intent of aligning the final form of the transfiguration story with the description of the clothing of the two men at the empty tomb in Luke 24:4, ἐσθῆτι ἀτραπτούσῃ.[125]

An influence on Luke's use of ἐξαστράπτων may be the LXX, where that participle occurs four times: Ezek 1:4,7; Nah 3:3; Dan 10:6.  Also, Luke was not the first writer to interchange ἐξαστράπτω and στίλβω.  Where στίλβοντος is found in Theodotion's version of Dan 10:6, the LXX has ἐξαστράπτων.  Also, in Nah 3:3 the two are found together: καὶ στιλβούσης ῥομφαίας καὶ ἐξαστραπτόντων ὅπλων.

The conclusions with regard to tradition and redaction in Luke 9:29 are: the familiar formula καὶ ἐγένετο + the dative of the articular infinitive with ἐν, resuming the reference to prayer in v 28, was constructed by Luke and yields no information regarding Luke's source.  The unusual expression τὸ εἶδος τοῦ προσώπου αὐτοῦ ἕτερον, however, indicates a non-Marcan source.  The second half of the verse, καὶ ὁ ἱματισμὸς αὐτοῦ λευκὸς ἐξαστράπτων, is Luke's redaction of

---

[119]Cadbury, Style, 118.

[120]Mark 9:3 is the only instance of it in the NT.

[121]Cadbury, Style, 182.

[122]The adverb λίαν is found in Mark 16:2, but is absent in the parallel Lucan passages: 4:42; 24:1. It also occurs in Mark 6:51, for which there is no Lucan parallel.  In Matthew, λίαν is found four times: 2:16; 4:8; 8:28; 27:14.  The first and last examples belong to peculiarly Matthean material. The Lucan parallel to Matt 4:8 (from Q) does not contain λίαν.  Either Luke omitted it, or it was not found in Q and Matthew added it, as he seems to have done to the Marcan tradition behind Matt 8:28.

[123]Luke 11:36; 17:24.  Only in the second example does the Matthean parallel (24:27) contain ἀστραπή.

[124]In Luke 17:24, where ἀστράπτουσα is found in the Lucan redaction of Q material, but is absent in the Matthean parallel (24:27); and in Luke 24:4, where ἀστραπτούσῃ may be attributable to L or Lucan redaction.

[125]To identify ἐξαστράπτων as Lucan redaction in order to align 9:29 with 24:4 does not preclude a special L source for ἄνδρες δύο in 9:30 which is also echoed in 24:4.  It is most probable that ἄνδρες δύο came from L in 9:29 and serves as Luke's inspiration for his repetition of the phrase in 24:4 and Acts 1:10, as shown above.

Mark 9:3 and was added secondarily by the evangelist to his special source when he combined this tradition with Mark's.

## Luke 9:30

In the analysis of the internal consistency of the narrative, it has been concluded that there is a redactional seam in v 30 and that the phrase οἴτινες ἦσαν Μωϋσῆς καὶ 'Ηλίας is a secondary addition by Luke. To his special source that told of two men who appeared in glory, Luke added the explanatory phrase οἴτινες ἦσαν Μωϋσῆς καὶ 'Ηλίας in order to identify the two men as the two OT figures that were named in Mark's account. He also added the phrase συνελάλουν αὐτῷ, patterned on Mark's συλλαλοῦντες τῷ 'Ιησοῦ. This hypothesis is confirmed by an examination of Luke's redactional habits.

The introductory καὶ ἰδοὺ is found twenty-six times in Luke's Gospel.[126] For the most part it occurs in material peculiar to Luke[127] and in Lucan redaction of Marcan material[128] and of Q material.[129] This abundant use of introductory καὶ ἰδοὺ in every type of Lucan material is most readily explained as coming from the hand of Luke. The same construction occurs frequently in the LXX, where it reflects either Hebrew wĕhinnēh or Aramaic wĕhā'.[130] As is the case with other Septuagintisms in Luke, καὶ ἰδοὺ in 9:30 was probably a touch from Luke's pen and reveals nothing about his source.

The noun ἀνήρ is found very frequently in Luke's Gospel and Acts.[131] In the Gospel, it occurs nine times in material peculiar to Luke,[132] four times in Luke's redaction of Q material,[133] and twelve other times in material that has a Marcan parallel.[134] Only twice do Mark and Luke coincide in using ἄνδρες.[135] Twice Luke substitutes ἄνδρες for Marcan ἄνθρωπος[136] and twice for Marcan εἷς.[137] In other instances, Luke expands on a Marcan description by adding a

---

[126]Luke 1:20,31,36; 2:25; 5:12,18; 7:12,37; 8:41; 9:30,38,39; 10:25; 11:31,32,41; 13:11,30; 14:2; 19:2; 23:14,15,50; 24:4,13,49. It is also found in Acts 5:28; 10:30; 27:24. The fuller phrase καὶ νῦν ἰδοὺ occurs in Acts 13:11; 20:22,25.

[127]Luke 1:20,36; 2:24; 7:12,37; 13:11; 14:2; 19:2; 23:14,15; 24:13,49.

[128]Luke 5:12,18: 8:41; 9:38,39; 10:25; 13:30; 23:50. There is no instance of καὶ ἰδοὺ in Mark's Gospel; ἰδοὺ is found in Mark 1:2; 3:32; 4:3; 10:28,33; 14:41,42.

[129]Luke 11:31,32,41. Only in the first instance does the Matthean parallel (Matt 12:42) also have καὶ ἰδοὺ.

[130]E.g., Gen 1:31; 15:17; 22:13. See Fitzmyer, Luke, 121; BDF §4 (2).

[131]It occurs twenty-seven times in the Gospel and 101 times in Acts.

[132]Luke 1:27,34; 2:36; 5:8; 17:12; 19:2,7; 22:63; 24:19.

[133]Luke 7:20; 11:31,32; 14:24. It is not found in any of the Matthean parallels.

[134]Luke 5:12,18; 6:8; 8:27,38,41; 9:14,38; 16:18; 23:50(2x); 24:4.

[135]Luke 9:14 = Mark 6:44; Luke 16:18 = Mark 10:12.

[136]Luke 6:8 = Mark 3:3; Luke 8:27 = Mark 5:20.

[137]Mark 5:22 = Luke 8:41; Mark 9:17 = Luke 9:38.

phrase with ἀνήρ.[138] Although ἀνήρ may be attributed to Luke's own hand in many instances, it was also present a number of times in Luke's special sources. Such is most probably the case for Luke 9:30, as shall be further demonstrated below.

Not only does Luke use ἀνήρ many more times than Mark or Matthew, but he also frequently employs ἰδού or καὶ ἰδού with ἀνήρ.[139] Similarly, καὶ ἰδού γυνή is found in Luke 7:37; 13:11 and καὶ ἰδοὺ ἄνθρωπος occurs in Luke 2:25; 7:34; 14:2.[140] The construction καὶ ἰδού with ἀνήρ, γυνή or ἄνθρωπος is a typically Lucan way of introducing characters. For Luke 9:30, the evangelist probably added καὶ ἰδού to ἄνδρες δύο in his source to create his favorite introduction of new characters.

That ἄνδρες δύο was found as such in Luke's non-Marcan source is likely for a number of reasons. It was demonstrated above that Luke's general pattern for introducing new characters is: καὶ ἰδοὺ + ἀνήρ (or γυνή or ἄνθρωπος) + ὀνόματι (or τὸ ὄνομα) + the proper name. The absence of this construction in 9:30 leads to the conclusion that ἄνδρες δύο οἳ ὀφθέντες ἐν δόξῃ was already so formulated in Luke's special source. A further reason to regard ἄνδρες δύο as an element from tradition is that Luke's general practice is to omit details of number.[141] There are nine instances in which Luke makes such an omission in his redaction of Marcan material[142] and one example in his treatment of Q.[143] An addition by Luke of δύο to a Marcan source would be contrary to his redactional habits.[144] A preferable explanation is that Luke's special source contained ἄνδρες δύο.

The verb συνλαλέω appears two other times in Luke's Gospel and once in Acts. In Acts it is pure conjecture to attribute συνλαλέω to either tradition or Lucan redaction. In Luke 4:36 and 22:4 the verb is specific to Luke's redaction of Marcan material. In the first instance Luke changes Mark's συζητεῖν (1:27) to συνελάλουν. In the second he adds συνελάλησεν, expanding Mark's account (14:10), which does not contain the verb συνλαλέω. In 9:30, συνελάλουν αὐτῷ can best be explained as a secondary addition by Luke patterned on Mark's ἦσαν συλλαλοῦντες τῷ Ἰησοῦ (9:4).

---

[138]E.g., Mark's ὁ λεπρός (1:40) becomes ἀνὴρ πλήρης λέπρας in Luke 5:12; Mark's ὁ δαιμονισθείς in Mark 5:18 becomes ὁ ἀνὴρ ἀφ᾽ οὗ ἐξεληλύθει τὰ δαιμόνια εἶναι in Luke 8:38; Mark's Ἰωσὴφ [ὁ] ἀπὸ Ἀριμαθαίας in Mark 15:43 results as καὶ ἰδοὺ ἀνὴρ ὀνόματι Ἰωσήφ . . . [καὶ] ἀνὴρ ἀγαθὸς καὶ δίκαιος in Luke 23:50.

[139]Luke 5:12,18; 8:41; 9:30,38; 19:2; 23:50; 24:4; Acts 1:10; 5:25; 8:27; 10:17,19,30; 11:11.

[140]Each of these examples of καὶ ἰδοὺ γυνή and καὶ ἰδοὺ ἄνθρωπος is found in L material with the exception of Luke 7:34 (= Matt 11:9), which is from Q.

[141]Cadbury (Style, 128-29) lists examples in which Luke eliminates details of number from his source. In the case of Luke 9:30 he regards δύο as an addition to the Marcan source that is due to Luke's use of a kind of formula for apparitions.

[142]Luke 8:8,15,33; 9:13,14; 18:30; 22:1,34,61.

[143]Luke 17:4.

[144]In contrast, Matthew creates two characters from Mark's single demoniac in Matt 8:28 and two blind men in Matt 9:27.

Luke's replacement of Mark's periphrastic construction with the imperfect is a stylistic change that he makes frequently.[145] Another indication that this phrase is a secondary insertion is that one would expect the description οἱ ὀφθέντες ἐν δόξῃ to follow more closely after ἄνδρες δύο. In other examples of heavenly messengers who are introduced as men, there is an immediate contextual clue describing their glorious raiment or appearance to give the indication that these figures are not mere mortals.[146]

It has been proposed above on the basis of the internal consistency of the narrative that the explanatory phrase οἵτινες ἦσαν Μωϋσῆς καὶ Ἡλίας was an editorial addition made by Luke when he joined his two strands of tradition. Luke's frequent addition of relative clauses supports this conclusion. Luke typically uses the indefinite relative for the definite relative to introduce such clauses.[147] Every instance of the use of ὅστις for ὅς in Luke occurs in material that is peculiarly Lucan[148] or in Luke's reformulation of his source.[149] In the case of Luke 9:30 the phrase with οἵτινες was formulated by Luke as a means to weave together his two sources.

There is no other instance in the NT in which Moses and Elijah are named together,[150] nor does either figure ever function as a heavenly messenger as in

---

[145]Cadbury (Style, 161) lists two examples: Luke 22:55; 23:51. Other examples where Luke has not retained a periphrastic imperfect construction from Mark are: Luke 5:21,33; 7:39; 8:23; 18:23; 22:53.

[146]Luke 24:4: καὶ ἰδοὺ ἄνδρες δύο ἐπέστησαν αὐταῖς ἐν ἐσθῆτι ἀστραπτούσῃ; Acts 1:10: καὶ ἰδοὺ ἄνδρες δύο παρειστήκεισαν αὐτοῖς ἐν ἐσθήσεσι λευκαῖς; Acts 10:30: καὶ ἰδοὺ ἀνὴρ ἔστη ἐνώπιόν μου ἐν ἐσθῆτι λαμπρᾷ; Ezek 40:3: καὶ ἰδοὺ ἀνήρ, καὶ ἡ ὅρασις αὐτοῦ ἦν ὡσεὶ ὅρασις χαλκοῦ στίλβοντος; 2 Macc 3:26: ἕτεροι δὲ δύο προσεφάνησαν αὐτῷ νεανίαι τῇ ῥώμῃ μὲν ἐκπρεπεῖς, κάλλιστοι δὲ τὴν δόξαν, διαπρεπεῖς δὲ τὴν περιβολήν; 2 Enoch 1:4-5: "Then two huge men appeared to me, the like of which I had never seen on earth. Their faces were like the shining sun; their eyes were like burning lamps; from their mouths fire was coming forth; their clothing was various singing [sic];" Gos. Pet. 9:36 (describing the scene at the empty tomb): "and they saw the heavens opened and two men come down from there in a great brightness and draw nigh to the sepulchre."

[147]In Hellenistic and biblical Greek the distinction between ὅς and ὅστις is no longer observed, especially in Luke. See BDF §293; Zerwick, Biblical Greek, §215-220; H. J. Cadbury, "The Relative Pronouns in Acts and Elsewhere," JBL 42 (1923) 150-57. In some instances Matthew uses ὅστις correctly: 5:39,41; 7:15; 10:33.

[148]Luke 1:20; 2:4,10; 7:37,39; 8:3; 10:42; Acts 5:16; 8:15; 9:35; 11:20,28; 12:10; 13:31,43; 16:12; 17:10; 21:4; 23:14,21,33; 24:1; 28:18.

[149]In Lucan redaction of Mark: Luke 8:26,43; 12:1; 23:19,55; and in Luke's version of Q material: Luke 14:15,27; 15:7.

[150]The two witnesses in Rev 11:1-13, although not named, are usually understood to be Moses and Elijah. See A. Y. Collins, The Apocalypse (NTM 22; Wilmington, DE: Glazier, 1979) 70-72; D. Haugg, Die zwei Zeugen. Eine exegetische Studie über Apk. 11,1-13 (NTAbh 17,1; Münster: Aschendorff, 1937); G. E. Ladd, A Commentary on the Revelation of John (Grand Rapids: Eerdmans, 1972) 155.

Luke 9:30.[151] In all other instances in which Moses is named in Luke's Gospel he is cited in the function of lawgiver. The Lucan references are to the Law of Moses,[152] to Moses and the prophets,[153] to Moses' writings,[154] and to his commands.[155] Mention of Elijah elsewhere in Luke's Gospel is in reference to his mighty deeds.[156] That Luke should have the same unusual combination of these two OT figures as Mark 9:4, and functioning in the same atypical manner, is best explained by Luke's having taken this element from Marcan tradition.

The preceding examination of Luke's tendencies in the treatment of his sources with regard to tradition and redaction confirm the conclusions drawn previously about the provenience of the material in Luke 9:30. In his non-Marcan source Luke found ἄνδρες δύο οἳ ὀφθέντες ἐν δόξῃ. The introductory καὶ ἰδού was from Luke's hand. The phrases συνελάλουν αὐτῷ and οἵτινες ἦσαν Μωϋσῆς καὶ Ἠλίας were inspired by Mark 9:4 and added secondarily by Luke when he joined the material from his particular source to the Marcan tradition.[157] The similarities between the two strands of tradition, each with two heavenly figures speaking to Jesus, contributed to Luke's joining the two narratives into one.

### Luke 9:31-33a

This section of Luke's narrative has no counterpart in Mark's account. The hypothesis proposed in this study attributes vv 31-33a to Luke's non-Marcan source, with the exception of the phrase ἦσαν βεβαρημένοι ὕπνῳ· διαγρηγορήσαντες δέ, which was a secondary addition made by Luke. The analysis of vv 31-33a will begin with οἳ ὀφθέντες ἐν δόξῃ.

Luke has a predilection for explanatory clauses introduced by a definite relative pronoun. Such constructions are found some eighty times in the Gospel and 135 times in Acts. In the Gospel they are found twenty-nine times in L material.[158] Luke preserves the definite relative from his Marcan source eleven times[159] and from Q five times.[160] In his redaction of Marcan material Luke

---

[151]On the function of Moses and Elijah as predicting angels, see below, chapter two, part IV on "Form" and detailed exegesis of v 30 in chapter three.

[152]In L material: Luke 2:22; 24:44.

[153]In L material: Luke 16:29,31; 24:27.

[154]Luke 20:28 = Mark 12:19; Luke 20:37 = Mark 12:26.

[155]Luke 5:14 = Mark 1:44.

[156]In L material: Luke 1:17; 4:25,26; from Mark: Luke 9:8,19.

[157]Schramm (Markus-Stoff, 138) draws the same conclusions for v 30, with the exception of καὶ ἰδού, which he attributes to Luke's special source.

[158]Luke 1:26,27,61,78; 2:11,15,25,31,37; 8:2(2x); 10:30; 11:27; 13:4,14,16; 14:33; 16:1; 17:7,12; 23:27,29(3x); 24:13,17,19,23,44.

[159]Luke 6:4,13,16; 7:27; 8:13; 18:29; 19:30; 20:47; 21:6; 22:22; 23:51.

[160]Luke 12:2(2x),42,43; 13:21.

introduces definite relative clauses twenty-four times.[161] In seven instances Luke's redaction of Q contains definite relative clauses where Matthew's version does not.[162] These data show widespread use of the definite relative by Luke in each kind of material found in the Gospel. The phrase οἳ ὀφθέντες ἐν δόξῃ, found in Luke's special source, was retained by him in accord with his consistent use of definite relative clauses.

The verb ὤφθη is used three other times by Luke for supernatural apparitions. It is used of the angel of the Lord who appeared to Zechariah in Luke 1:11; of the strengthening angel at the agony scene in 22:43;[163] and of the risen Jesus in his appearance to Simon in Luke 24:34. There are nine similar examples in Acts.[164] Each of these instances occurs in material peculiar to Luke. In the case of 9:31 the greatest probability is that οἳ ὀφθέντες ἐν δόξῃ was found in Luke's special source.

As for δόξα, this is a favorite noun of Luke. It appears thirteen times in his Gospel and four times in Acts,[165] as compared with only three times in the Gospel of Mark.[166] Three times Luke has retained δόξα from his source,[167] six times it occurs in material peculiar to Luke,[168] and twice it is peculiar to Luke's redaction of his source.[169] In 9:31 it is most likely that ἐν δόξῃ was found in Luke's special source. The whole phrase οἳ ὀφθέντες ἐν δόξῃ makes clear that the two men are heavenly messengers. Like the men in Luke 24:4, ἄνδρες δύο . . . ἐν ἐσθῆτι ἀστραπτούσῃ, and in Acts 1:10, ἄνδρες δύο . . . ἐν ἐσθήσεσι λευκαῖς, and Acts 10:30, ἀνὴρ . . ἐν ἐσθῆτι λαμπρᾷ, it is their glorious apparel that distinguishes them from ordinary mortals.

---

[161]Luke 5:3,10,17,18,21,29; 6:3,14; 8:13,17(2x),35,38,41; 11:22; 13:30(2x); 18:30; 19:30; 21:4,6,15; 22:7,10.

[162]Luke 6:49; 7:2,4; 12:24,48; 19:15,20.

[163]The authenticity of Luke 22:43-44 remains a highly debated question. For a comprehensive survey of the arguments for and against see B. D. Ehrman and M. A. Plunkett, "The Angel and the Agony: The Textual Problem of Luke 22:43-44," *CBQ* 45 (1983) 401-16. J. Neyrey (*The Passion According to Luke. A Redaction Study of Luke's Soteriology* [Theological Inquiries; N.Y.: Paulist, 1985] 49-68) argues persuasively for Lucan authorship.

[164]In Acts it is used of angelic appearances in 7:30,35; of the appearances of the risen Christ in 9:17; 13:31; 26:16; of the appearance of the tongues of fire in 2:3; or the appearance of the glory of God in 7:2; and of a vision to Paul in 16:9. In one instance, Acts 7:26, ὤφθη is used of Moses appearing to his fellow Israelites in a natural way. See further BAGD, 578. The only instance of ὤφθη in both Mark and Matthew is in their respective accounts of the transfiguration.

[165]Luke 2:9,14,32; 4:6; 9:26,31,32; 12:27; 14:10; 17:18; 19:38; 21:27; 24:26; Acts 7:2,55; 12:23; 22:11.

[166]Mark 8:38; 10:37; 13:26.

[167]Luke 9:26; 21:27 from Mark; Luke 12:27 from Q.

[168]Luke 2:9,14,32; 14:10; 17:18; 24:26.

[169]Luke 4:6 from Q; Luke 19:38 from Mark.

**Luke 9:31b**

The unusual noun ἔξοδος occurs only twice elsewhere in the NT, and nowhere else in Lucan writings.[170] The best explanation for its appearance in Luke 9:31 is that Luke retained it from his special source.

The verb μέλλω is often used by Luke.[171] For the most part, it is found in material specific to Luke[172] or in his particular redactions of Marcan tradition[173] and of Q.[174] There is one instance in which it came to Luke from Mark (Luke 21:7)[175] and one in which Luke retained it from Q (Luke 3:7). These data are inconclusive regarding the provenience of the verb μέλλω. Sometimes it comes from Luke's own hand, and frequently it is found in his sources. There is no evidence that runs counter to the proposition that in Luke 9:31 ἤμελλεν was found in Luke's non-Marcan source.

The verb πληρόω occurs eight other times in Luke's Gospel and sixteen times in Acts.[176] In every instance in the Gospel, it is found in L material. So too in Luke 9:31 πληροῦν is attributable to Luke's special source.[177]

The use of the form 'Ιερουσαλήμ is most typical of Luke.[178] This form, which is almost a transcription of the Hebrew name, occurs twenty-six times in Luke's Gospel and thirty-nine times in Acts. Mark always uses the Greek spelling 'Ιεροσόλυμα as does Matthew.[179] In almost every instance, 'Ιερουσαλήμ is

---

[170]It is found in Heb 11:22 and 2 Pet 1:15. Luke does frequently use ὁδός, but there is no certain instance in his Gospel in which it derives from Lucan composition. In Luke 8:5,12; 9:3; 18:35; 19:36; 20:21 Luke takes it over from Mark. In Q material, twice Luke and Matthew both have ὁδός (Luke 12:58 = Matt 5:25; Luke 14:23 = Matt 22:10); twice (Luke 9:57; 10:4) Luke has it but not Matthew (8:18; 10:9). Seven times ὁδός occurs in L material: Luke 1:76,79; 2:44; 10:31; 11:6; 24:32,35. There are three instances in which ὁδός appears in a Lucan quotation of the OT. Luke 3:4 is a quotation of Isa 40:3, which Luke shares with Matthew (3:3). Luke alone extends the quotation to include Isa 40:4-5 (= Luke 3:5-6), which contains another instance of ὁδός. Luke 7:27 is a quotation of Mal 3:1, which is also found in Mark 1:2 and Matt 11:10. One instance of εἴσοδος appears in Acts 13:24.

[171]Twelve times in the Gospel and thirty-three times in Acts.

[172]E.g., Luke 13:9; 19:4; 21:36; 24:21.

[173]Luke 9:44; 22:23.

[174]Luke 7:2; 10:1; 19:11.

[175]The only other occurrence of μέλλω in Mark is in 10:32. In Luke's redaction the verb is omitted.

[176]Luke 1:20; 2:40; 3:5; 4:21; 7:1; 21:24; 22:16; 24:44; Acts 1:16; 2:2,28; 3:18; 5:3,28; 7:23,30; 9:23; 12:25; 13:25,27,52; 14:26; 19:21; 24:27. In Mark it is found twice: Mark 1:15; 14:49. In neither instance is there a corresponding parallel in Luke.

[177]So also Schramm, Markus-Stoff, 138.

[178]See J. K. Elliott, "Jerusalem in Acts and in the Gospels," NTS 23 (1976-77) 462-69; J. Jeremias, "'ΙΕΡΟΥΣΑΛΗΜ/'ΙΕΡΟΣΟΛΥΜΑ," ZNW 65 (1974) 273-76.

[179]The only exception is Matt 23:37. Luke has 'Ιεροσόλυμα four times. Once he retains it from Mark (Luke 19:28 = Mark 11:1), and three times it is found in L material: Luke 2:22; 13:22, 23:7.

found in material from Luke's special sources.[180] It also occurs in his own composition and redaction of his sources.[181] Only twice does ʼΙερουσαλήμ occur as a Lucan alteration of Mark's ʼΙεροσόλυμα,[182] and once it derives from Q.[183] Although the evidence for the provenience of ʼΙερουσαλήμ is mixed, because of the great number of times in which it is found in material that comes from Luke's particular sources, it is most probable that for 9:31 ʼΙερουσαλήμ should be regarded as coming from Luke's non-Marcan source.

The whole phrase ἣν ἤμελλεν πληροῦν ἐν ʼΙερουσαλήμ, like many Lucan clauses introduced with a definite relative pronoun, came from Luke's special source.[184] In sum, the whole of v 31, was found in the non-Marcan source, as is evident from its two definite relative clauses, the unusual noun ἔξοδος, and vocabulary typical of Luke's special sources: πληρόω and ʼΙερουσαλήμ.

### Luke 9:32

The expression ὁ δὲ Πέτρος καὶ οἱ σὺν αὐτοῦ resumes the mention of the three disciples in Luke 9:28 and most probably was found as such in Luke's special source. The preposition σύν is a favorite of Luke and is found very frequently in his Gospel and Acts with a connotation of personal association.[185] There is only one instance (Luke 23:32) in which σύν is taken by Luke from Mark.[186]z Four times Luke substitutes σύν + the dative for Marcan μετά + the genitive.[187] In one instance σύν occurs in a Lucan redaction of Mark (Luke 20:1) and once in the Lucan version of Q material (Luke 7:6). The remaining occurrences of σύν are found in passages from Luke's own sources.[188]

Furthermore, the same syntactical construction, καί + the definite relative + σύν + the personal pronoun, is found two othercan also times in L material.[189] There is adequate reason, then, to suppose that καὶ οἱ σὺν αὐτῷ in Luke 9:32

---

[180]Luke 2:25,38,41,43,45; 9:53; 10:30; 13:4,33; 17:11; 23:28; 24:13,18,33,47,52.

[181]Luke 4:9; 5:17; 9:51; 19:11; 21:20,24.

[182]Luke 6:17 = Mark 3:8; Luke 18:31 = Mark 10:33. In other instances where ʼΙεροσόλυμα is found in Mark (Mark 3:22; 7:1; 10:32; 11:11,15,27; 15:41) Luke omits the mention of the city in his redaction. The only exception is Luke 19:28 = Mark 11:1, mentioned above, where Luke retains ʼΙεροσόλυμα.

[183]Luke 13:34 = Matt 23:37.

[184]See above, on οἵτινες ἦσαν Μωϋσῆς καὶ ʼΗλίας for data on definite relative clauses in Luke.

[185]Seventeen of the twenty times that σύν occurs in the Gospel it is with this connotation; all fifty-two instances in Acts have this sense. The six times that σύν is found in Mark it denotes personal association, as also three times in Matthew. In the one remaining example of σύν in Matthew, the preposition connotes material association.

[186]In other instances where σύν occurs in Mark (Mark 2:26; 4:10; 8:34; 15:32) Luke eliminates or alters it in his corresponding passages.

[187]Luke 8:38,51; 22:14,56.

[188]Luke 1:56; 2:5,13; 5:9; 7:12; 8:1; 23:11; 24:10,24,29,33,44.

[189]Luke 5:9, καὶ πάντας τοὺς σὺν αὐτῷ, and 24:33, καὶ τοὺς σὺν αὐτοῖς.

belonged to the non-Marcan source. Moreover, as was demonstrated earlier, the designation οἱ σὺν αὐτῷ is unusual for characters already named, and points to the provenience of the phrase ὁ δὲ Πέτρος καὶ οἱ σὺν αὐτῷ from a special source.

The phrase ἦσαν βεβαρημένοι ὕπνῳ· διαγρηγορήσαντες δὲ is an element that was a later insertion into the narrative, acquired from association with the Gethsemane tradition.[190] Luke uses the same construction of ἦσαν + a participle[191] that is in Mark's Gethsemane tradition, ἦσαν . . . καταβαρυνόμενοι (Mark 14:40), but he replaces the compound verb καταβαρύνω (a *hapax* in the NT) with the perfect participle passive of βαρέομαι. The verb βαρέομαι is also used by Luke in 21:34. The noun ὕπνος appears another time in Lucan writings (Acts 20:9) and the related verb ἀφυπνόω is found in Luke 8:23. In the latter instance, the verb comes from Luke's redactional hand. Neither the verb βαρέομαι nor any form of ὑπνόω is found in Mark's Gospel. Their presence in Luke 9:32 can be attributed to his editorial hand.

As for διαγρηγορήσαντες, although Luke 9:32 is the only instance of the compound verb in the NT, the verb γρηγορέω does occur in Luke 12:37, in a passage peculiar to Luke, and in Acts 20:31.[192] The parts of the verses that contain γρηγορέω in Mark's Gethsemane account (Mark 14:34,37,38) are absent in Luke's account of the agony. This is not due to a tendency of Luke to avoid the verb, since he does use it elsewhere, but rather it has been transferred to the transfiguration story. Luke has a special affinity for compound verbs, especially with the prefix δια-[193] and it is in accord with this stylistic preference that he converted γρηγορέω from the Gethsemane tradition to διαγρηγορήσαντες for his addition to the transfiguration account.

The aorist indicative of the verb ὁράω is found six other times in Luke's Gospel. Twice it occurs in L material (15:20; 24:24); once in the Lucan version of Q material (10:24 = Matt 13:17); and three times in Lucan redaction of Mark (19:37; 21:1,2). These data are inconclusive for indicating the provenience of εἶδον in 9:32. There is no evidence that it was not contained in Luke's special source.

Among the synoptic evangelists, Luke is particularly noted for his use of

---

[190]See above, section II.B.4.

[191]This construction appears many times in material unique to Luke, e.g., 9:53; 14:1; 15:1; 21:37; 23:8; 24:13,27,32.

[192]The verb γρηγορέω is found six times in Mark's Gospel. It occurs three times in Mark's conclusion to the parable of the fig tree (Mark 13:34,35,37) but Luke has no parallel to this pericope. Although Luke 12:40 bears some resemblance to Mark 13:35, it is evident from the parallel in Matt 24:44 that its provenience is from Q and not Mark. See Fitzmyer, *Luke*, 1231.

[193]E.g., διανοίγω (4x in Luke; 3x in Acts); διατάσσω (4x in Luke; 5x in Acts); διέρχομαι(10x in Luke; 20x in Acts). See Plummer, *Luke*, lii-liii. In many instances these verbs are found in L material, and may be from Luke's hand. E.g., διανοίγω in 2:23; 24:31,32; διατάσσω in 3:13; 17:9,10; διέρχομαι in 2:15,35; 17:11; 19:1,4; διερμενεύω in 24:27; διαβαίνω in 16:26; διαβάλλω in 16:1; διαγγέλλω in 9:60; διαγογγύζω in 19:7 and possibly 15:2; διαιρέω in 15:12; διαλαλέω in 1:65; διαλογίζομαι in 1:29; 12:17; διαμαρτύρομαι in 16:28; διαμένω in 1:22 and possibly 22:28; διανεύω in 1:22; διαπεράω in 16:26; διασείω in 3:14; διασκορπίζω in 1:51; 15:13; 16:1; διαταράσσομαι in 1:29; διατερέω in 2:51.

δόξα. Not only are the occurrences of δόξα most frequent in Luke's Gospel,[194] but also the connotations it has there are more varied. In Mark's Gospel, δόξα always refers to the future glory of the Son of Man (Mark 8:38; 10:37; 13:26). In Matthew's Gospel, there are four instances where δόξα has this connotation[195] and two examples in which the meaning of δόξα is "splendor," "magnificence."[196] As in Mark and Matthew, there are examples in Luke in which δόξα refers to the future glory of the Son of Man.[197] In two examples from Q material,[198] δόξα is found with the connotation "splendor." In addition there are two meanings that occur only in Lucan material: "radiance" or "glory" associated with God,[199] and "fame" or "honor."[200] Particularly characteristic of Luke is the expression "give glory to God" as a response to a divine manifestation, using either the verb δίδωμι with δόξα[201] or the formula δοξάζω τὸν θεόν.[202] The occurrence of δόξα in Luke 9:32 is the only instance in the synoptic gospels in which δόξα is used of Jesus where it is not explicitly spoken of as a future glory into which he will enter. The uniqueness of this example and the frequent occurrence of δόξα in special L material lead to the conclusion that for 9:32 Luke found δόξα in his non-Marcan source.[203] With his affinity for δόξα in various connotations, Luke easily incorporated this example from his special source into his narrative. The element δύο ἄνδρας was present in Luke's special source. The reasons for this assertion have already been outlined in the treatment above of ἄνδρες δύο in v 30.

Luke 9:32 contains the only occurrence in the synoptic gospels of the verb συνίστημι and it is the only instance in the NT where that verb is used intransitively with a present meaning of "stand with or by someone."[204] The unusual use of the verb is due to Luke's having taken συνεστῶτας from his particular source.[205]

The conclusion reached for v 32 is that the whole of the verse, with the

---

[194]See above, on v 31.

[195]Matt 16:27 = Mark 8:38; Matt 24:30 = Mark 13:26; Matt 19:28; 25:31. These last two examples are found in material peculiar to Matthew.

[196]Matt 4:8; 6:29 in Q material.

[197]Luke 9:26 = Mark 8:38; Luke 21:27 = Mark 13:26. Also, Luke 24:26, from L. In this last example, δόξα is said to belong to the Christ rather than to the Son of Man.

[198]Luke 4:6 = Matt 4:8; Luke 12:27 = Matt 6:29.

[199]Luke 2:9; Acts 7:2; 22:11. Luke 9:31 is probably to be understood similarly, as Moses' and Elijah's sharing in God's glory.

[200]In L material: Luke 2:14,32; 14:10; 17:18; Acts 12:23; in a Lucan redaction of Mark: Luke 19:38.

[201]Luke 17:18; Acts 12:23.

[202]In L material: Luke 2:20; 7:16; 13:13; 17:15; in Lucan redaction of Mark: Luke 5:25,26; 18:43; 23:47. In only one instance is the expression found in Mark (2:12), which Luke keeps in 5:26.

[203]Schramm (Markus-Stoff, 138) draws the same conclusion.

[204]Elsewhere in the NT συνίστημι is found in Rom 3:5; 5:8; 16:1; 2 Cor 3:1; 4:2; 5:12; 6:4; 7:11; 10:12,18; 12:11; Gal 2:18; Col 1:17; 2 Pet 3:5.

[205]See Schramm, Markus-Stoff, 138.

exception of the phrase ἦσαν βεβαρημένοι ὕπνῳ· διαγρηγορήσαντες δὲ, was found in Luke's special non-Marcan source. The unusual use of συνίστημι and δόξα, as well as the indefinite references οἱ σὺν αὐτῷ and δύο ἄνδρας after those individuals had been given proper names, point to the use of a special source by Luke. The vocabulary of βαρέομαι, ὕπνος, διαγρηγορέω is not foreign to Luke, and the phrase ἦσαν βεβαρημένοι ὕπνῳ· διαγρηγορήσαντες δὲ is recognizable as Luke's redaction of traditional material from the Gethsemane story.

### Luke 9:33a

As was discussed in the treatment of v 29, the construction καὶ ἐγένετο followed by ἐν + the dative of the articular infinitive and a personal pronoun in the accusative is a characteristically Lucan formulation. In the L source was contained the detail of the departure of the two men, expressed with the verb διαχωρίζω. The only occurrence of διαχωρίζω in the NT is Luke 9:33. Most frequently compound verbs with δια- come from Luke's special sources.[206] In his reformulation of his source for v 33a, Luke employs a favorite construction: καὶ ἐγένετο ἐν τῷ διαχωρίζεσθαι αὐτοὺς ἀπ' αὐτοῦ. Following this, the narrative of the L source concluded, εὑρέθη Ἰησοῦς μόνος (v 36b).

In sum, vv 31-33a came substantially from Luke's special source and are not a piece of Lucan composition elaborating on what was contained in the Marcan tradition of the transfiguration. Luke's redactional hand is detected in the phrase ἦσαν βεβαρημένοι ὕπνῳ· διαγρηγορήσαντες δὲ and in the formulation of the construction καὶ ἐγένετο ἐν τῷ διαχωρίζεσθαι αὐτούς. The remainder was found essentially as is in Luke's non-Marcan source.

### Luke 9:33b-35

From the analysis of the internal consistency of Luke's narrative, it was concluded that Luke 9:33b-35 belonged to a different source from 9:28-33a. It is in vv 33b-35 that Luke's account of the transfiguration most closely resembles Mark's. We have proposed that in this section Luke was dependent on Marcan tradition. A detailed examination of these verses will show that in Luke 9:33b-35 are found typical Lucan redactional tendencies that appear in other passages where Luke is dependent on Marcan tradition.

### Luke 9:33b

Luke's εἶπεν in v 33b is easily understandable as a deliberate alteration of Mark's καὶ ἀποκριθεὶς . . . λέγει. When Luke joined his two sources, he created one of his favorite constructions: καὶ ἐγένετο + a finite verb (εἶπεν) in the indicative. Although Luke frequently uses the participle ἀποκριθείς,[207] he does not retain it from Mark in this instance, since he chose to construct instead the καὶ

---

[206]See above on διαγρηγορέω, v 32.

[207]E.g., Luke 1:19,35,60; 3:11; 4:8. The aorist participle appears thirty-six times in Luke's Gospel.

ἐγένετο + a finite verb formula when he spliced together the two traditions.[208] The change from Mark's historic present, λέγει, to the aorist, εἶπεν is a consistent trait of Lucan redaction.[209]

Luke's πρὸς τὸν Ἰησοῦν in place of Mark's τῷ Ἰησοῦ can also be explained as a typical touch of Lucan redaction. There are nintey-nine instances in his Gospel in which Luke uses πρός with the accusative after a verb of speaking.[210] In twenty-seven of these instances, Luke has substituted πρός with the accusative for the simple dative of his Marcan source.[211] Its appearance in Luke 9:33 can be regarded as another such example.[212] This construction is rare in the Gospels of Mark and Matthew and occurs only occasionally in classical and Hellenistic Greek. It does appear frequently in the LXX as a translation for Hebrew lĕ- or 'el and can be considered another of Luke's Septuagintisms.[213]

Peter's address to Jesus is ἐπιστάτα in Luke 9:33, as compared with ῥαββί in Mark 9:5. Luke never uses the title ῥαββί in his Gospel. In the two other instances in which there is a Lucan parallel to a pericope in which Mark uses ῥαββί as an address to Jesus, Luke does not employ it. Once Luke omits the address altogether (Luke 22:47 = Mark 14:45) and once Luke changes the address from Mark's Ραββουνι to κύριε (Luke 18:41 = Mark 10:51).

The term ἐπιστάτης is peculiar to Luke in the NT and occurs only in the vocative. Twice it is found in material unique to Luke (Luke 5:5; 17:13), and twice Luke substitutes it for the Marcan διδάσκαλε (Luke 8:24; 9:49). There is one instance in which Luke adds ἐπιστάτης where the Marcan parallel does not have any title of address (Luke 8:45). These data support the assertion that Luke consciously avoids the title ῥαββί[214] and that he substituted his preferred ἐπιστάτης in 9:33 for the title he found in the Marcan tradition.

Luke reverses Mark's position of the adjectival numerals in v 33. He places

---

[208]There are two standard forms of the Lucan formula: καὶ ἐγένετο/ἐγένετο δὲ + a finite verb in the indicative, and καὶ ἐγένετο/ἐγένετο δὲ + καί + a finite verb in the indicative. An intervening participle such as ἀποκριθείς never occurs in this kind of Lucan construction. See further Fitzmyer, Luke, 119.

[209]E.g., Luke 4:43; 5:20,22,24,27,31,33. See Neirynck, Agreements, 224-28, for a complete list.

[210]It occurs abundantly in Acts (fifty-two times) as well. See J. C. Hawkins, Horae Synopticae. Contributions to the Study of the Synoptic Problem (2d ed.; Oxford: Clarendon, 1968) 45-46, for examples.

[211]See Cadbury, Style, 203, for examples.

[212]J. J. O'Rourke ("The Construction with a Verb of Saying as an Indication of Sources in Luke," NTS 21 [1975] 421-23) has studied the percentage of times that πρός + the accusative with a verb of saying is found in Luke's Gospel as compared with the occurrences of the simple dative. In his investigation he questions whether this construction is indicative of sources for Luke. O'Rourke's point is well taken, but it is still a demonstrable tendency of Luke to replace the simple dative of his Marcan source with πρός + the accusative.

[213]Fitzmyer, Luke, 116.

[214]Cadbury (Style, 156-57) suggests this is due to Luke's tendency to translate Semitic words. See further O. Glombitza, "Die Titel διδάσκαλος und ἐπιστάτης für Jesus bei Lukas," ZNW 49 (1958) 275-78.

τρεῖς after σκηνάς and μίαν before σοί, Μωϋσεῖ, and Ἠλίᾳ. With regard to the first instance, Luke does have a tendency to change the syntax of his Marcan source so that an adjectival numeral follows the noun it modifies.[215] Examples of such are found in Luke 4:2; 8:43; 9:13,14,17; 23:32. The position of τρεῖς following σκηνάς in Luke 9:33 can be regarded as another such instance. However, this is not a hard and fast pattern in Lucan writings, and there are also many examples in which an adjectival numeral precedes the noun or pronoun it modifies. In some instances Luke has retained this order from his source,[216] and in other cases it is found in material peculiar to Luke.[217] There are also examples in Lucan redaction in which an adjectival numeral precedes the noun or pronoun.[218] Luke's placement of μίαν before σοί, Μωϋσεῖ, and Ἠλίᾳ is similar to the construction found in Luke 18:22: ἐν σοι λείπει, which is Lucan redaction of Mark,[219] and is simply a stylistic variation of Mark 9:5.

Luke's μὴ εἰδὼς ὃ λέγει is his version of Mark's οὐ γὰρ ᾔδει τί ἀποκριθῇ. There are numerous instances in which Luke omits the particle γάρ in his redaction of Marcan material.[220] Luke 9:33 can be considered another such example.[221] The perfect participle εἰδώς occurs two other times in Lucan redaction of Marcan material[222] and can be attributed to Luke's hand in 9:33 as well.

Just as Mark frames Peter's speech with the verb ἀποκρίνομαι (ἀποκριθείς at the beginning of v 5 and ἀποκριθῇ in v 6) so Luke does with the verb λέγω. Luke introduces Peter's speech with εἶπεν and concludes it with ὃ λέγει.[223]

The phrase μὴ εἰδὼς ὃ λέγει is strikingly close to Luke 22:60: οὐκ οἶδα ὃ λέγεις, Peter's assertion to the man in the courtyard who tries to identify Peter with Jesus after Jesus' arrest. It may be that Luke's phrasing in 9:33 is a foreshadowing of Luke 22:60. In both instances it is Peter who does not know what is being said. Central to the scene in both cases is Jesus' identity as the Messiah who must suffer and the attendant implications of that for his disciples. In both Luke 9:33 and 22:60 the Lucan formulation differs from Mark's and can be attributed to Luke's editorship.

Luke has moved the element of fear to v 34, associating it with the cloud rather than giving it as the motive for Peter's not knowing what to say. In v 32, with the inclusion of the detail of the sleepiness of the disciples, Luke has already

---

[215]Cadbury, *Style*, 153-54.

[216]From Mark in Luke 9:3,16; from Q in Luke 16:3.

[217]E.g., Luke 2:24; 3:11; 7:41; 15:11.

[218]Luke 5:2; 19:13,16,17,18.

[219]Mark 10:21 has ἕν σε ὑστερεῖ.

[220]E.g., Luke 4:32,43; 5:28,29,42; 6:14,17; 9:43,46; 12:40; 18:27; 20:21,35; 21:10; 22:27.

[221]Cadbury (*Style*, 136) lists Luke 9:33 among examples in which Luke replaces Marcan clauses containing γάρ with a participle.

[222]Luke 9:47; 11:17; also in Acts 2:30; 5:7; 20:22; 24:22.

[223]Cadbury (*Style*, 139) lists ὃ λέγει of Luke 9:33 among examples that illustrate a Lucan tendency to alter indirect questions found in Marcan tradition.

suggested an explanation for Peter's not knowing what he was saying. Perhaps, too, Luke senses the incongruity of Mark's close juxtaposition of καλόν ἐστιν ἡμᾶς ὧδε εἶναι and ἔκφοβοι γὰρ ἐγένοντο and so postpones the motif of fear until a new element is introduced, the overshadowing cloud.[224]

### Luke 9:34

Luke 9:34 opens with the genitive absolute phrase ταῦτα δὲ αὐτοῦ λέγοντος followed by ἐγένετο. Mark has simply καὶ ἐγένετο.[225] It is not unusual for Luke to substitute a genitive absolute for another expression of Mark.[226] Likewise, the genitive absolute is found in Luke's redaction of Q material[227] and in material that is peculiarly Lucan.[228] On the whole, Luke's use of the genitive absolute comes from his own editorial hand[229] and frequently occurs in introductory or transitional verses of Luke's own composition.[230] The expressions that most closely resemble that of Luke 9:34 are: ταῦτα λέγων (Luke 8:8), καὶ ταῦτα λέγοντος αὐτοῦ (Luke 13:17), and ταῦτα δὲ αὐτῶν λαλούντων (Luke 24:36). The last two examples belong to L material; the first is Luke's redaction of Mark's ἔλεγεν (Mark 4:9). The preceding examples supply ample evidence to attest that ταῦτα δὲ αὐτοῦ λέγοντος in Luke 9:34 is Lucan redaction of the Marcan tradition.

Luke's use of ἐπεσκίαζεν in place of Mark's ἐπισκιάζουσα is in accord with several other examples in which Luke replaces a Marcan participle with the finite verb.[231] The finite verb ἐπεσκίαζεν also fits Luke's stylistic intent for v 34, in which the disciples' fear is provoked by the overshadowing cloud. The sequence of actions in Luke 9:34-35 is expressed with four finite verbs: ἐγένετο νεφέλη, ἐπεσκίαζεν αὐτούς, ἐφοβήθησαν, and φωνὴ ἐγένετο. In contrast, Mark has connected the disciples' fear with their not knowing in the previous verse and the action in Mark 9:7 focuses on the coming of the cloud, ἐγένετο νεφέλη and the coming of the voice, ἐγένετο φωνή. In Mark, the overshadowing of the cloud is only mentioned parenthetically with the participial phrase. The action of overshadowing does not have the same role in Mark as it is given by Luke. A further influence on this particular redactional change may be from the LXX, where

---

[224]Best, "Redaction," 47.

[225]On Mark's frequent use of introductory καὶ ἐγένετο, see Reiser, *Syntax*, 89.

[226]Cadbury (*Style*, 133-34) cites these examples: Luke 4:42; 8:23,45; 9:34,42,43; 19:36,37; 22:55,60; 24:5. One may also add Luke 8:8; 11:14,29.

[227]Luke 3:15; 6:48; 9:57.

[228]Luke 13:17; 24:36.

[229]One exception is Luke 8:49 where Luke adopts the expression from Mark (5:35).

[230]E.g., Luke 3:15; 4:42; 9:57; 11:14,29.

[231]E.g., ἔλεγον in Luke 4:22 for λέγοντες in Mark 6:2; ἔτιλλον in Luke 6:1 for τίλλοντες in Mark 2:23; ἑστήκασιν in Luke 8:20 for στήκοντες in Mark 3:31; ἔκλαιον in Luke 8:52 for κλαίοντας in Mark 5:38; ἐξήτουν in Luke 11:16 for ζητοῦντες in Mark 8:11; λύετε in Luke 19:33 for λύοντες in Mark 11:5; ἀπεκρίθησαν in Luke 20:7 for ἀποκριθέντες in Mark 11:33; προσεδέχετο in Luke 23:51 for προσδεχόμενος in Mark 15:43.

the same form of the verb is used in reference to the cloud at Sinai in Exod 40:35, ἐπεσκίαζεν ἐπ' αὐτὴν ἡ νεφέλη. This influence may also account for Luke's use of the accusative αὐτούς[232] in place of Mark's dative αὐτοῖς.[233]

The verb φοβέομαι is found frequently throughout Luke's Gospel in material from each of his sources.[234] There are several other instances where it appears in the aorist passive, ἐφοβήθησαν.[235] Its occurrence in Luke 9:34 can be explained as Luke's reformulation of Mark's ἔκφοβοι, a rare word in the NT.[236]

The phrase ἐν τῷ εἰσελθεῖν αὐτοὺς εἰς τὴν νεφέλην is an addition by Luke that may be intended as an allusion to Exod 24:18: καὶ εἰσῆλθεν Μωυσῆς εἰς τὸ μέσον τῆς νεφέλης. The construction ἐν + the dative of the articular infinitive is typically Lucan, as has been demonstrated in vv 29, 33. The verb εἰσέρχομαι appears a number of times in other examples of Lucan redaction of Mark.[237] It is reasonable to conclude that Luke has formulated the phrase ἐν τῷ εἰσελθεῖν αὐτοὺς εἰς τὴν νεφέλην in imitation of the LXX, as he does elsewhere, and with it makes specific the motive for the disciples' fear.

## Luke 9:35

In Luke 9:35 the word order of Mark's ἐγένετο φωνή is inverted. The combination γίνομαι + φωνή occurs four times in Luke's Gospel and four times in Acts.[238] The word order in Luke 9:35 can be explained as an editorial change by Luke of the Marcan tradition reflecting his tendency to alter his source so that the subject is followed by the verb.[239]

Another characteristic of Luke is to insert the participial form of λέγω before direct discourse. The participle λέγουσα in v 35 has been added by Luke, as in

---

[232]Neirynck ("Transfiguration," 264) explains Luke's use of the accusative αὐτούς as "linked with his representation of the cloud, not hanging over the disciples and overshadowing them, but involving reality in which they enter."

[233]Luke does not reproduce the whole LXX phrase since that would make a monotonous three-fold repetition of νεφέλη within one verse.

[234]Luke retains it from Mark in Luke 8:25,35,50; 9:45; 20:19; it is found in Lucan redaction of Mark in Luke 22:2. It comes from Q in Luke 12:4,5(2x),7; and is found in Lucan redaction of Q in: Luke 12:32; 19:21. It occurs in L material: Luke 1:13,30,50; 2:9,10; 5:10; 18:2,4; 23:40.

[235]Luke 2:9; 8:35 (= Mark 5:15); 20:19 (= Mark 12:12); Acts 16:38; 22:29.

[236]The only other occurrence of ἔκφοβός is in Heb 12:21, which is a quote from Deut 9:19.

[237]E.g., Luke 8:30,41,51; 9:46; 11:37; 18:25; 22:3,10,40,46.

[238]Luke 1:44; 3:22; 9:35,36; Acts 2:6; 7:31; 10:13; 19:34. This last example has the same word order, φωνὴ ἐγένετο, as Luke 9:35. But the reverse, ἐγένετο φωνή, occurs in Luke 1:44; Acts 7:31; 10:13.

[239]In addition to Luke 9:35, Cadbury (Style, 152-53) lists these examples as illustrations of such a tendency of Luke: 4:8; 5:13,14,24,34; 9:40; 12:30,34,58; 13:35; 17:2,37; 18:39; 19:36; 20:19,20,25,38; 21:11; 22:61,71; 23:3. On the Marcan order, see Reiser, Syntax, 77-79, 95.

many other instances when he is working from Marcan tradition.[240]

In Luke's version of the transfiguration, the voice from the cloud calls Jesus ὁ ἐκλελεγμένος[241] rather than Mark's designation, ὁ ἀγαπητός. Twice Luke retains ἀγαπητός in his redaction of Marcan tradition.[242] The verb ἐκλέγομαι is used three other times in Luke; twice in L material[243] and once in Luke's redaction of Mark.[244] The adjective ἐκλεκτός is found in Luke 18:7 (in L material) and 23:35 (Lucan redaction of his sources for the passion narrative). Lucan redaction of Mark also accounts for the participial adjective form of ἐκλέγομαι in Luke 9:35.

In v 35 there is another inversion of Mark's word order: the directive of the voice from the cloud is expressed as αὐτοῦ ἀκούετε. This reversal can be explained as a Lucan modification of the Marcan tradition.[245] As is often the case, Luke aligns his wording more closely with that of the LXX, which has αὐτοῦ ἀκούσεσθε in Deut 18:15.[246] Furthermore, Luke may have placed αὐτοῦ in the emphatic position so as to stress the person of Jesus as the greater authority to whom obedience is due.

In sum, all of the differences between Luke 9:33b-35 and Mark 9:5-7 can be accounted for in terms of Lucan redactional changes of the Marcan tradition.

## Luke 9:36

It has been observed that the shift in focus from the disciples back to Jesus in v 36 betrays a seam in Luke's weaving together of his two sources. Verse 36a, καὶ ἐν τῷ γενέσθαι τὴν φωνήν, is of Luke's own composition; v 36b, εὑρέθη Ἰησοῦς μόνος, belonged to the non-Marcan source and was originally joined to v 33a.[247]

The temporal phrase καὶ ἐν τῷ γενέσθαι τὴν φωνήν replaces Mark's v 8a in

---

[240]Examples in which Luke adds a participial form of λέγω before direct discourse to his Marcan source are: Luke 4:21; 7:39; 9:38; 10:25; 13:25; 18:18; 19:38; 20:2,14; 23:3,21.

[241]The best MSS (P⁴⁵·⁷⁵ ℵ B L Ξ 892. 1241 pc vgˢᵗ syˢ·ʰᵐᵍ co) read ἐκλελεγμένος. Some have ἐκλεκτός (Θ 1 pc), but this is a scribal harmonization with Luke 23:35. Others read ἀγαπητός (A C* R W f¹³ M it vgʷʷ sy⁽ᶜ⁾·ᵖ·ʰ Mcion Cl) or ἀγαπητός ἐν ᾧ εὐδόκησα (C³ D Ψ pc boᴹˢ), but this too is due to assimilation with Mark 9:7 and Matt 17:5. The preferred reading is ἐκλελεγμένος since it is the harder reading and is attested in the best MSS. See B. Metzger, *A Textual Commentary on the Greek New Testament* (New York: UBS, 1971) 148.

[242]Luke 3:22 = Mark 1:11; Luke 20:13 = Mark 12:6. It also occurs once in Acts (15:25).

[243]Luke 10:42; 14:7. It also occurs in Acts 1:2,24; 6:5; 13:17; 15:7,22.

[244]In the account of the choosing of the twelve, Luke's rendition is: καὶ ἐκλεξάμενος ἀπ᾿ αὐτῶν δώδεκα (6:13). Mark's account reads: καὶ ἐποίησεν δώδεκα (3:14).

[245]Other instances in which Luke reverses Mark's order to object followed by verb are: Luke 5:21; 8:13,25; 9:5. For a complete list see Neirynck, *Agreements*, 258-59.

[246]Luke's quotation of Deut 18:15 in Acts 3:22 has the wording αὐτοῦ ἀκούσεσθε.

[247]The remainder of v 36 is Luke's summary of Mark 9:9-13, an episode that Luke omits. It is not part of the transfiguration story proper.

order to make a smooth transition to v 36b, which had originally followed the same kind of construction. Luke composed the phrase, as in v 29a, with his frequent formulation, ἐν + the dative of the articular infinitive, and resumed the combination γίνομαι with φωνή from v 35.[248] This follows the same style Luke employed in v 29a. These are clear indications that v 36a is a piece of Lucan composition.

It is not surprising, given Luke's editorial preferences, that he retains nothing of Mark's v 8a. Luke generally avoids emphatic words such as ἐξάπινα[249] as well as compound negatives such as οὐκέτι οὐδένα.[250] Nor does he usually retain the verb περιβλέπομαι when it appears in his Marcan source.[251]

Verse 36b, εὑρέθη Ἰησοῦς μόνος, is best explained as coming from Luke's non-Marcan source. The progression of thought is much better if v 36b is connected with v 33a, as has been proposed. The result of such a connection is that the statement that Jesus was found alone follows the indication of the departure of Moses and Elijah. As for the vocabulary in v 36b, the verb εὑρίσκω is very common in Luke's Gospel and Acts.[252] It is found in material from each of Luke's sources.[253] These data do not provide an indication of the source of εὑρέθη in 9:36. However, the three other examples of the aorist passive of εὑρίσκω in Luke occur in peculiarly Lucan material.[254] In these instances, as well as in 9:36, it is most likely that εὑρέθη was found in Luke's special source.[255]

Luke did not alter the ending of his special source to match that of the Marcan story. He typically avoids using the reflexive pronoun ἑαυτοῦ, and so does not incorporate Mark's μεθ᾽ ἑαυτῶν.[256]

---

[248]Other examples where ἐν + the dative of the articular infinitive are used to resume an immediately preceding phrase with the same verb are found in Luke 8:5; 9:19; 24:15,51.

[249]Cadbury (Style, 118) lists the following as other examples in which Luke omits or tones down emphatic words that are found in Mark: μεγάλη is omitted in Luke 8:23,24,32,56; μέγαν is omitted in Luke 8:25; πολύς is omitted in Luke 4:40, 8:40,42,43.

[250]Cadbury, Style, 201. Other examples in which Luke alters or omits a double negative found in his Marcan source are: Luke 5:14; 8:51; 19:30; 20:21,40; 22:18.

[251]Of the six times Mark uses this verb (Mark 3:5,34; 5:32; 9:8; 10:23; 11:11), Luke keeps it only once (Luke 6:10 = Mark 3:5).

[252]In the Gospel it is found forty-six times and in Acts thirty-four times, in contrast to only ten times in Mark's Gospel.

[253]E.g., from Mark: Luke 19:30,32; 22:13,45; from Q: Luke 7:9; 11:9,10; 12:43; 15:5; from L: Luke 1:30; 2:12,45,46; 4:17; 15:8,9,24,32; 17:18; 18:8; 23:14; 24:23,33; also in Lucan redaction of Mark: Luke 5:19; 6:7; 8:35; 9:12; 19:48; 23:2,4,22; and of Q: Luke 15:4,6.

[254]Luke 15:24,32; 17:18. Also, there are two examples in Acts: 5:39; 8:40.

[255]There may be Septuagintal influence in Luke's use of εὑρέθη, reflecting the Hebrew passive nimsāʾ with the connotation of "be" or "prove to be," as in Luke 17:18. But this observation is inconclusive for determining Luke's source.

[256]Examples in which Luke omits ἑαυτοῦ from Mark are: Luke 5:22; 8:13; 9:12; from Q: Luke 11:26. See further Cadbury, Style, 195.

## G. CONCLUSION

The preceding analyses of Luke's redactional habits confirm the hypothesis that Luke joined two separate traditions to form his version of the story of the transfiguration. Many of the elements in the first half of Luke's narrative (vv 28-33a) are very difficult to explain as conscious redactions by Luke of the Marcan tradition. These elements include unusual vocabulary: ἔξοδος, συνίστημι, διαχωρίζω; atypical expressions: τὸ εἶδος τοῦ προσώπου αὐτοῦ ἕτερον, εἶδον τὴν δόξαν αὐτοῦ, a noncharacteristic formulation for the introduction of Moses and Elijah, indefinite references to characters already named: οἱ σὺν αὐτῷ, and δύο ἄνδρας, and inexplicable differences from Mark: ἡμέραι ὀκτώ, ἀνέβη, ἄνδρες δύο, and αὐτῷ for τῷ Ἰησοῦ. There are no obstacles to the hypothesis that these came from a separate Lucan source. There are three secondary additions in the first half of the narrative. Verses 29c (καὶ ὁ ἱματισμὸς αὐτοῦ λευκὸς ἐξαστράπτων) and 30b (συνελάλουν αὐτῷ) were inspired by the Marcan transfiguration tradition and formulated by Luke to interweave the two separate sources. Verse 32b (ἦσαν βεβαρημένοι ὕπνῳ· διγρηγορήσαντες δε) is Luke's insertion of an element from the Gethesemane tradition.

In the second half of Luke's narrative (vv 33b-35), all the differences from the Marcan account are easily explained as Lucan modifications of Mark's tradition. The conclusion of the Lucan story, v 36b (εὑρέθη Ἰησοῦς μόνος), originally belonged to the non-Marcan source, and was joined by a piece of Lucan composition, v 36a (καὶ ἐν τῷ γενέσθαι τὴν φωνὴν) to the material from the Marcan source. The similarities betweeen the separate traditions that stood behind Luke 9:28-33a,36b and Mark 9:2-4,8b were coincidental agreements that caused Luke to bring the two strands of tradition together to create his composite story of the transfiguration.

From the preceding analyses it is now possible to delineate more precisely the elements that came from the special Lucan tradition and those attributable to Luke's redaction or composition. Those elements that are Lucan redaction of Marcan tradition are underlined.

| L TRADITION | LUCAN REDACTION/COMPOSITION |
|---|---|
| (28) | ἐγένετο δὲ μετὰ τοὺς λόγους τούτους ὡσει |
| ἡμέραι ὀκτὼ παραλαβὼν Πέτρον καὶ Ἰωάννην καὶ Ἰάκωβον ἀνέβη εἰς τὸ ὄρος προσεύξασθαι. | [καὶ] |
| (29) | καὶ ἐγένετο ἐν τῷ προσεύχεσθαι αὐτὸν |
| τὸ εἶδος τοῦ προσώπου αὐτοῦ ἕτερον | καὶ ὁ ἱματισμὸς αὐτοῦ λευκὸς ἐξαστράπτων. |

| L TRADITION | LUCAN REDACTION/COMPOSITION |
|---|---|
| (30) καὶ ἰδοὺ | |
| ἄνδρες δύο | συνελάλουν αὐτῷ |
| | οἵτινες ἦσαν Μωϋσῆς καὶ Ἠλίας |
| (31) οἳ ὀφθέντες ἐν δόξῃ | |
| ἔλεγον τὴν ἔξοδον αὐτοῦ | |
| ἣν ἤμελλεν πληροῦν | |
| ἐν Ἰερουσαλήμ | |
| (32) ὁ δὲ Πέτρος καὶ οἱ σὺν αὐτῷ | ἦσαν βεβαρημένοι ὕπνῳ· |
| | διαγρηγορήσαντες δὲ |
| εἶδον τὴν δόξαν αὐτοῦ | |
| καὶ τοὺς δύο ἄνδρας | |
| τοὺς συνεστῶτας αὐτῷ. | |
| (33) | καὶ ἐγένετο ἐν τῷ |
| διαχωρίζεσθαι αὐτοὺς ἀπ᾽ αὐτοῦ | εἶπεν ὁ Πέτρον πρὸς τὸν Ἰησοῦν· |
| | ἐπιστάτα, καλον ἐστιν ἡμᾶς ὧδε εἶναι |
| | καὶ ποιήσωμεν σκηνὰς τρεῖς, |
| | μίαν σοὶ καὶ μίαν Μωϋσεῖ καὶ μίαν |
| | Ἠλίᾳ, μὴ εἰδὼς ὃ λέγει. |
| (34) | ταῦτα δὲ αὐτοῦ λέγοντος |
| | ἐγένετο νεφέλη |
| | καὶ ἐπεσκίαζεν αὐτούς· |
| | ἐφοβήθησαν δὲ ἐν τῷ εἰσελθεῖν αὐτοὺς |
| | εἰς τὴν νεφέλην. |
| (35) | καὶ φωνὴ ἐγένετο |
| | ἐκ τῆς νεφέλης λέγουσα· |
| | οὗτός ἐστιν ὁ υἱός μου |
| | ὁ ἐκλελεγμένος, |
| | αὐτοῦ ἀκούετε. |
| (36) | καὶ ἐν τῷ γενέσθαι τὴν φωνὴν |
| εὑρέθη Ἰησοῦς μόνος. | |

The conclusion that Luke combined two sources for his account of the transfiguration is supported by the fact that there are other instances in the third gospel where the evangelist fuses more than one source. For example, Luke 4:16-30 appears to be inspired by Mark 6:1-6, from which the wording for Luke 4:16,22,24 is taken, but then is combined with material from a special Lucan source or Lucan composition.[257] Luke 5:1-11 is another example of a pericope that seems to combine both L material and redacted Marcan material.[258]

---

[257]Bultmann, *Geschichte*, 30-31; Fitzmyer, *Luke*, 526-27.

[258]Fitzmyer, *Luke*, 560-61. Perry (*Sources*, 6) regards this example as well as Luke 4:16-30 and 7:36-50 as instances in which Luke has chosen a non-Marcan version of the tradition and substituted it for the Marcan rendition. Perry holds that where two sources contained divergent accounts of the same event, Luke typically selected the one that seemed more reliable rather than attempt to preserve

Likewise, it is possible that Luke 7:36-50 is a story that came essentially from L and that Luke combined this story with details from Mark 14:3-9.[259] Another composite section is Luke 22. M. Soards[260] has demonstrated the complexity of Luke's redactional and compositional technique of combining in this chapter Marcan material with little or no changes, thoroughly redacted Marcan material, oral tradition drawn on by Luke, and Lucan composition. What is evident from these and other examples in Luke's Gospel is that a Lucan pericope that has a Marcan parallel is not always a simple reworking of Mark's tradition by Luke. Rather, Luke sometimes combines material from his own sources with that of Marcan tradition. The hypothesis that this same kind of combining of sources was done by Luke for 9:28-36 is consistent with the evangelist's redactional habits.

## IV. FORM

In addition to the above analyses from the perspective of literary source and redaction/composition criticism, a form-critical examination of Luke 9:28-36 also contributes a crucial piece to the understanding of the tradition history. The transfiguration story is not easily categorized form-critically, as is evident from the lack of scholarly consensus.

### A. PAST ATTEMPTS AT FORM CLASSIFICATION

To classify the transfiguration as a myth is problematic.[258] The same is true of the theory that the transfiguration is a resurrection-appearance story that has been retrojected into the Galilean ministry.[259] Nor is Luke 9:28-36 a Lucan ascension story.[260] Bultmann identifies it as a legend.[261] But the transfiguration story does not have as its purpose purely biographical interest in Jesus as an extraordinary person, as personal legends generally do. Rather, the story, in its final form, aims at conveying the significance of the event for the life and interests of the disciples.

V. Taylor categorizes Luke 9:28-36 as a story about Jesus.[262] Since these stories have, by definition, no common structural form, the usefulness of such a

---

exception, for which Luke did conflate separate sources.

[259]Schramm, *Markus-Stoff*, 44-45. Fitzmyer (*Luke*, 684-85) proposes that although Luke 7:36-50 has many similarities to Mark 14:3-9, the passage is derived on the whole from L and was already conflated in Luke's source.

[260]*The Passion According to Luke. The Special Material of Luke 22.* JSNTSup 14; Sheffield: JSOT, 1987.

[258]See above, chapter one, part III.

[259]See above, chapter one, part II.

[260]See above, chapter one, part V, section C on the theories of R. H. Gause and J. G. Davies.

[261]*Geschichte*, 260-81.

[262]*The Formation of the Gospel Tradition* (London: Macmillan, 1964) 150. Fitzmyer (*Luke*, 795) also adopts this classification.

classification is negligible. The same is true of the identification of the transfiguration as an epiphany story, or as a Christophany.[263] Apart from the element of supernatural disclosure, there is no common factor in NT narratives so classified.[264] Such a vague concept is of little help in form-critical analysis of the transfiguration account.

## B. A NEW PROPOSAL: PREDICTIVE ANGELOPHANY

None of the previous attempts at identifying the form of the transfiguration account is satisfactory for Luke 9:28-36. Past studies have failed to distinguish between source and redaction, and/or have misunderstood the nature and function of the narrative. In the case of the Lucan version, two different forms must be recognized. The story found in the L tradition is a predictive angelophany. The final version created by Luke's combination of his special source with the Marcan tradition is a pronouncement story. Discussion of this final form of Luke 9:28-36 is taken up at the end of chapter three. An analysis of the form of the L material behind Luke 9:28-36 follows.

Throughout biblical tradition and in early Jewish literature, stories abound in which angels figure. First we will outline the identifying terms and characteristics of angels. Then form classifications will be discussed according to the function of the angel.

### 1. Terminology

The most frequently used term for "angel" in the OT is *mal'āk*, "messenger," or *mal'āk YHWH*, "angel of the LORD." In the LXX and in the NT the term is ἄγγελος or ἄγγελος κυρίου. The root meaning of the word is "messenger," i.e., one sent. When the term *mal'āk* or ἄγγελος is used in the OT and the NT, it is immediately understood that the messenger is a heavenly being sent by God.[265]

In some cases the figure that appears is alternatively identified as an angel and as God. For example, in Gen 16:11 the angel of the Lord speaks to Hagar. But in v 13 Hagar names "the LORD who spoke to her." Similarly, in the story of the call of Moses (Exod 3:1-4:16), an angel of the Lord appears to Moses in fire flaming out of a bush (3:2). Then, Gen 3:4 says the Lord saw Moses coming over to look at it, and called out to him from the bush. Likewise, in Judg 6:11-24, the "angel of the LORD," (vv 11,12,20,21[2x],22) alternates with "the LORD," (vv

---

[263]E.g., F. Hahn, *The Titles of Jesus in Christology* (N.Y.: World, 1969) 334-335; Schulz, *Stunde*, 57. Other stories in the same category would be the walking on the water (Mark 6:45-52 and parr.), and the feeding accounts (Mark 6:30-44; 8:1-10 and parr.).

[264]Kee, "Epiphany or Apocalyptic Vision," 151 n.14.

[265]The few exceptions are instances in the OT in which *mal'āk* refers to a prophet (Hag 1:13; Isa 44:26; 2 Chr 36:15), or priest (Mal 2:7) as a messenger of God. Three times in the NT ἄγγελος refers to human messengers: the scouts sent by Joshua to Jericho (Jas 2:25); those sent by John to Jesus to ascertain whether he was the one who was promised (Luke 7:24); and those sent by Jesus to Samaria to prepare for his reception there (Luke 9:52).

14,16,23).

There are a number of examples in which ἀνήρ, often ἄνδρες δύο, or sometimes ἄνθρωπος, denotes a heavenly envoy. In Genesis 18-19 God and two angels appear to Abraham with the message that Sarah would bear him a son. That the τρεῖς ἄνδρες referred to in 18:2 (LXX) are God and two angels becomes clear from 18:1,33; 19:1. Gen 18:1 says that God appeared, and in v 33, that the Lord went on his way. Meanwhile, 19:1 narrates that the two angels (οἱ δύο ἄγγελοι) went on to Sodom. Then throughout chapter 19, the two are referred to interchangeably as ἄνδρες (vv 5,10,12) and ἄγγελοι (vv 1,15,16). This same exchange between ἄνθρωπος/ἀνήρ and ἄγγελος is also found in Josh 5:13, where a man, ἄνθρωπος, appears to Joshua before the battle of Jericho. He then identifies himself as the commander of the Lord's army, i.e., a divine envoy.

In Judg 13:3 "an angel of the LORD" appeared to Samson's mother. In reporting this to her husband, she says, "a man of God came to me" (v 6). She further describes him as having "the appearance of an angel of God, terrible indeed." This alternation between "angel" (Judg 13:9,13,15,16,18,20,21) and "man" (Judg 13:10,11) continues throughout the narrative. In *1 Enoch* 46:1 the heavenly interpreter is first described as "one whose face was like that of a human being." He is then said to be "one from among the angels" (v 2). In Dan 3:95 (LXX) the fourth man of the ἄνδρας τέσσαρας (v 92) is identified as an angel of God.

Heavenly messengers seen by mortals appear in human form. In many cases an angel is identified by radiance or brilliant dress. For example, the man, ἀνήρ, who shows Ezekiel the vision of the restored temple and land (Ezek 40:3,4), is known to be a heavenly messenger by his "appearance . . . of bronze." In 2 Macc 3:26 the two young men, δύο νεανίαι, "remarkably strong, strikingly beautiful, and splendidly attired," are recognizable as agents of God. In *2 Enoch* 1:4, two men appear to Enoch to interpret his dream. The description of them, with shining faces and clothing, the like of which Enoch had not seen on earth (vv 4-5), makes it clear that these are heavenly beings.

In a very few instances the angel is identified by name. In Dan 8:15, one having the appearance of a man, ὡς ὅρασις ἀνθρώπου (LXX)/ἄνδρος (Θ), comes to Daniel to interpret his vision. He is then identified as Gabriel (v 16). This is the same angel who announces the birth of John to Zechariah in Luke 1:8-20 and the birth of Jesus to Mary in Luke 1:26-38. In the book of Tobit (5:4) it is the angel Raphael, appearing as a "young man," who guides Tobiah (5:5).

In Luke-Acts, there are several examples where ἀνήρ connotes angel. In Luke 24:4 the two men, ἄνδρες δύο, at the empty tomb are revealed to be heavenly beings by their brilliant apparel, ἐν ἐσθῆτι ἀστραπτούσῃ. Furthermore, in 24:23 the women's encounter with the two is explicitly called a vision of angels, ὀπτασίαν ἀγγέλων. In the parallel account in Mark 16:5, the figure is a young man, νεανίσκος, identified as a heavenly messenger by his white robe, περιβεβλημένον στολὴν λευκήν. Matthew's messenger (28:2-3) is an angel of the Lord, ἄγγελος κυρίου. In Acts 1:10, two men, ἄνδρες δύο, are heavenly messengers who interpret the ascension. Again, their brilliant clothing, ἐν ἐσθήσεσι λευκαῖς, identifies them as angels. In Acts 10, in Cornelius' vision, a heavenly interpreter is identified alternately as ἄγγελος/ἀνήρ. In Acts 10:3,7 the messenger is first called an angel of God, ἄγγελος τοῦ θεοῦ. But in Cornelius' retelling of the event in 10:30, the figure is described as a man in bright apparel, ἀνήρ . . . ἐν ἐσθῆτι λαμπρᾷ.

It is clear that ἄνδρες, often in a pair, are understood throughout biblical tradition as angels or messengers of God. In the special L source for Luke 9:28-36 the two figures, ἄνδρες δύο, were originally anonymous angels.[266]

## 2. Types of Angelophanies

Stories involving angels can be classified according to the function of the divine envoy. At times angels simply act on God's behalf toward human beings;[267] at other times they speak a message from God. The following analysis will treat only those stories in which divine messengers speak and are said to appear or to be seen. These angelophanies can be further classified according to the nature of the angel's message: a. Mandatory Angelophany; b. Interpretative Angelophany; c. Predictive Angelophany.

### a. Mandatory Angelophany

In mandatory angelophanies the divine messenger is seen and delivers a command from God.[268] There are five elements: (1) Introduction; (2) the angel is seen (expressed with ὁράω in the LXX and NT); (3) the one who sees the angel falls prostrate or reacts in fear; (4) the angel speaks God's command and may give the reason for it; (5) the person to whom it is directed obeys. Examples of such include: the command to Lot to take his family away from Sodom before its destruction (Gen 19:1-22); the mandate of the captain of the host of the Lord to Joshua (Josh 5:13-15); the command to Gad to tell David to erect an altar on the threshing floor of Ornan the Jebusite (1 Chr 21:15-30); and the instruction to Cornelius to summon Peter from Joppa (Acts 10:1-8):

| (1) Introduction | (2) Appearance | (3) Prostration/Fear |
|---|---|---|
| Gen 19:1a | Gen 19:1b | Gen 19:1c |
| Josh 5:13a | Josh 5:13b | Josh 5:14b |
| 1 Chr 21:14-15 | 1 Chr 21:16a | 1 Chr 21:16b |
| Acts 10:1-2 | Acts 10:3 | Acts 10:4 |

---

[266]See Bultmann, *Geschichte*, 279-337.

[267]In the majority of instances, God's angels act to assist human beings, e.g., Gen 24:7,40; Exod 14:19; 23:20-23; 32:34; 33:2; Num 20:16; Ps 91:11-12; Zech 12:8; Dan 3:49; 6:23; Mark 1:13; Matt 4:11; Luke 22:43; Acts 12:6-11. Only in a few examples does God's angel act as an agent of punishment or destruction, e.g., 1 Sam 24:16-17; Acts 12:23. Several NT passages speak of angels who will separate the wicked from the righteous in the end times, e.g., Matt 13:39,41,49; 24:31; Mark 13:27; Rev 14:14-20.

[268]There are angelic command stories in which no visual perception of the angel is narrated, e.g., Gen 21:17-19; 22:9-14; 31:13; 1 Kgs 19:4-8; 2 Kgs 1:3-4,15-16; Acts 5:19-21; 8:26-27.

| (4) Command | (5) Fulfillment |
|---|---|
| Gen 19:12-13,15,17 | Gen 19:14,16 |
| Josh 5:15a | Josh 5:15b |
| 1 Chr 21:18 | 1 Chr 21:19-26 |
| Acts 10:5 | Acts 10:7-8 |

A variation of this type of story is one in which the command involves a call. The pattern for call narratives identified by N. Habel includes these six elements: (1) divine confrontation; (2) introductory word; (3) commission; (4) objection; (5) reassurance; (6) sign.[269] In the case of Exod 3:1-12, the call of Moses, and Judg 6:11-17, the call of Gideon, the divine confrontation is begun with an angelic appearance.

Another variation of mandatory angelophanies is the angelic dream appearance. R. E. Brown has identified the pattern of these stories as found in Matt 1:20-21,24-5; 2:13-15a; 2:19-21.[270] The basic elements are: (1) an introductory resumptive clause that connects the appearance with what precedes (Matt 1:20; 2:13,19); (2) the apparition of an angel of the Lord in a dream (Matt 1:20; 2:13,29); (3) a command given by the angel (Matt 1:20-21; 2:13,20); (4) a reason offered for the command (Matt 1:20-21; 2:13,20); (5) the fulfillment of the command by Joseph, who gets up and does exactly what the angel directed (Matt 1:24-25; 2:14-15a,21).

The function of mandatory angelophanies is to show that God directs the course of salvation history. Through heavenly envoys, God actively intervenes in

---

[269]"The Form and Significance of the Call Narratives," *ZAW* 77 (1965) 297-323. Habel recognizes this pattern in the calls of Moses (Exod 3:1-12), Gideon (Jdg 6:11b-17), Jeremiah (Jer 1:4-10), Isaiah (Isa 6:1-13), Ezekiel (Ezek 1:1-3:15), and Second Isaiah (Isa 40:1-11). See also B. O. Long, "Prophetic Call Traditions and Reports of Visions," *ZAW* 84 (1974) 494-500. B. J. Hubbard (*The Matthean Redaction of a Primitive Apostolic Commissioning: An Exegesis of Matthew 28:16-20* [SBLDS 19; Missoula, MT: Scholars, 1974]) compares the work of Habel with that of J. K. Kuntz (*The Self-Revelation of God* [Philadelphia: Westminster, 1967] and K. Baltzer ("Considerations Regarding the Office and Calling of the Prophet," *HTR* 61 [1968] 567-91) on the form of call stories, and finds that in all stories of this genre there are three essential parts: (1) all have a moment of confrontation between the deity or God's messenger and the individual; (2) all emphasize the word spoken, i.e., the commissioning or call; (3) all view the deity or the divine messenger as in some way giving reassurance or support to the one commissioned. According to him, most stories of this genre have the following elements: (1) introduction; (2) confrontation between the deity and the individual; (3) reaction; (4) commission (this is the central element); (5) protest; (6) reassurance; (7) conclusion. In his work on Matthew, Hubbard applies this schema to Matt 16:16-20 and recognizes its basic form in Matt 28:1-8 and 28:8-10. In a later work, "Commissioning Stories in Luke-Acts: A Study of their Antecedents, Form and Content," *Semeia* 8 (1977) 103-26, Hubbard outlines these seven elements in 29 commission stories from the Hebrew Scriptures, in ten examples from Ancient Near Eastern literature, and in twenty-five NT pericopae, sixteen of which are from Luke-Acts. T. Y. Mullins ("New Testament Commission Forms, Especially in Luke Acts," *JBL* 95 [1976] 603-14) makes a similar analysis of 27 passages from Luke-Acts.

[270]R. E. Brown, *The Birth of the Messiah* (Garden City, N.Y.: Doubleday, 1977) 108. See also G. M. Soares Prabhu, *The Formula Quotations in the Infancy Narrative of Matthew* (AnBib 63; Rome: Biblical Institute, 1976).

the human faith community, calling forth specially chosen agents, and giving specific commands for the well-being of God's people. By formulating these experiences in terms of angelophanies, the biblical writers present the happenings as objective ones,[271] even while an aura of the mystery of the transcendent envelops the scene. The fulfillment of the divine mandates assures the believer of the faithfulness of God, whose word is always brought to completion.

## b. Interpretative Angelophany

In this type of story, angels impart to human beings the divine interpretation of past or present happenings. These stories contain the following six elements: (1) Introduction; (2) the angel appears/is seen; (3) the person falls prostrate or reacts in fear; (4) the divine interpretation is given;[272] (5) other witnesses are mentioned; (6) the departure of either the angel or the recipient(s) of the interpretation. Stories exhibiting this form include: Balaam's journey with the princes of Balak (Num 22:31-35); the encounter of Heliodorus with the angel (2 Macc 3:22-34); the interpretation of the birth of Jesus to the shepherds (Luke 2:8-15);[273] the announcement of the resurrection of Jesus (Matt 28:1-8; Mark 16:1-8; Luke 24:1-9);[274] and Jesus' ascension (Acts 1:6-12).[275]

---

[271]Mullins, "Commission," 612.

[272]Sometimes this is accompanied by a command to tell what one has been given to understand, as in Num 22:35; 2 Macc 3:34; Matt 28:7; and Mark 16:7.

[273]Mullins ("Commission Forms," 603-14) and Hubbard ("Commisioning Stories," 103-26) classify Luke 2:8-20 as a commission form. There is, however, no commission given to the shepherds in the story, but rather an announcement and explanation of the meaning of the birth of Jesus.

[274]In John 20:1-18 the two angels do not interpret the event; rather it is Jesus (v 17) who does so. In her analysis of the empty tomb traditions in Matt 28:1-8; Mark 16:1-8; Luke 24:1-12; John 20:1-13, Perkins (*Resurrection*, 91-93) has charted the common elements found in these stories. The structure that emerges is: a temporal designation is given in the introduction; the recipients of the appearance are named; the place destination is mentioned; a remark is made about the stone; an angelic appearance occurs; there is a description of the clothing of the angel(s); a message is given; the recipients of the appearance depart. Boismard makes a similar analysis of the gospel accounts of the appearances of the resurrected Jesus ("Le réalisme des récits évangéliques," *LumVie* 109 [1972] 31-41) and finds the same schema in them as in the numerous OT angelic appearance stories. Dillon (*Eye-Witnesses*, 184-85) also identifies the angelophany model as operative in Luke 24:36-43. In their classification of Matt 28:1-8 as a commission form, Hubbard ("Commissioning Stories, 103-26) and Mullins ("Commission Forms," 603-14) do not account for the interpretative element of the angel's message. So also for Mark 16:1-8 (Hubbard) and Acts 1:6-12 (Mullins). Neither include Luke 24:1-9 in their analyses.

[275]A related, but slightly different genre are the visions in Ezekiel 40-48; Dan 8:15-12:13; and Zech 1:7-6:15 in which an angel talks with the prophet, interpreting what he sees. Likewise, the angel Raphael in the book of Tobit serves as an interpreting guide to Tobias throughout the entire narrative. In *1 Enoch* and *2 Esdras* are also narrated a series of visions in which an angel accompanies the seer and interprets throughout. Also similar to these examples is the angel that accompanies Hermas, interpreting his visions and parables (*Herm. Vis.* 5:4 through *Sim.* 10.4.5).

| (1) Introduction | (2) Appearance | (3) Prostration/Fear |
|---|---|---|
| Num 22:31a | Num 22:31b | Num 22:31c |
| 2 Macc 3:22-24 | 2 Macc 3:25,26,33 | 2 Macc 3:27 |
| Matt 28:1 | Matt 28:3 | Matt 28:4,5 |
| Mark 16:1-4 | Mark 16:5 | Mark 16:5 |
| Luke 2:8 | Luke 2:9a,b | Luke 2:9c |
| Luke 24:1-3 | Luke 24:4 | Luke 24:5 |
| Acts 1:6-9 | Acts 1:10 | |

| (4) Interpretation | (5) Witnesses[276] | (6) Departure |
|---|---|---|
| Num 22:32-33 | Num 22:35 | Num 22:35 |
| 2 Macc 3:33-34 | 2 Macc 3:34 | 2 Macc 3:34 |
| Matt 28:6 | Matt 28:7,8 | Matt 28:8 |
| Mark 16:6 | Mark 16:7 | Mark 16:8 |
| Luke 2:10b-12 | Luke 2:13 | Luke 2:15 |
| Luke 24:6-7 | Luke 24:9 | Luke 24:9 |
| Acts 1:11 | Acts 1:13-15 | Acts 1:12 |

The function of an interpretative angelophany is to clarify the meaning of some past or present occurrence in the divine drama of salvation and to emphasize its importance. The appearance of an angel conveys the impression of an objective experience, thus making the interpretation given by the angel indisputable. Furthermore, the heavenly messenger relates the divine perspective on the earthly happenings. In this way the biblical author makes it eminently clear to the readers what explanation of the narrated events they are to adopt. The addition of other witnesses to the one(s) to whom the disclosure is originally made serves to further ratify the truth of the divine interpretation.

### c. Predictive Angelophany

Predictive Angelophanies follow essentially the same form as Interpretative Angelophanies but are distinct from the latter in that the event being interpreted is future, rather than past or present. The first three elements are the same:
(1) Introduction; (2) the angel appears/is seen; (3) the person falls prostrate or reacts in fear. The fourth element combines both prediction and interpretation of the future event. Two additional components are found in this form:
(5) protestation or questioning of the prediction; and (6) reassurance, sometimes involving a sign. The narrative concludes with (7) the mention of further witnesses; and (8) departure.
Belonging to this category are: the prediction of the birth of Ishmael (Gen

---

[276]In 2 Macc 3:34 the witnesses are those who will hear the proclamation that Heliodorus is commanded to make. Similarly in Mark 16:7 and Matt 28:7,8 the disciples to whom the women will tell the good news are the further witnesses.

16:1-16); the announcement of the birth of Isaac to Abraham and Sarah (Gen 18:1-
16); the announcement of the birth of Samson (Judg 13:2-23); the prediction of
Enoch's ascension (2 Enoch 1:1-10); the announcement of the birth of John the
Baptist (Luke 1:5-23); and the announcement to Mary of Jesus' birth (Luke 1:26-
38).[277]

| (1) Introduction | (2) Appearance | (3) Prostration/Fear |
|---|---|---|
| Gen 16:1-6 | Gen 16:7,13 | |
| Gen 18:1 | Gen 18:1,2 | Gen 18:2 |
| Judg 13:2 | Judg 13:3a,20 | Judg 13:20,22 |
| 2 Enoch 1:1-3 | 2 Enoch 1:4-6 | 2 Enoch 1:7 |
| Luke 1:5-10 | Luke 1:11 | Luke 1:12 |
| Luke 1:26-27 | Luke 1:28 | Luke 1:29 |

| (4) Prediction/Interpretation | (5) Protestation/Questioning |
|---|---|
| Gen 16:10-12,14 | Gen 16:13 |
| Gen 18:10,14 | Gen 18:12 |
| Judg 13:3-5 | Judg 13:12,17 |
| 2 Enoch 1:8b | |
| Luke 1:13b-17 | Luke 1:18 |
| Luke 1:31-33,35 | Luke 1:34 |

| (6) Reassurance | (7) Witnesses[278] | (8) Departure |
|---|---|---|
| | Gen 16:15 | |
| Gen 18:14 | Gen 18:18 | Gen 18:16 |
| Judg 13:20,23 | Judg 13:6 | Judg 13:20 |
| | 2 Enoch 1:9 | 2 Enoch 1:10 |
| Luke 1:19-20 | Luke 1:21-22 | Luke 1:23 |
| Luke 1:35-37 | Luke 1:36 | Luke 1:38 |

A predictive angelophany, like an interpretative angelophany, enables the
reader to understand a future event as mandated by God and as playing a crucial
role in the divine plan for salvation. Often the prediction concerns the birth of a
key salvific figure, and interprets his role, as in Gen 16:1-16; Gen 18:1-16; Judg

---

[277]The foretelling of the safe landing for Paul and his fellow sailors in the shipwreck off the coast
of Malta in Acts 27:21-31 exhibits essentially the same form. We do not include this example
because the visual perception of the angel is not recounted. Mullins ("Commission," 603-14) and
Hubbard ("Commissioning Stories," 115-23) identify Luke 1:5-23 and 1:26-38 as commission
stories. However, this classification fails to account for the interpretive element in the angel's
proclamation.

[278]In 2 Enoch 1:9 the witnesses are those who will hear the proclamation that Enoch is commanded
to make.

13:2-23; Luke 1:5-23,26-38.[279] The elements of questioning or protestation highlight the improbability of the predicted event in human terms; the reassurance underlines the awesome power of God who will accomplish it. Thus, the reader is directed to move from dismay and doubt to the affirmation, "nothing will be impossible for God" (Luke 1:37). These two elements are not prevalent in interpretative angelophanies, since in those, the event is already at hand or past. There is no incredulity regarding its occurrence; it is the meaning that must be explained. In predictive angelophanies, both the possibility of the event as well as its significance are at issue.

The L material of Luke 9:28-33a,36b is precisely in the form of a predictive angelophany.[280] (1) The introduction in v 28 sets the stage for (2) the appearance of the two heavenly beings in vv 30-31. Appearing as men (ἄνδρες δύο), they are recognizable as angels by their glorious appearance (οἳ ὀφθέντες ἐν δόξῃ). (3) The element of prostration or fear is not found in this story. It is inappropriate for Jesus to fear or bow down before angels.[281] (4) The prediction and divine interpretation are found in v 31, where the two envoys speak of Jesus' "exodus" that is to be fulfilled in Jerusalem. (5-6) The elements of questioning and reassurance are lacking. Luke reserves these for his agony scene, where Jesus kneels and prays that the cup be taken away from him. An angel appears to strengthen him (22:41-43). (7) The witnesses are Peter and those with him (v 32; in v 28 "those with him" were identified as John and James). (8) The departure of the messengers is related in v 33a.

---

[279]R. E. Brown has identified a formulaic pattern for angelic appearances that are annunciations of birth (*Birth*, 155-59. See Table VIII on p. 156). In his analysis of Gen 16:7-12; 17:1-21; 18:1-12; Judg 13:3-23; Luke 1:11-20,26-37; Matt 1:20-21, he discerns five standard elements: (1) the appearance of the Lord/an angel of the Lord; (2) a reaction of fear or prostration; (3) the divine message; (4) an objection or a request for a sign; (5) the giving of a sign. Within component (3) Brown delineates eight other recurring elements (*Birth*, 156). See also S. Muñoz-Iglesias, "Los Evangelios de la Infancia y las infancias de los héroes," *EstBib* 16 (1957) 329-83, who finds the same literary pattern in these birth announcements and in the stories of the calls of Moses (Exod 3:1-12) and Gideon (Judg 6:11-17).

[280]Murphy-O'Connor ("Transfiguration," 17) rightly identifies the two men in Luke 9:30,32 as "explaining angels." To better understand the function of the story that stood in the L source, we distinguish between stories in which angels explain past or present happenings (Interpretative Angelophanies) from those in which the event interpreted lies in the future (Predictive Angelophanies). See the following who have recognized the function of Moses and Elijah as interpreting angels: M. Goguel, "Notes d'histoire évangélique. Esquisse d'une interprétation du récit de la transfiguration," *RHR* 81 (1920) 150; Léon-Dufour, "Transfiguration," 115; P. Seidensticker, *Die Auferstehung Jesu in der Botschaft der Evangelisten. Ein traditionsgeschichtlicher Versuch zum Problem der Sicherung der Osterbotschaft in der apostolischen Zeit* (SBS 27; Stuttgart; Katholisches Bibelwerk, 1967) 49 n. 4. E. Grässer (*Das Problem der Parusieverzögerung in den synoptischen Evangelien und in der Apostelgeschichte* [BZNW 22; Berlin: Töpelmann, 1957] 185) sees their role as divine messengers.

[281]Heb 1:5-14 elaborates the theme of Christ's superiority to the angels.

The recognition of Luke 9:28-33a,36b as a predictive angelophany[282] confirms the source analysis made above.   It also provides an important understanding of the original intent of the story.   The angelophany is a literary device that emphasizes the importance and clarifies the meaning of Jesus' "exodus" in the divine drama of salvation.[283]   The heavenly messengers signal the advent of this crucial event and interpret it as mandated by God.   Luke's reader is thus given to understand that the anomaly of a Messiah who must suffer (Luke 24:26) is exactly in accord with the plan of God.

Another important aspect of this narrative is the portrait of Jesus that it puts forth.   Jesus is not fearful at the appearance of the heavenly messengers.   Being himself God's messenger *par excellence*, he is quite at home in the world of heavenly envoys.   Nor is there protestation or questioning on his part, because the function of these elements is to show the unreadiness of the recipient of the message.   The story portrays Jesus' readiness to take the next step of his mission: he will set his face toward Jerusalem (Luke 9:51), where his "exodus" will be accomplished.

In its final form Luke's account is no longer purely a predictive angelophany. By incorporating details from the Marcan tradition, Luke has converted his narrative into a pronouncement story.   This final form and function will be discussed in the following chapter.

## V. MARK VIS-A-VIS LUKE

With the assertion that two separate sources stand behind Luke 9:28-36, the question arises whether these two sources represent two different stages of development of the same underlying tradition, or whether they were entirely unrelated on a literary level before they were brought together by Luke.

An hypothesis that explains the tradition history of the Lucan narrative in terms of layers of development of the same basic tradition rather than the fusing of entirely separate traditions is that of Murphy-O'Connor.[284]

He proposes that Luke 9:28-33a,36b reflects the most primitive version of the transfiguration story.   It consists of two basic parts, a factual part that tells of Jesus' face changing (v 29) and an interpretive part (v 31) that explains the reason for the change.   Murphy-O'Connor suggests that Mark became aware of this primitive account in a somewhat garbled form, that contained this much of the story: "Accompanied by a small group of disciples, Jesus went up a mountain; there

---

[282]See P. Fiedler's examination of the formula καὶ ἰδού (*Die Formel "und siehe" im Neuen Testament* [STANT 20; Munich: Kösel, 1969] 37), which demonstrates that Luke's use of the phrase is deliberately evocative of OT apparitions that are also introduced with καὶ ἰδού.

[283]When the two figures, ἄνδρες δύο, and then later, Moses and Elijah, are understood as a literary device used to clarify and highlight the significance of what is being narrated, a host of questions on the level of the historicity of the event disappears.   Such questions as how the two men, or Moses and Elijah, got there, or how the disciples recognized them as the two long-dead characters from the OT, are not relevant.

[284]"Transfiguration," 8-21.

he underwent a luminous change and encountered two men who spoke with him."[285] The layers of fact and interpretation were no longer distinguished in this version, and, according to Murphy-O'Connor, Mark added another layer of interpretation to the story to fill it out. In this added interpretation Mark brings the disciples to the fore, portrays the change in Jesus' face as affecting his whole person, extending even to his clothes, identifies the two men as Elijah with Moses, and gives an apocalyptic flavor to the whole story. To explain the present form of Luke's story in 9:28-36, Murphy-O'Connor proposes that a later editor added Marcan details to the original Lucan story to bring it into line with Mark's.

This hypothesis has several points in its favor. To begin with, it eliminates the need to explain the number of verbal similarities between Luke 9:28-30 and Mark 9:2-4 as coincidental. According to Murphy-O'Connor's hypothesis, these similarities would exist because the two accounts are redactions of the same basic tradition. This hypothesis would explain, for example, the provenience of ὤφθη in Mark 9:4, which appears nowhere else in Mark's Gospel.

Also supporting Murphy-O'Connor's thesis is the ability to explain most details in Mark 9:2-4 in terms of Marcan redaction of the tradition that stands behind Luke 9:28-33a,36b. For example, in Mark 9:2, a change of ἡμέραι ὀκτώ to ἡμέρας ἕξ can be explained as an intended allusion to the length of time Moses spent on Mount Sinai, suggested by the mention of ὄρος. The verb παραλαμβάνει could be Mark's editorial alteration of παραλαβών, reflecting his consistent preference for the historical present[286] and for finite verb forms.[287] The specification of ὁ Ἰησοῦς as the subject in Mark 9:2 is consistent with Marcan style. The name of Jesus appears eighty times in Mark's Gospel and could be an addition by Mark in this instance, as well as in v 4. As for the definite article τόν, in several other instances where the names of Peter, James, and John appear in Mark's Gospel in the accusative, τόν precedes them.[288] This use of the definite article could be attributed to Marcan redaction. A change of ἀνέβη to ἀναφέρει αὐτούς could be accounted for in terms of Mark's frequent use of φέρω and its compounds.[289]

The addition of the pronoun αὐτούς can be explained by a theological motive of shifting the focus of the story to the disciples. This shift could also account for ἔμπροσθεν αὐτῶν in v 2 and ὤφθη αὐτοῖς in v 4.[290] Mark's penchant for vivid

---

[285]*Ibid.*, 19. That Mark knew the complete primitive version contained in Luke 9:28-33a,36b Murphy-O'Connor considers very unlikely, since no good reason can be given for Mark's elimination of the references to prayer, the mention of Jesus' face, and the content of the conversation between Jesus and the two figures.

[286]See BDF §321.

[287]Of the six instances that the verb παραλαμβάνω appears in Mark's Gospel, five times it is found in the finite form: 4:6; 5:40; 7:4; 9:2; 14:33. The aorist participle occurs once in 10:32.

[288]Mark 5:37; 14:33,67.

[289]Mark 1:32; 2:3; 4:8; 6:27,28; 7:32; 8:22; 9:17,19,20; 11:2,7; 12:15,16; 15:1,22.

[290]Murphy-O'Connor ("Transfiguration," 14-15) regards this shift in focus as a telltale sign that the story is later than that behind Luke 9:28-33a,36b. The tendency of the tradition, he says, is that a

details makes it plausible that he would add the adjective ὑψηλός to describe ὄρος. The phrase κατ᾽ ἰδίαν can also be attributed to Marcan redaction. This phrase appears six other times in Mark's Gospel.[291] The combination of κατά + μόνος would not be unusual for Mark, as 4:10 shows. It is also possible to understand μετεμορφώθη as a Marcan expansion of τὸ εἶδος τοῦ προσώπου αὐτοῦ ἕτερον. To extrapolate from the face to the whole person is quite understandable.[292] There are instances where πρόσωπον denotes "form" or "figure"[293] since the face controls the whole appearance. Also, one might note the close association of the nouns εἶδος and μορφή in classical Greek. The two were nearly synonymous and could be interchanged.[294] They were frequently used together to express the concept of kind and form, with μορφή denoting the form of the appearance and εἶδος the appearance as a whole.[295] Perhaps by this association Mark could have converted a change in εἶδος into a change in μορφή.

Once having specified the change in Jesus as something other-worldly with the term μετεμορφώθη, the way would have been paved for Mark to expand on the description with apocalyptic elements. In 9:3, the expression καὶ τὰ ἱμάτια αὐτοῦ ἐγένετο στίλβοντα λευκὰ λίαν could well have been inspired by other descriptions of glistening garments in Jewish apocalyptic.[296] The noun ἱμάτιον is a frequent one in Mark's Gospel,[297] and is used three other times by Mark to refer to Jesus' clothing.[298] Mark 9:3 is the only instance of the verb στίλβω in the NT, but it appears in the apocalyptic imagery of Dan 10:6 (Θ) and Nah 3:3, from which Mark may have adopted it. The adjective λευκός is also found frequently in apocalyptic literature. White garments are tokens of heavenly existence and symbolize victory and purity.[299] For Mark to add such a description of Jesus' clothes in his redaction of the transfiguration story would be quite understandable against this background. The adverb λίαν could also be attributed to Mark's hand; it occurs

---

more primitive story about an incident that happened to Jesus is reinterpreted in later tradition in light of its meaning and impact on disciples.

[291]Mark 4:34; 6:31,32; 7:33; 9:28; 13:3.

[292]See above, on 9:29 for expressions where πρόσωπον connotes the whole person or personal presence.

[293]See E. Lohse, "πρόσωπον," TDNT 6 (1968) 769.

[294]H. Cremer, Biblisch-theologisches Wörterbuch des neutestamentlichen Griechisch (rev. J. Kögel; Stuttgart: Perthes, 1923) 389, 736. See LSJ, 482, 1147. Also nearly synonymous are ὄψις, which appears in Theodotion's version of Dan 3:19, where the LXX has μορφή, and ὅρασις, which appears in LXX Dan 5:6, where Θ has μορφή.

[295]E.g., Plato, Rep. 2. 380, ἀλλάττειν τὸ αὑτοῦ εἶδος εἰς πολλὰς μορφάς; Plutarch, Mor. 1013 C, ἡ δὲ μορφὴν καὶ εἶδος τῷ γενομένῳ παρέσχε. See also John 5:37, where εἶδος is translated as "form" in the NRSV and NAB. The NJB erroneously translates it "shape."

[296]E.g., Dan 7:9; Herm. Vis., 1,2,2; Sim. 8,2,3; 1 Enoch 62:16; 2 Enoch 22:8; 2 Esdr 2:39-44.

[297]Mark 2:21; 5:27,28,30; 6:56; 9:3; 10:50; 11:7,8; 13:16; 15:20,24.

[298]Mark 6:56; 15:20,24.

[299]E.g., Rev 3:5; 7:9.

three other times in his Gospel.[300]   Mark's description continues with οἶα
γναφεὺς ἐπὶ τῆς γῆς οὐ δύναται οὕτως λευκᾶναι. A clause introduced with οἶα
may be identifiable as Marcan, since another such example is found in Mark 13:19.
Likewise, the expression ἐπὶ τῆς γῆς, the verb δύναμαι, and the adverb οὕτως
could be regarded as Marcan.[301]  Thus the whole of Mark 9:3 could be explained
as Marcan redaction of Luke's special tradition.

Mark's identification of the two figures as Elijah and Moses in 9:4 is
explained by Murphy-O'Connor as having been suggested by ὄρος. The mountain
would call to mind Mount Sinai, with which both Moses and Elijah were associated
(Exod 19:34; 1 Kings 19). The placement of Elijah's name before that of Moses
paves the way for the discussion about the coming of Elijah in Mark 9:9-10.
Mark's frequent use of the periphrastic imperfect[302] explains the provenience of
the expression ἦσαν συλλαλοῦντες.

According to Murphy-O'Connor, vv 5-8 are Mark's interpretation of the
sketchy form of the story he received.   Mark moves the disciples to the forefront
of the story so that the import of the event for Jesus' followers becomes clearer.
He borrows the idea of tents (v 5) and the cloud (v 7) as symbols for God's
presence, from the Exodus narrative (15:13; 16:10; 19:9; 26:21). He also adds his
favorite theme of the lack of comprehension of the disciples (v 6). The voice and
its message are taken from the baptism tradition (Mark 1:11).   Most of the
vocabulary from vv 5-8 is found in other instances in Mark's Gospel.[303]   These
data could be used to support the proposition that vv 5-8 were composed by Mark
as his interpretation of the same tradition that underlies Luke 9:28-33a,36b.

In sum, a comparison of the differences between Mark 9:2-4 and Luke
9:28-33a,36b shows that most variations in Mark could be attributed to Marcan
redaction of the L tradition behind Luke 9:28-33a,36b. Some exceptions remain,
most notably, the references to Jesus' prayer (Luke 9:28,29) and the content of the
conversation between Jesus, Moses, and Elijah (Luke 9:31-33a). Since Mark
makes mention of Jesus' prayer elsewhere (1:35; 6:46; 14:32,35,38,39), it is
unlikely that he would omit such a reference if it were contained in his source.
Similarly, no good explanation can be given as to why Mark would eliminate the
conversation between Jesus, Moses, and Elijah, since it contains important

---

[300]Mark 1:35; 6:51; 16:2.

[301]The expression ἐπὶ τῆς γῆς occurs nine other times in Mark: 2:10; 4:1,26,31(2x); 6:47; 8:6;
9:20; 14:35. In the accusative, ἐπὶ τὴν γῆν, it is found in 4:20; 6:53; 15:33. The verb δύναμαι
appears thirty-two other times: 1:40,45; 2:4,7,19; 3:20,23,24,25,26,27; 4:32,33; 5:3; 6:5,19;
7:15,18,24; 8:4; 9:22,23,28,29,39; 10:26,38,39; 14:5,7; 15:31. There are nine other instances of
οὕτως in Mark: 2:7,8,12; 4:26; 7:18; 10:43; 13:29; 14:59; 15:39.

[302]BDF §353.

[303]The formulation ἀποκριθείς. . . λέγει is found in Mark 3:33; 8:29; 9:19; 10:24; 11:22,33; 15:2;
ῥαββί in 10:51; 11:21; 14:45; καλός in 4:8,20; 7:27; 9:42,43,45,47,50; 14:6,21; ὧδε in 6:3; 8:4;
9:1; 11:3; 13:2,21; 14:32,34; 16:6; περιβλέπομαι in 3:5,34; 5:32; 10:23; 11:11; οὐκέτι + οὐδείς
in 5:3; 7:12; 12:34; 15:5. Examples of οὐδείς with other negatives are found in 3:27,37; 6:5; 11:2;
12:14,60,61; 15:4; 16:8. Two other instances of οὐκέτι are: Mark 10:8; 14:25. The phrase μεθ'
ἑαυτῶν also occurs in 8:14; 14:7.

theological development. The best explanation is that these details were absent from the form of the tradition that Mark received, as Murphy-O'Connor asserts.

## VI. AGREEMENTS OF LUKE AND MATTHEW AGAINST MARK

Having reached the conclusion that Luke was dependent on both the Marcan tradition and a special Lucan source, a question remains whether there was any direct relationship between Luke and Matthew in the formulation of their respective versions of the transfiguration.

What prompts speculation that there was cross-influence between Luke and Matthew is that there are a number of apparent agreements between the two against Mark. These are as follows:

**Luke 9:28 / Matt 17:1**

- lack of τόν before the names Ἰωάννην and Ἰάκωβον;
- lack of μόνους;

**Luke 9:29 / Matt 17:2**

- mention of Jesus' face: τοῦ προσώπου αὐτοῦ / τὸ πρόσωπον αὐτοῦ;
- a different formulation from Mark's ἐγένετο στίλβοντα λευκὰ λίαν: to ἐγένετο λευκὸς ἐξαστράπτων / ἐγένετο λευκὰ ὡς τὸ φῶς;
- lack of Mark's phrase οἷα γναφεὺς ἐπὶ τῆς γῆς οὐ δύναται οὕτως λευκᾶναι;

**Luke 9:30 / Matt 17:3**

- introductory καὶ ἰδού rather than Mark's καί
- placement of Μωϋσῆς before Ἠλίας;
- use of καί rather than σύν to connect the names of Moses and Elijah;
- συνελάλουν / συλλαλοῦντες rather than Mark's periphrastic ἦσαν συλλαλοῦντες
- a pronoun, αὐτῷ / μετ᾽ αὐτοῦ, rather than Mark's τῷ Ἰησοῦ

**Luke 9:33 / Matt 17:4**

- use of εἶπεν rather than Mark's λέγει;
- another title of address, ἐπιστάτα / κύριε, than Mark's ῥαββί;

**Luke 9:34 / Matt 17:5**

- use of a genitive absolute construction: ταῦτα δὲ αὐτοῦ λέγοντος / ἔτι αὐτοῦ λαλοῦντος;
- a finite form, ἐπεσκίαζεν / ἐπεσκίασεν, rather than Mark's participle ἐπισκιάζουσα;
- αὐτούς where Mark has αὐτοῖς;

**Luke 9:34 / Matt 17:6**

- use of ἐφοβήθησαν in contrast to Mark's ἔκφοβοι ἐγένοντο;

**Luke 9:35 / Matt 17:5**

- introductory formula with λέγουσα;
- variation from Mark's ὁ ἀγαπητός:
  ὁ ἐκλελεγμένος / ὁ ἀγαπητός, ἐν ᾧ εὐδόκησα;

**Luke 9:36 / Matt 17:8**

- lack of Mark's ἐξάπινα, οὐκέτι, ἀλλά, μεθ᾽ ἑαυτῶν

How are these apparent agreements to be explained? This question is part of a larger problem of how agreements of Matthew and Luke against Mark are to be accounted for in the context of the whole source problem for the synoptic gospels. The solutions offered are as varied as the number of hypotheses for the resolution of the synoptic problem.[304] The agreements have been explained in terms of coincidental independent redactions by Luke and Matthew of Mark,[305] reliance by Luke and Matthew on a common non-Marcan source,[306] dependence of Luke and Matthew on a different recension of Mark[307] or a proto-Marcan text,[308] accidental corruption of the Marcan text,[309] conflation by Mark of the texts of Matthew and Luke,[310] dependence of Matthew on Luke,[311] dependence of Luke on Matthew,[312] and influence from oral tradition.[313]

---

[304]For a more complete survey, see T. A. Friedrichsen, "The Matthew-Luke Agreeements Against Mark. A Survey of Recent Studies: 1974-1989," *L'Évangile de Luc* (Ed. F. Neirynck; Leuven: University Press, 1989) 335-91 and Neirynck, *Agreements*, 11-48.

[305]E.g., Fitzmyer, *Luke*, 792; Neirynck, "Transfiguration," 253-66; J. Schmid, *Matthäus und Lukas: Eine Untersuchung der Verhältnisse ihrer Evangelien* (Freiburg: Herder, 1930).

[306]Schramm, *Markus-Stoff*, 72-77.

[307]Hawkins, *Horae*, 208-12; W. Sanday, "The Conditions Under Which the Gospels Were Written, in their Bearing Upon Some Difficulties of the Synoptic Problem," *Studies in the Synoptic Problem* (ed. W. Sanday; Oxford: Clarendon, 1911) 21.

[308]Boismard, *Synopse* 1. 30-32, 2. 252.

[309]B. H. Streeter, *The Four Gospels: A Study in Origins* (London: Macmillan, 1964) 315-16.

[310]Mann, *Mark*, 52-53.

[311]For some passages: C. G. Wilke, *Der Urevangelist, oder exegetisch-kritische Untersuchung über das Verwantschaftsverhältnis der drei ersten Evangelien* (Dresden: Fleischer, 1838) 460-62.

[312]B. C. Butler, "St. Luke's Debt to St. Matthew," *HTR* 32 (1939) 237-308; A. Farrer, "On Dispensing With Q," *Studies in the Gospels. Essays in Memory of R. H. Lightfoot* (ed. D. E. Nineham; Oxford: Blackwell, 1955) 55-86; Gundry, *Matthew*, 346; N. Turner, "The Minor Verbal Agreements of Matthew and Luke against Mark," *International Congress on "The Four Gospels in 1957," Oxford, 1957* (SE 1; TU 73; Berlin: Akademie, 1959) 223-34.

With regard to the transfiguration accounts, all of the similarities listed are minor, although there are two that are generally given more attention than the others: the mention of Jesus' face: τοῦ προσώπου αὐτοῦ (Luke 9:29) / τὸ πρόσωπον αὐτοῦ (Matt 17:2); and the genitive absolute constructions: ταῦτα δὲ αὐτοῦ λέγοντος (Luke 9:34) / ἔτι αὐτοῦ λαλοῦντος (Matt 17:5). A close examination of these two expressions shows them to be only apparent agreements.[314]

In the reference to Jesus' face, the wording and description in the two accounts is quite different. Matthew's description of Jesus' face shining like the sun elaborates on Mark's brief μετεμορφώθη.[315] Luke's statement is that Jesus' facial expression changed. Luke says nothing about Jesus' face shining; his description is not a development of μετεμορφώθη. Matthew's καὶ ἔλαμψεν τὸ πρόσωπον αὐτοῦ ὡς ὁ ἥλιος is best explained as a piece of Matthean redaction that is an echo of Matt 13:43, with possible allusions to Exod 34:29-30,35; Rev 1:16; and Dan 10:6.[316] The provenience of Luke's τὸ εἶδος τοῦ προσώπου αὐτοῦ ἕτερον is most plausibly explained in terms of a separate non-Marcan source.

The genitive absolute constructions used by Matthew and Luke are also worded quite differently[317] and have distinct functions. Luke's formulation uses the verb λέγω, whereas Matthew's employs λαλέω. Matthew's particle ἔτι links the genitive absolute expression closely to the preceding direct speech and emphasizes the abruptness of the arrival of the cloud. Luke's version, on the other hand, begins with ταῦτα. Without ἔτι the simultaneity conveyed by Matthew's formulation is not emphasized quite as much. Furthermore, the connection with Peter's speech is interrupted in Luke's account by the intervening μὴ εἰδὼς ὃ λέγει. Luke's genitive absolute designates the beginning of a new section and thus functions quite differently from Matthew's. There are enough differences in these two Matthean and Lucan constructions to outweigh the similarities and to support

---

[313]A. G. DaFonseca, Quaestio Synoptica (3d ed.; Institutiones biblicae; Rome: Biblical Institute, 1952); Kümmel, Introduction, 76-80; Marshall, Luke, 381.

[314]Neirynck, "Transfiguration," 253-66; Schmid, Matthäus und Lukas, 122. Streeter (Gospels, 315-16) attributes these two agreements to textual corruption. In the first example, he proposes that the original Marcan text had: καὶ ἐγένετο στίλβον τὸ πρόσωπον καὶ τὰ ἱμάτια αὐτοῦ λευκὰ λίαν. As for the genitive absolute, he hypothesizes that it represents a line in the original text of Mark that has dropped out. Lagrange (Luc, lxxi-lxxiii) regards this latter agreement as an exceptional case of Matthean dependence on Luke. Both of these explanations seem forced.

[315]S. McLoughlin ("Les accords mineurs Mt-Lc contre Mc et le problème synoptique: Vers la théorie de deux sources," De Jésus aux évangiles: Tradition et rédaction dans les évangiles synoptiques [BETL 25; ed. I. de la Potterie; Gembloux: Duculot, 1967] 29-30) argues that Mark's text needs correction. He maintains that to say that Jesus was transfigured and then to immediately describe his clothing is rather odd. More expected would be a depiction of his person or his face. Streeter (Gospels, 316) also remarks on the strangeness of the lack of mention of Jesus' face in Mark's account.

[316]See above, chapter one, part IV.B for the parallels identified by Sabbe between Matt 17:1-9 and Daniel 10. See also Boismard, Synopse 2.250, and Murphy-O'Connor, "Transfiguration," 12.

[317]Actually, the only word the two have in common is αὐτοῦ. As McLoughlin ("Accords," 27) remarks, if Matthew and Luke are using a common source, one of them did not follow it very carefully.

the conclusion that each evangelist redacted his sources independently.

The same can be said for other so-called agreements. In many of the supposed agreements, the formulations of Matthew and Luke are far from identical. In Luke the definite article τόν is absent before all three proper names; in Matthew it is present before Πέτρον. Both Matthew and Luke describe Jesus' clothing in a way different from Mark, but their descriptions are quite distinct. Matthew and Luke do not have the same verb tense of συνλαλέω, nor do they have they same case of the pronoun found in place of Jesus' name in their parallels to Mark 9:4. The title of address on the lips of Peter to Jesus is different for Matthew and Luke. The forms used by the two evangelists of the verb ἐπισκιάζω are not identical, nor is the wording for the description of the disciples' fear. The variations from Mark's ὁ ἀγαπητός are not the same, and the final verses in Matthew's and Luke's versions are not formulated alike.

The supposed agreements between Luke and Matthew against Mark in the transfiguration narratives are very few and most are only apparent and superficial. If there were some cross-influence between Matthew and Luke, one would expect a much closer correspondence between the two accounts than is evident. In the preceding analyses of the accounts of Matthew and Luke, each of the elements listed as a so-called agreement has been adequately explained in terms of the individual evangelist's treatment of his sources. There is no compelling reason to resort to a hypothesis of cross-influence between Matthew and Luke. The best explanation remains that the supposed minor agreements between Matthew and Luke against Mark in the transfiguration accounts are only apparent and are due to coincidental independent redaction by Matthew and Luke of their sources. That two authors from like backgrounds living in a similar milieu and writing at approximately the same time would formulate some analogous expressions is not surprising.

## VII. CONCLUSION

The analysis of the internal consistency of Luke 9:28-36 revealed several tensions and inconsistencies in Luke's narrative with regard to the focus, the means of referring to the two figures, the unclarity of who perceived whose glory, and the sleepiness of the disciples. These are indications of redactional seams which provide the evidence that Luke combined two separate sources for his narrative of the transfiguration. Behind vv 28-33a,36b stands a non-Marcan tradition unique to Luke. To this Luke joined the Marcan tradition of the transfiguration, which is reflected in vv 33b-35. To weave together the two separate traditions, he also composed several linking phrases.

A verse-by-verse comparison of Luke's account vis-à-vis Mark's confirmed the hypothesis that Luke used two separate traditions for his transfiguration story. Most of the variations between Luke 9:28-33a,36b and Mark 9:2-4,8b are not satisfactorily explained as Lucan redactional changes of Mark. A better solution is that Luke was using a different source for these verses. On the other hand, the differences between Luke 9:33b-36a and Mark 9:5-8a can be adequately explained in terms of Lucan composition and redaction of Mark.

The hypothesis of a separate L source for 9:28-33a,36b was confirmed by a form-critical analysis. This revealed that the peculiarly Lucan story conforms to the pattern of a predictive angelophany. The question of whether the two sources behind Luke 9:28-36 were related on a literary level before they were brought together by Luke was examined. It was found that many of the differences between Mark 9:2-8 and Luke 9:28-33a,36b could be explained in terms of Marcan redaction and composition. Thus, it is possibile that Mark 9:2-8 and Luke 9:28-33a,36b represent two different stages of development of the same underlying tradition.

As for the relationship between Luke and Matthew, an examination of their supposed agreements against Mark showed that these are actually very few and are, for the most part, only apparent. Similarities between the narratives of Luke and Matthew as opposed to Mark are due to coincidental independent redaction of their sources by the two evangelists.

The question of how Luke understood the traditions that he combined for his transfiguration story will be the subject of the next chapter. The context and function of the final form of Luke 9:28-36 will be discussed, followed by a detailed exegesis of each verse.

# CHAPTER THREE

## EXEGESIS OF LUKE 9:28-36

### I. INTRODUCTION

In the preceding chapter the analysis of the tradition history of Luke 9:28-36 led to the conclusion that Luke combined two separate sources to create his version of the transfiguration story. This chapter will deal with the question of how Luke understood the two traditions that he fused and what meaning he intended to convey through his composite narrative. A discussion of the context, function, and final form of the narrative precedes the verse-by-verse exegesis.

### II. CONTEXT AND FUNCTION

In the wide context of Luke-Acts, angelic appearances are used to signal events of great import that occur at significant turning points. Angelophanies mark the annunciation of the birth of John the Baptist (1:5-23), the birth of Jesus (1:26-38; 2:8-20), his resurrection (24:1-11), and his ascension (Acts 1:6-12). So too the transfiguration, set in the form of a predictive angelophany, announces an important turning point in the Gospel, one that concerns Jesus' ministry. In the Gospel of Luke, Jesus' ministry is divided into three phases: the Galilean ministry (4:14-9:50), the journey to Jerusalem (9:51-19:27), and the Jerusalem ministry (19:28-21:38).[1] The transfiguration narrative is the hinge between the first and second of these phases. In Acts 1:6-12 and 10:1-8 the same device of an angelic appearance is used by Luke to mark turning points in the ministry of Jesus' first followers. At the ascension (1:6-12) the disciples learn that a new stage is beginning in which they must take Jesus' mission "to the ends of the earth" without Jesus being bodily present. The appearance of the angel in Cornelius's vision (10:1-8) heralds the beginning of Peter's mission to the gentiles. So too the transfiguration episode, situated at a turning point in Jesus' ministry, provides essential clues to the meaning of his mission.

There are important links between Luke's transfiguration story and other key episodes in his Gospel.[2] There are obvious correlations between the transfiguration story and the account of Jesus' baptism (3:21-22). In both Jesus is at prayer (3:21; 9:28,29), the heavenly voice calls Jesus "Son" (3:22; 9:35), and the term εἶδος appears (3:22; 9:29). The temptation account (4:1-13) sounds chords that will resound in the transfiguration story. In both, Jesus' sonship and how that is to be understood are at the root of the episode. The devil's concept of "Son of God" is

---

[1] H. Conzelmann, *The Theology of St. Luke* (Philadelphia: Fortress, 1961) 193-94.

[2] These have been highlighted by A. Trites in "The Transfiguration in the Theology of Luke: Some Redactional Links," in *The Glory of Christ in the New Testament. Studies in Christology* (Ed. L. D. Hurst and N. T. Wright; Oxford: Clarendon, 1987) 71-81. Trites points out that these correlations are evident particularly in Lucan redactional material and therefore are not accidental.

one who is able to perform miraculous works in order to satisfy his own needs (4:3) and who will not have to undergo death because God's angels would guard him from any harm (4:9-11). By contrast, in the transfiguration account, God's heavenly messengers are precisely the ones who underscore that Jesus' death is the fulfillment of his sonship (9:31,35).

References to glory are prominent in both passages. There is a contrast drawn between the false glory of all the kingdoms of the world (4:6) and that of God's chosen one (9:32) and God's heavenly agents (9:31). Luke also links the nativity story (2:9,14,32), the entrance into Jerusalem (19:38), and the coming of the Son of Man at the parousia (9:26; 21:27) with references to δόξα. Jesus' entrance into each phase of his mission is marked with glory: his incarnation, his final days of earthly existence, and his coming again. The transfiguration signals the beginning of Jesus' journey toward the final phase of his mission, wherein the necessity of suffering in order to enter into his glory (24:26) is made clear.

The transfiguration strongly echoes elements of the episode of Peter's declaration of Jesus as Messiah (Luke 9:18-22). The prayerfulness of Jesus is highlighted (9:18; 28) and the necessity of his passion (9:22,31) figure prominently in both. Both occur in the company of some of Jesus' disciples (9:18,28). In both, the meaning of Jesus' identity and mission is the crux of the pericope (9:18-20,22,31,35). In both the disciples are silent about the revelation (9:21,36).

The links of the transfiguration story with the agony scene are strong, particularly in the emphasis on Jesus' prayer (9:28,29; 22:40,41,44,45,46), the sleepiness of the disciples (9:32; 22:45), and the imminence of Jesus' passion (9:31; 22:40,42).

The resurrection accounts also recall elements from the transfiguration story: two men (9:30; 24:4), dazzling apparel (9:29; 24:4), the understanding of Jesus' messiahship as the way through suffering and death to glory (9:31; 24:26,46), the role of Moses and the prophets as interpreters (9:30,31; 24:27), the desire of the disciples to remain (9:33; 24:29), the theme of fulfillment (9:31; 24:44), the importance of listening to Jesus (9:36; 24:27,32,44,45) and the centrality of Jerusalem (9:31; 24:33,47,49). This careful construction of links backward and forward throughout the whole of the Gospel shows the centrality of the transfiguration story and provides the framework for understanding the Lucan Jesus' identity and mission.

In the immediate context of Luke's chapter nine, the transfiguration episode comprises one of several responses to Herod's question, "Who is this?" (Luke 9:9).[3] The question of Jesus' identity had been recurring since 5:21, where it was first posed by Pharisees and teachers of the law. In 7:19-20, it is reiterated by John the Baptist's disciples; in 7:49, by those who were at table in the home of Simon the Pharisee; and in 8:25, by Jesus' disciples, after the calming of the storm. The answers to this question are given, some explicitly and some implicitly, in the nine episodes in Luke 9 that follow Herod's question.

---

[3]See further J. A. Fitzmyer, "The Composition of Luke, Chapter 9," *Perspectives on Luke-Acts* (ed. C. H. Talbert; Special Studies Series 5; Danville, VA: Association of Baptist Professors of Religion, 1978) 139-52; Ellis, "Composition," 193-200.

In the first episode, the feeding of the five thousand (vv 10-17), an implicit answer is given by way of the miracle. The feeding demonstrates what is stated in Acts 2:22: that Jesus is "a man attested by God with mighty works and wonders and signs." In the second episode, Peter's confession (vv 18-21), an explicit answer is given: Jesus is the anointed one of God, ὁ χριστὸς τοῦ θεοῦ. In the third segment, the first announcement of the passion and the sayings about discipleship (vv 23-27), the further answer provided to Herod's question is that Jesus is the suffering Son of Man. Closely linked with the previous episode, this identification serves as a corrective to the notions that the disciples had of Jesus' messiahship.

The transfiguration, the fourth episode (vv 28-36), gives both an implicit and an explicit answer to Herod's question. The voice from the cloud in v 35 gives the explicit identification of Jesus as "my chosen Son." The implicit identification is found in the juxtaposition of Jesus with Moses and Elijah: Jesus stands in continuity with these OT figures, yet now supersedes them as the one in whom God's saving action is manifest.

In the fifth episode, the cure of the possessed boy (vv 37-43a), the same implicit answer is given in this miracle as in the first episode: Jesus is the one in whom the majesty of God is made manifest. The sixth scene, the second announcement of the passion (vv 43b-45), reiterates the answer given in episode three: Jesus is the Son of Man who is to be handed over. The seventh vignette, the argument among the disciples over greatness (vv 46-48), supplies an implicit identification of Jesus as one who is sent and who nevertheless identifies himself with the lowliness of a child. In the eighth episode, concerning the strange exorcist (vv 49-50), Jesus is called ἐπιστάτης, a title that implies his mastery and authority. The final segment, the introduction to the travel account that relates the disciples' reaction to the inhospitable Samaritans (vv 51-56), provides a concluding answer to Herod's question with the title κύριος.

Thus the nine episodes in Luke 9:10-56 produce a series of christological statements in answer to Herod's question, "Who is this?" Some of the answers are implicit and others are explicit; some are exclusively Lucan, and some reflect Luke's reworking of Marcan motifs. The transfiguration account, like the episode of Peter's confession, stands out as containing some of the most important christological affirmations in this string of episodes. Just as the annunciation of Jesus' passion in 9:22 serves as a corrective to Peter's declaration of Jesus' messiahship in 9:20, so too the transfiguration scene confirms Jesus' identity as ὁ χριστὸς τοῦ θεοῦ but also corrects the disciples' understanding of what Jesus' messiahship entails. Followers of Jesus are to comprehend that his sonship is played out as the servanthood of God's chosen one, whose way through suffering and death leads to glory. The two heavenly figures confirm Jesus' identity as God's unique chosen one and herald a turning point in Jesus' ministry. Jesus is now to embark on the path to Jerusalem, where his "exodus" will fulfill God's saving plan.

## III. FORM

The final form of Luke 9:28-36 is that of a pronouncement story. Pronouncement stories were first defined by V. Taylor as stories that "culminate in a saying of Jesus which expresses some ethical or religious precept."[4] More recently, R. Tannehill has examined the rhetorical function of these stories, and provides this definition: "A pronouncement story is a brief narrative in which the climactic (and often final) element is a pronouncement which is presented as a particular person's response to something said or observed on a particular occasion of the past."[5] Tannehill delineates two main parts of a pronouncement story: "the pronouncement and its setting, i.e., the response and the situation provoking that response. The movement from the one to the other is the main development in these brief stories."[6] Everything in the story points to the climactic pronouncement, which "makes a final impression on the reader or hearer, without the distraction of statements which qualify or contradict."[7]

Tannehill identifies six types of pronouncement stories: (1) correction stories; (2) commendation stories; (3) objection stories; (4) quest stories; (5) inquiry stories; (6) description stories. There are also "hybrids" that combine elements from more than one of the subtypes. Although neither Tannehill nor Taylor classify the transfiguration as a pronouncement story, it does correspond in every way to the first type, the correction pronouncement story.[8] In this type of story two attitudes are contrasted. In the stimulus part of the narrative, someone takes a position that may seem innocent or even commendable. The story reaches its culmination as this position is corrected by the responder. Located in the climactic final position, this correction makes the lasting impression, thus inviting the reader or hearer to align their position with that of the corrector. The function of such a story is to challenge one to move from one value stance to another.[9]

In Luke 9:28-36, the setting is provided in vv 28-33a. The trip up the mountain, the change in Jesus, and the conversation with Moses and Elijah lead to Peter's statement in v 33b, "Master, it is good that we are here; let us make three tents: one for you and one for Moses and one for Elijah." The attitude reflected by Peter's exclamation is that Jesus is on a par with the OT giants Moses and Elijah.[10] The pronouncement in v 35, "This is my chosen Son; listen to him," uttered by the voice from the cloud, corrects Peter's position. It challenges him and the subsequent hearers and readers of the transfiguration story not to see Jesus only as one more in the long line of Jewish prophets and leaders, but to adopt the divine position, understanding Jesus as the unique, chosen one, and to pledge sole

---

[4]*Formation*, 63.

[5]R. C. Tannehill, "Introduction: The Pronouncement Story and Its Types," *Semeia* 20 (1981) 1.

[6]*Ibid.*, 1.

[7]*Ibid.*, 3.

[8]In Taylor's definition, the pronouncement is made by Jesus. The transfiguration, with its pronouncement made by the heavenly voice, is classified by Taylor as a "story about Jesus," which has no real standard form. Tannehill, who looks not only at NT pronouncement stories, but also stories in Greek literature of the Roman period, does not define the type in terms of Jesus doing the pronouncing. By his definition, the transfiguration episode fits the type on all counts.

[9]R. C. Tannehill, "Varieties of Synoptic Pronouncement Stories," *Semeia* 20 (1981) 105.

[10]See below in the detailed exegesis of 9:33.

allegiance to him.

## IV. DETAILED EXEGESIS

In the ensuing verse-by-verse exegesis, attention will be given to the meaning and function of each detail of the narrative. At times details in 9:28-33a,36b take on a different significance in the final form of the narrative than they had in their original form in the non-Marcan tradition. Such differences will be discussed, while at the same time the aim will be to achieve an overall understanding of the pericope as it now stands.

### Luke 9:28

The opening phrase of Luke's story, ἐγένετο δὲ, is a frequently used Lucan introduction and sets the narrative off as a distinct new pericope. The expression that follows, μετὰ τοὺς λόγους τούτους, can be understood in two different ways: "after these sayings," or "after these things." The latter translation would reflect Semitic influence, giving λόγους the broader connotation that corresponds with the Hebrew děbārîm.[11] Luke uses λόγος in this sense in Luke 1:4; Acts 8:21; 15:6. However, in the case of 9:28, it is probable that the more literal meaning was intended, "after these words/sayings." Immediately preceding the transfiguration narrative, there is in Luke 9:21-27, a string of sayings of Jesus that expands on the passion prediction and its implications for his disciples. The expressions τοὺς ἐμοὺς λόγους in 9:26 and τοὺς λόγους τούτους in 9:44 refer literally to Jesus' words. With the close connection to these two references, it is more likely that the same literal connotation is intended for τοὺς λόγους τούτους in 9:28.[12]

The translation of the phrase τοὺς λόγους τούτους as "these words/sayings" also serves to make the transfiguration narrative itself more cohesive in its final form. The story begins with a reference to Jesus' words in v 28 and then reaches its climax with the heavenly instruction to listen to/obey him in v 35. There are many times in Luke's Gospel where λόγος is used to refer to Jesus' words,[13] but the connection between his words and the word of God is not always stated explicitly. It is a connection that becomes clear only as the gospel story unfolds. Amazement and wonderment by all at Jesus' words in Luke 4:22,32,36 prepare the way for the link between Jesus' words and the word of God to be made in 5:1; 8:21; and 11:28.

The importance of Jesus' words is stressed in Luke 6:47; 9:26,44; 21:33; 24:44, where Jesus gives his disciples fuller instruction on his words themselves. The proper response of a disciple who hears (ἀκούει) Jesus' words is to do/obey (ποιεῖν) them (6:47; 8:21). Two examples of believers who adhere to Jesus' words

---

[11]As also Luke's use of ῥήματα in 1:65; 2:19,51; Acts 5:32; 13:42 and the singular ῥῆμα in Luke 1:37; 2:15.

[12]The translations of the NRSV, "after these sayings," the NAB, "after he said this," and the NJB "after this had been said," all reflect this understanding.

[13]4:22,32,36; 6:47; 7:7; 9:26,44; 10:39; 20:20; 21:33; 24:19,44.

are the centurion whose request of Jesus is simply "say the word," εἰπὲ λόγῳ (7:7), and Mary, who listens to his word, ἤκουεν τὸν λόγον αὐτοῦ (10:39). These figures contrast with the scribes and chief priests and their spies in 20:20, who take hold of Jesus' words in order to deliver him up to the governor. The theme of hearing and doing/obeying the word of God as perceived in Jesus' words is graphically emphasized by the reference in 9:28 to Jesus' words, τοὺς λόγους τούτους, and the command of the heavenly voice, αὐτοῦ ἀκούετε, in 9:35.

Several attempts at a theological interpretation of Luke's time designation have been made. B. D. Chilton suggests that ἡμέραι ὀκτὼ clinches a connection with the Sinai events.[14] In the Jerusalem Targum of Exod 24:11 it is said of Nadab and Abihu, Moses' companions, that after seeing the glory of the Lord, a stroke awaited them on the eighth day for a retribution to destroy them. Chilton sees Luke's "eight days" as a deliberate redactional change of Marks's "six days" intended to evoke this targumic interpretation of the Sinai tradition. This explanation strains the limits of credibility. The date of the Targum is much later than that of the Gospel of Luke and cross-influence from that tradition is highly questionable. Furthermore, even if one were to grant such an influence, it is difficult to see what kind of parallel this would be. And, if Luke intended an allusion to the Sinai event, why would he make it so obscure? Why would he not adopt "six days" as in the Marcan tradition?

Another interpretation is that ἡμέραι ὀκτὼ fits a Lucan schema of emphasis on a theology of the eighth day. The importance of this day is reflected in several OT customs. The rite of circumcision was prescribed for the eighth day after birth.[15] Offerings to God from the fullness of one's harvest were to be made on the eighth day (Exod 22:29-30). The obligations for the feast of Tabernacles included the provision that on the eighth day a holy convocation be held and an offering by fire be presented to God (Lev 23:36). The eighth day (Num 6:10) marks the end of the period of purification for a Nazirite who has become defiled. Luke mentions a similar period of purification in Acts 21:27.

One other reference to eight days in the NT is found in John 20:26, where μεθ' ἡμέρας ὀκτὼ is used to situate the resurrected Jesus' appearance to Thomas and the disciples. The phrase is translated as "a week later"[16] by a method of reckoning that includes the beginning and end of a period. This understanding is reinforced for John 20:26 by sy[s] which adds the Syriac equivalent of the Greek τῇ μιᾷ ἑτέρων σαββάτων to μεθ' ἡμέρας ὀκτὼ, explicitly interpreting μεθ' ἡμέρας ὀκτὼ as the first day of the next week, that is, the next Sunday. The phrase may well reflect the liturgical practice of the early Christian community,[17] which had

---

[14]"Transfiguration," 121. The opposite suggestion has also been made (Danker, *Jesus and the New Age*, 197), that Luke deliberately changed ἡμέρας ἕξ to avoid an analogy to Moses, since Jesus is not portrayed as a second Moses in Luke's Gospel. But then the question remains: why the change to "eight"?

[15]See Gen 17:12; 21:4. Luke reflects this in 1:59.

[16]Brown, *John*, 2. 1025; R. Schnackenburg, *The Gospel According to St. John* (3 vols.; New York: Seabury, 1968, 1980, 1982) 3. 331.

[17]Schnackenburg, *John*, 3. 331.

established Sunday, the first day (= the eighth day), as the Lord's day in contrast to the Jewish sabbath.[18] In light of this Johannine example, the suggestion can be made that ἡμέραι ὀκτὼ in Luke 9:28 has a similar significance.

These attempts at a theological explanation for ἡμέραι ὀκτὼ are not persuasive. The transfiguration narrative has no connection with circumcision, or an offering of firstfruits, or a period of purification. An allusion to the feast of Tabernacles is unlikely in light of the fact that the way Peter's proposition about erecting tents is expressed in Luke 9:28-36 implies that the suggestion was made at the end of the festivities instead of at the beginning.[19] Nor is there anything else in Luke's transfiguration story that indicates that the evangelist intended to reflect early Christian liturgical practice as is suggested for John 20:26.

There are further reasons why a reference to the eighth day of resurrection such as John 20:26 is unlikely. First, there is no resurrection appearance narrated by Luke that is said to take place after eight days such as that in John. In Luke, the announcement of the resurrection to the women takes place on the first day of the week, τῇ δὲ μιᾷ τῶν σαββάτων (24:1). The appearance to the two on the way to Emmaus also happens that very day, ἐν αὐτῇ τῇ ἡμέρᾳ (24:13), as does the final appearance to the disciples. This last appearance occurs as the two who encountered Jesus on the way to Emmaus are still reporting the happening to the others, ταῦτα δὲ αὐτῶν λαλούντων αὐτὸς (24:36). Thus μετὰ ἡμέραι ὀκτὼ in 9:28 would not evoke a Lucan reference to a resurrection appearance.

Nor is the expression an allusion to the resurrection itself, which is always referred to as occurring on the third day (9:22; 18:33). Furthermore, such a reference runs counter to Luke's redactional activity with regard to the material following the transfiguration account. Luke has omitted the Marcan sequel to the story (Mark 9:9-10 = Matt 17:9) in which the topic of resurrection from the dead is brought to the fore. Although resurrection is mentioned by Luke in 9:22, the primary emphasis in the sayings preceding and following the transfiguration (9:21-29 and 9:44) is on the passion. In sum, these theological explanations of ἡμέραι ὀκτὼ, based on the presupposition that Luke changed ἡμέρας ἓξ of Mark, are not tenable.

A much simpler explanation is that Luke retained ἡμέραι ὀκτώ from his special source, and added ὡσεὶ to construct a phrase that links the transfiguration story to the preceding episode of Peter's confession of faith and to Jesus' subsequent instruction to his disciples. The adverb ὡσεί indicates that the time reference is approximate, as also in Luke 22:59 and 23:44. The whole phrase ὡσεὶ ἡμέραι ὀκτώ is an imprecise time designation meaning "about a week later." The sy[s] MS of John 20:26, as explained above, supports this interpretation. Interestingly, in current colloquial speech in modern Greece, the same expression

---

[18] A later pseudepigraphical writing contains a similar reference. *Barn.* 15:9 asserts: διὸ καὶ ἄγομεν τὴν ἡμέραν τὴν ὀγδόην εἰς εὐφροσύνην, ἐν ᾗ καὶ ὁ Ἰησοῦς ἀνέστη ἐκ νεκρῶν καὶ φανερωθεὶς ἀνέβη εἰς οὐρανούς, "We celebrate with gladness the eighth day in which Jesus also rose from the dead and appeared and ascended into heaven."

[19] Danker, *Jesus and the New Age*, 198.

is still so used.[20]

Luke frequently introduces new pericopae with temporal designations expressed in terms of ἡμέραι.[21] These time markers are imprecise, i.e., they are not to be interpreted as giving a factual, historical chronology.[22] They simply serve to aid the flow of the narration. In the case of ὡσεὶ ἡμέραι ὀκτώ in 9:28, it, too, is an inexact time reference that forms part of the introductory setting for the narrative.[23]

The remainder of v 28, [καὶ] παραλαβὼν Πέτρον καὶ 'Ιωάννεν καὶ 'Ιάκωβον ἀνέβη εἰς τὸ ὄρος προσεύχεσθαι, completes the setting of the stage for the story. The focus is on Jesus' action of ascending the mountain to pray. This is accomplished by the use of the verb ἀνέβη in the singular and the subsequent description of what happens to Jesus. The basic meaning of the verb ἀναβαίνω is spatial and it is so used elsewhere in Luke. In 2:4, it is used for Joseph's going up to Judea; in 2:42; 18:31 and 19:28 for going up to Jerusalem;[24] in 18:10 for going up to the temple; in 5:19, for ascending the roof with the paralytic; and in 19:4 for Zacchaeus' climbing of the tree. In 24:38, ἀναβαίνω occurs in a figurative sense for questions that arise.

The expression εἰς τὸ ὄρος occurs four other times in Luke's Gospel: 6:12; 21:21,37; 22:39. In the last two examples, it refers specifically to the Mount of Olives. In the other instances, τὸ ὄρος is probably a stereotyped phrase meaning "the mountains," or "the hill country," rather than one particular mountain.[25] In

---

[20]*Ibid.*, 198.

[21]E.g., 1:5: ἐγένετο ἐν ταῖς ἡμέραις 'Ηρῴδου; 1:24: μετὰ δὲ ταύτας τὰς ἡμέρας; 1:39; 6:12: ἐν ταῖς ἡμέραις ταύταις; 2:1: ἐν ταῖς ἡμέραις ἐκείναις; 2:22: ὅτε ἐπλήσθησαν αἱ ἡμέραι; 4:16: ἐν τῇ ἡμέρᾳ τῶν σαββάτων; 4:42: γενομένης δὲ ἡμέρας; 5:17; 8:22; 20:1: ἐν μιᾷ τῶν ἡμερῶν; 9:37: τῇ ἐξῆς ἡμέρᾳ; 9:51: ἐν τῷ συμπληροῦσθαι τὰς ἡμέρας τῆς ἀναλήμψεως; 22:66: ἐγένετο ἡμέρα; 24:13: ἐν αὐτῇ τῇ ἡμέρᾳ.

[22]Thus, attempts to identify the mountain by the distance able to be traveled in eight days from Caesarea Philippi are erroneously based.

[23]Some scholars have interpreted the phrase as a precise dating, the only such found in a pericope outside of the passion and resurrection narratives. They conclude from this that the narrative was originally part of a tradition about a postresurrection appearance. However, even if ὡσεὶ ἡμέραι ὀκτὼ were interpreted as a precise date, the premise that it is the only exact temporal reference given in the Gospel outside of the passion and resurrection narratives is incorrect. In Luke 2:21 is found καὶ ὅτε ἐπλήσθησαν αἱ ἡμέραι ὀκτὼ, in 2:46 μετὰ ἡμέρας τρεῖς, and in 4:2 ἡμέρας τεσσεράκοντα. For further reasons why the transfiguration account was not originally a resurrection-appearance story, see above, chapter one, part II.

[24]There is still a basically spatial meaning involved in these references, since Jerusalem is a city on a hill. J. Schneider ("ἀναβαίνω," *TDNT* 1 [1964] 519-22) sees a cultic nuance as well, following the use of the Hebrew *'âlâ*.

[25]In Luke, ὄρος is always accompanied by the definite article, but this does not denote a particular mountain. See Zerwick, *Biblical Greek*, §167 on εἰς τὸ ὄρος as a stereotyped phrase for "hill country." The traditional site of the transfiguration is Mount Tabor, but this tradition goes back only to the fourth century C.E. The presence of a fortress there is mentioned by Josephus in *J.W.* 2.20.6; 14.1.8 and poses a challenge to its identification as a place for solitude and prayer. Other suggestions include Mount Hermon and Mount Meron. However, any identification of a specific

the Galilean setting of the transfiguration story, τὸ ὄρος designates the hilly ring surrounding Lake Gennesaret. In Luke 6:12 and 22:39-46, as in 9:28, τὸ ὄρος is a place of prayer. Elsewhere in Luke, mountains function as an obstacle to the Lord's coming (3:5),[26] a place from which the Nazarenes want to throw Jesus (4:29), a place where swine graze (8:32), a place of refuge (21:21), and either a covering in time of catastrophe or a destructive force (23:30).

The Mount of Olives is represented by Luke as the point of entry into Jerusalem (19:29,37), the place where Jesus would lodge for the night after teaching all day in the temple (21:37, and implied in 22:39), the place of the ascension (implied in 24:50 and made explicit in Acts 1:12), and as a place of prayer (22:39-46).

The one other mountain mentioned in Lucan writings is Mount Sinai (Acts 7:30-38), which is described as the place of the apparition of an angel to Moses, where he heard the voice of the Lord and received living oracles. It is possible that in the final form of the transfiguration narrative, with its mention of Moses and Elijah in vv 30,33, τὸ ὄρος is meant as an evocation of Mount Sinai. Such a reference would place the revelation at the transfiguration over against those that took place on Mount Sinai for Moses and Elijah. In this way, what Luke would convey would be both a continuity with and a replacement of the former covenant.

Whether or not there is an allusion to Mount Sinai, τὸ ὄρος does connote a place of close proximity to God. Pagan sanctuaries were customarily built upon hills or mountains (e.g., Deut 12:2). Many encounters with God are portrayed as taking place on mountains in the OT.[27] In the NT, in Mark 6:46; Matt 14:23; Luke 6:12; 9:28, Jesus is said to go to the mountain/hill country, εἰς τὸ ὄρος, to pray. Luke makes it explicit in 9:28 that τὸ ὄρος is intended as a place for encounter with God. The hill country provides solitude and separation from the crowd, as 9:37 indicates, for a time of more intense communion with God.

The mention of τὸ ὄρος can also carry an apocalyptic connotation. This dimension comes to the fore in the Book of Revelation.[28] Mark (13:3) and Matthew (24:3) use the Mount of Olives as the setting for Jesus' apocalyptic discourse. Luke 23:30 speaks of mountains in an apocalyptic context. In the transfiguration narrative, τὸ ὄρος can be regarded as one of many apocalyptic elements, among which are also apparitions, brilliant clothing, a heavenly voice, fear, mysterious dialogues, sleep, and divine esteem for elect visionaries.[29]

Jesus' desire for prayer is given as the motive for his ascent into the hill country. The theme of prayer, both that of Jesus and that of pious Jews before him and Christian disciples after him, is a predominant one in Luke-Acts. The opening scene of the Gospel takes place in the context of Jewish communal prayer (1:10).

---

mountain is pure conjecture and is not necessary if τὸ ὄρος is understood generally as "hill country."

[26]Luke 3:5 is an allusion to Isa 40:4, where mountains are an obstacle to the returning exiles.

[27]E.g., Exod 19:20; 34:2,29; Deut 10:1; 11:29; 1 Sam 7:1; 1 Kgs 18:42; 1 Chr 16:39-40.

[28]E.g., 6:14; 8:8; 16:20; 17:9; 21:10.

[29]See above, chapter one, part IV. B. on Jewish Apocalyptic, for specific references for these apocalyptic elements.

Following that, pious individuals are depicted at prayer, such as Zechariah (1:8-23) and Anna (2:36-38). In 5:33, the prayer of John the Baptist's disciples is mentioned. Jesus himself is portrayed by Luke as being at prayer in 3:21; 5:16; 6:12; 9:18,28; 10:21-23; 22:32; 23:39-46. Jesus' instruction to his disciples on prayer is relayed in 6:28; 10:2; 11:1-4; 20:45-47; 21:36; 22:40,46, and in parables in 11:5-13; 18:1-8,9-14. In Acts, the early Christians are portrayed as constantly at prayer (Acts 1:14,24; 2:42,46,47; 3:1; 6:4,6; 8:15; 9:11,40; 10:9,30; 11:5; 12:12; 13:3; 14:23; 16:25; 20:36; 21:5; 22:17; 28:8).[30]

In the Gospel, Luke shows Jesus at prayer especially at critical turning points: at his baptism (3:21), before his choice of the twelve (6:12), before Peter's confession of him as the Messiah (9:18), at the transfiguration (9:28), before his arrest on the Mount of Olives (22:39-46), and on the cross (23:46). In this way, Luke emphasizes Jesus' intimate union with God and the unfolding of the course of Jesus' life and ministry in accord with God's saving plan. In his writings, Luke converts a practice of Jewish piety into a prime characteristic of Christian life.[31]

The motive for Jesus' ascent to the mountain is explictly given as that of Jesus' own prayer. What transpires at the transfiguration is placed in the context of Jesus' communion with God. The disciples are on the periphery. The participle παραλαβών makes Peter, John, and James parenthetical to the main action, of which Jesus is the subject. This trio of disciples appears two other times in Luke. In 5:10, at the call of the first disciples, James and John are introduced as Simon's partners, and in 8:51, these three are the only ones permitted to enter Jairus's house with Jesus. Although Peter, John, and James are more frequently singled out in Mark's Gospel,[32] Luke does preserve the tradition in 8:51 and 9:28 that these three are particularly privileged witnesses.

In Luke 8:51; 9:28; Acts 1:13, the Lucan order of the names, with John preceding James, may reflect the fact that Luke is writing after John has become the better known,[33] since James has already died (Acts 12:2). Luke's juxtaposition of John's name with Peter's reflects the close association of the two in the early church, as seen in Acts 3:1,3,4; 4:13,19; 8:14.[34] Luke also pairs Peter and John in the Gospel in 22:8, where Jesus sends the two to prepare for the passover supper.

Some commentators see a parallelism between Jesus' selection of Peter, John, and James and Moses' selection of Aaron, Nadab, and Abihu as his companions in

---

[30]See R. O'Toole, *The Unity of Luke's Theology. An Analysis of Luke-Acts* (Good News Studies 9; Wilmington, DE: Glazier, 1984) 72-73.

[31]See further Fitzmyer, *Luke*, 244-47 and his bibliography on the Lucan theme of prayer, 268-69.

[32]In 4:38, in the incident of the healing of Peter's mother-in-law, Luke does not name the three as does Mark in his parallel pericope (1:29). This may be so because in Luke's Gospel the disciples have not yet been called. Nor are the three singled out in Luke's account of the agony (22:39-46) as they are in Mark 14:33. One more instance of the trio's being treated separately occurs in Mark 13:3, where their question prompts Jesus' apocalyptic discourse.

[33]Plummer, *Luke*, 250.

[34]Fitzmyer, *Luke*, 749, 798.

Exod 24:1,9.[35]   This allusion is possible in the final form of the narrative. However, the question then arises whether this symbolism is supposed to be operative in every instance in which Peter, John, and James appear together, a very unlikely proposition.

In the tradition behind Luke 9:28-33a,36b, Peter, John, and James functioned simply as witnesses of a transformation that took place in Jesus during an experience of his communion with God in prayer. In the final form of the story, they become active participants in the drama (vv 33b-35) and the revelation becomes directed to them.

## Luke 9:29

The opening phrase καὶ ἐγένετο ἐν τῷ προσεύχεσθαι αὐτὸν resumes προσεύξασθαι from v 28. The backdrop has been set for the happening that takes place: τὸ εἶδος τοῦ προσώπου αὐτοῦ ἕτερον.

It is often suggested that Luke's description of Jesus' face is an explicit allusion to Exod 34:29, δεδόξασται ἡ ὄψις τοῦ χρώματος τοῦ προσώπου αὐτοῦ, where it is said that Moses' face shone after his encounter with God.[36] However, this interpretation has a number of difficulties. The only phrase that is common to Exod 34:29 (LXX) and Luke 9:29 is τοῦ προσώπου αὐτοῦ. The descriptions of what happened to each face are quite different. If Luke intended an allusion to Moses' face, one wonders why he would have made it so abstruse. Why would he not have used the verb δοξάζω with reference to Jesus' face as in Exod 34:29 if that parallel was what he wanted to convey? An avoidance of δοξάζω is especially puzzling in light of the occurrence of δόξα in vv 31-32. Furthermore, it is questionable whether any typology of Jesus as a new Moses is operative in Luke's Gospel.[37] Rather, when Moses is mentioned explicitly in Luke's Gospel, it is in connection with the role that he played in redemptive history as the mediator of the Law.[38] A more detailed look at expressions with εἶδος and πρόσωπον in Luke and the LXX yields a more likely interpretation.

The noun εἶδος occurs one other time in Luke's Gospel, in 3:22, at Jesus' baptism, where the holy Spirit descends upon him in bodily form, σωματικῷ εἴδει. In that example as well as in 9:29, εἶδος denotes "form, outward appearance," "the

---

[35]E.g., Ziesler, "Transfiguration," 265. McNeile (*Matthew*, 249) sees a comparison with David (2 Sam 23:8-11), who also had an inner circle of three men.

[36]H. Schürmann, *Das Lukasevangelium* (HTKNT 3; Freiburg: Herder, 1969) 556; Marshall, *Luke*, 383; R. O'Toole, "The Parallels Between Jesus and Moses," *BTB* 20 (1990) 22-23. For a different interpretation of Exod 34:29, that the skin of Moses' face was burnt or disfigured rather than glorified, see W. H. Propp, "The Skin of Moses' Face---Transfigured or Disfigured?" *CBQ* 49 (1987) 375-86.

[37]Conzelmann (*Theology*, 166-67) says there is no suggestion of such; O'Toole ("Parallels," 22-29), on the contrary, asserts that Luke has drawn numerous parallels between the two.

[38]There are five references to the Law of Moses (Luke 2:22; 5:14; 20:28,37; 24:44) and three to Moses and the prophets (Luke 16:29,31; 24:27), a summary way of referring to the OT.

total visible appearance; what may be perceived and known by others."[39]    In the LXX, εἶδος most frequently translates *mar'eh* ("appearance") or *tō'ar* ("form, appearance"). It is used of God in Gen 32:31; Exod 24:17; Num 12:8. It is used to describe people of beautiful appearance in such expressions as καλὸς τῷ εἴδει (e.g., Gen 29:17; 39:6; Deut 21:11; 2 Sam 11:2; 13:1), or ἀγαθὸς τῷ εἴδει (e.g., 1 Sam 16:18; 25:3). Other descriptions are given with εἶδος + a genitive, such as ὡς εἶδος λέπρας (Lev 13:43); ὡς εἶδος πυρὸς (Num 9:15,16); and εἶδος κρυστάλλου (Num 11:7).[40]    In Exod 26:30; Num 8:4, εἶδος has the connotation "plan, pattern."

The expression τὸ εἶδος τοῦ προσώπου is not found anywhere in the LXX, but a similar expression, ὁμοίωσις τῶν προσώπων αὐτῶν is found twice in Ezekiel (1:10; 10:22). The references are to the faces of the living creatures that Ezekiel saw in visions. Similarly, in Dan 3:19 (LXX) is found ἡ μορφὴ τοῦ προσώπου αὐτοῦ (in Theodotion's version, ἡ ὄψις τοῦ προσώπου αὐτοῦ), referring to Nebuchadnezzar's countenance.

Regarding the noun πρόσωπον, its usage in the NT follows closely that of the LXX, which corresponds to the Hebrew usage of *pānîm* and *'ap*. In Lucan writings, πρόσωπον appears twelve other times in the Gospel, and eleven times in Acts. In most instances πρόσωπον is part of an idiomatic expression.[41]    Only in Luke 9:29 and Acts 6:15 does πρόσωπον carry a literal connotation of "face, countenance."[42]

The adjective ἕτερος appears frequently in Luke-Acts. It is a dual adjective used to denote the "other" of two, to contrast a definite person or thing with another,[43] or to designate "another" of more than two.[44]    It also occurs in the plural, ἕτεροι as "others."[45] It is also used in lists.[46] In the expression τῇ ἑτέρᾳ, it is used to designate "the next day."[47]    In Acts 13:35, ἐν ἑτέρῳ denotes "in

---

[39]BAGD, 221; Behm, "μορφή," 743. This same connotation is found in John 5:37, where εἶδος αὐτοῦ is used of God. There are two other instances in which εἶδος is found in the NT, but with slightly different connotations. In 2 Cor 5:7, where εἶδος appears in the expression διὰ πίστεως . . . οὐ διὰ εἴδους it is rendered "sight" (*NRSV, NAB, NJB*). In 1 Thess 5:22, εἶδος carries the connotation "kind" (BAGD, 221), as reflected in the *NAB* (1986) translation of the phrase ἀπὸ παντὸς εἴδους πονηροῦ, "from every kind of evil." However, the nuance of "form," or "appearance" is also operative in this example, thus the *NRSV* and *NJB*, render εἶδος as "form;" the *NAB* (1970 translation) as "semblance."

[40]Other similar expressions are found in Exod 24:10; Num 11:7; Jdgs 8:18; 13:6; Sir 43:1; 45:11; Ezek 1:16,26.

[41]See above, chapter two, on 9:29.

[42]So defined in BAGD, 720. See also LSJ, 1533, for the full semantic range of πρόσωπον.

[43]Luke 5:7; 7:41; 14:31; 16:13; 17:34,35; 18:10; Acts 23:6. This and the subsequent definitions of ἕτερος are from BAGD, 315.

[44]Luke 6:6; 9:56,59,61; 16:18; Acts 1:20 (= Ps 108:8) 7:18 (= Exod 1:8); 8:34.

[45]Luke 3:18; 4:43; 8:3; 10:1; 11:26; 22:65; 23:32; Acts 2:13; 27:1.

[46]Luke 8:6,7,8; 11:16; 14:19,20; 16:7; 19:20; 20:11; 22:58.

[47]Acts 20:15; 27:3.

another place" (in scripture). As a substantive, ἕτερος appears in the expression οὐδὲν ἕτερον in Acts 17:21. In Luke 9:29, the connotation of ἕτερος is "another, different from what precedes,"[48] the only instance of such a nuance in Luke-Acts.[49]

The whole phrase, τὸ εἶδος τοῦ προσώπου αὐτοῦ ἕτερον in Luke 9:29 says simply that the visible appearance of Jesus' face changed. For clues to the significance of this expression, a search for other expressions describing a change in countenance yields some enlightening data. These will be examined with a view to identifying what it was that caused the change in facial expression in each case and what that change signifies.

There are no examples in the LXX of ἕτερος used with πρόσωπον to describe a change in facial expression. But there are several instances in which such a change is expressed with the verb ἀλλοιόω + πρόσωπον.[50] One such example is found in Judith 10, where the process of how Judith beautified herself for her mission is described. When the ancients of the city saw her (v 7), they noted that her face was changed, ἦν ἠλλοιωμένον τὸ πρόσωπον αὐτῆς, as well as her garments, καὶ τὴν στολὴν μεταβεβληκυῖαν αὐτῆς. The transformation of Judith is one that is deliberately effected by her own devices, as described in 10:3-4 and recalled in 16:8-9, in preparation for her encounter with the Assyrian commander Holofernes.

In Sir 12:18, ἀλλοιώσει τὸ πρόσωπον αὐτοῦ is said of an enemy whose true face will be revealed in time of adversity. The expression is found in a section containing advice not to trust in appearances. It admonishes that in prosperity enemies appear to be friends; it is only in adversity that their faces change and their true character is revealed. In the following chapter of the same book, in Sir 13:25, is another saying about a change in countenance. There it is said that the heart of a person is what changes one's countenance, whether it be for good or evil, καρδία ἀνθρώπου ἀλλοιοῖ τὸ πρόσωπον αὐτοῦ, ἐάν τε εἰς ἀγαθὰ ἐάν τε εἰς κακά. A similar example is found in Sir 25:17, in a section of sayings on wicked and virtuous women. It states that wickedness changes one's appearance, πονηρία γυναικὸς ἀλλοιοῖ τὴν ὅρασιν αὐτῆς καὶ σκοτοῖ τὸ πρόσωπον αὐτῆς ὡς ἄρκος.

One example in Isa 29:22 uses the verb μεταβάλλω, a synonym of ἀλλοιόω, with πρόσωπον. Here it is said that Jacob shall no more be ashamed, neither shall he now change countenance, οὐ νῦν αἰσχυνθήσεται Ιακωβ οὐδε νῦν τὸ πρόσωπον μεταβαλεῖ. This expression occurs in the context of an oracle of redemption and signifies that the house of Jacob will no longer be afflicted or in fear.

There are several instances in Daniel in which a change of countenance is expressed with ἀλλοιόω + μορφή rather than πρόσωπον. In Dan 3:19 (LXX), μορφή translates the Aramaic selem 'anpôhî, connoting "face." In this instance, the expression ἡ μορφὴ τοῦ προσώπου αὐτοῦ ἠλλοιώθη refers to King Nebuchadnezzar, whose wrath toward Shadrach, Meshach, and Abednego caused

---

[48]As also in Mark 16:12; Rom 7:23; 1 Cor 15:40; Gal 1:6; Jas 2:25.

[49]See further J. K. Elliott, "The Use of ἕτερος in the New Testament," *ZNW* 60 (1969) 140-41.

[50]In several MSS of Luke 9:29 (D e sy^{a.c.p} co) ἠλλοιώθη is found in place of ἕτερον.

his change of face. Nebuchadnezzar's previously favorable attitude toward them changed to fury when they refused to worship his golden statue. In Daniel 5:6,9,10; 7:28 (Θ), μορφή translates the Aramaic zîw, which means "brightness of countenance." The change of countenance described in 5:6,9,10 reflects the great fear of King Belshazzar at the appearance of the fingers of a hand that wrote on the wall. In 7:28, it is Daniel's facial expression that is said to be altered, because of his being troubled over his night visions. A similar example is found in *Herm. Man.* 12.4.1, where a change in the appearance of the shepherd, expressed as ἡ μορφὴ αὐτοῦ ἠλλοιώθη, is due to his anger. Earlier in the work (*Herm. Vis.* 5.4), a change in the form of the shepherd, ἠλλοιώθη ἡ ἰδέα αὐτοῦ enables Hermas to recognize the angel of penance to whom he had been entrusted.

Although neither ἀλλοιόω nor μεταβάλλω is used in Gen 31:2,5, another formulation with πρόσωπον is found there, expressing a change of face: καὶ εἶδεν Ιακωβ τὸ πρόσωπον τοῦ Λαβαν, καὶ ἰδοὺ οὐκ ἦν πρὸς αὐτὸν ὡς ἐχθὲς καὶ τρίτην ἡμέραν. Jacob perceives that Laban's attitude, or face, is not the same as before. Laban's previously favorable attitude changes when he sees that Jacob has outwitted him with regard to the livestock.

In 2 Macc 3:16 a change of face is expressed with the verb παραλλάσσω in conjunction with the nouns ὄψις ("face") and χρόα ("color" of the skin; complexion). The phrase ἡ γὰρ ὄψις καὶ τὸ τῆς χρόας παρηλλαγμένον ἐνέφαινεν τὴν κατὰ ψυχὴν ἀγωνίαν describes the change in the high priest: "His countenance and the changing of his color declared the inward agony of his mind." Similar vocabulary is used in Exod 34:29-30 to describe the change in Moses' face following his encounter with God on Mount Sinai, δεδόξασται ἡ ὄψις τοῦ χρώματος τοῦ προσώπου αὐτοῦ, "the skin of his face had become radiant."

In 1 Sam 1:9-18 a change in Hannah's face occurs after her prayer of lament over her childlessness. In the course of her prayer, she is given assurance that her petition will be answered. In response, she goes on her way and her countenance is no longer sad, τὸ πρόσωπον αὐτῆς οὐ συνέπεσεν ἔτι (1 Sam 1:18, LXX).

In 1QapGen 2:16-17 is found another example that speaks of a change in countenance. The text deals with the birth of Noah and Lamech's anxiety about whether Lamech is, indeed, the real father of the child. Bitenosh, Lamech's wife, attempts to reassure him, and queries, [*lm ' slm*] *'npyk kdn ' 'lyk sn ' wsht wrwhk kdn 'lyb '*, "[Why is the expression] of your face so changed and deformed? Why is your spirit so depressed?"[51]

Two examples in 2 *Enoch*[52] tell of a change of countenance in the visionary. In 2 Enoch 1:7 Enoch's reaction to the two huge men sent by God is described,

---

[51]See further J. A. Fitzmyer, *The Genesis Apocryphon of Qumran Cave I* (2d ed.; BibOr 18A; Rome: Biblical Institute, 1971) 53, 90-91.

[52]There are widely divergent views on the date and provenience of 2 *Enoch*. Dates assigned to the work range from pre-Christian times to the late Middle Ages; the provenance from Hellenized Jewish first-century Alexandria to ninth-century Byzantium. See further F. I Andersen, "2 (Slavonic Apocalypse of) Enoch," *The Old Testament Pseudepigrapha* (2 vols.; ed. J. H. Charlesworth; Garden City, NY: Doubleday, 1983) 1. 94-97.

". . . I was terrified; and the appearance of my face was changed because of fear."[53] In 2 Enoch 22:1-6, Enoch is permitted to see and stand in front of the face of God forever. That this encounter leaves an effect on the face of Enoch himself is evident from chapter 37, where an angel of God chills Enoch's face before he is returned to the earth, since otherwise, as God explains, "no human being would be able to look at your face."[54]

There is one instance, in Job 14:20, in which it is said that God changes a person's countenance, šānâ pānîm.[55] This expression occurs in the context of a poem on the misery and brevity of life, in which the phrase is interpreted as a graphic description of death, or even rigor mortis,[56] i.e., the ultimate change of countenance.

In these examples of phrases that express a change of countenance, there are several reasons given for the alteration of facial expression. In the case of Judith, the change was brought about by her own devices for the purpose of her mission. Many of the examples tell of a change of face that reflects a change in one's emotions. In Dan 3:19 the alteration is caused by wrath; in Herm. Man. 12.4.1 by anger; in Isa 29:22; Dan 5:6,9,10; 2 Enoch 1:7 by fear; in Dan 7:28; 1QapGen 2:16-17 by anxiety; in 2 Macc 3:16 by anguish of soul; in Gen 31:2,5 by disfavor. The maxims in Sirach speak of adversity changing the face to reveal one's true character (12:18), the heart changing one's countenance (13:25), and wickedness changing one's appearance (25:17). And in Job 14:20 it is death that effects the change.

Several of the examples describe a change in countenance as a result of prayer or encounter with God. The most famous instance is that of Moses' radiant face (Exod 34:29-30) following his meeting with God on Mount Sinai. In 1 Sam 1:18 it is implied that the change in Hannah's facial expression is brought about by what transpired during her communion with God in her time of distress. In the case of Judith, although her change of face is accomplished by her own efforts,[57] the

---

[53]So the J recension. The A recension says, "the appearance of my face was glittering because of fear" (Andersen, "2 Enoch," 106-107).

[54]This reference is from the longer (J) recension. The shorter (A) recension also tells of God allowing Enoch to stand in front of God's face forever in chap. 22, but is more sparse in the description of the "chilling" of Enoch's face in chap. 37. This account simply says that one of God's senior angels "refreshed my face, because I could not endure the terror of the burning of the fire." For discussion on the two recensions of 2 Enoch, see Andersen, "2 Enoch," 92-94.

[55]The LXX understood this verse differently and reads: ἐπέστησας αὐτῷ τὸ πρόσωπον, "you set your face against him." Elsewhere in the OT, the expression ἐφίστημι τὸ πρόσωπον translates nātān pānîm or śîm pānîm.

[56]S. Driver and G. B. Gray, A Critical and Exegetical Commentary on the Book of Job (ICC; Edinburgh: Clark, 1950) 131.

[57]This is implicit in chap. 10, but made explicit in chap. 16. The description of Judith's activity of beautification in 10:3-4 focuses on her manner of clothing herself and applying exterior ornaments. But what draws attention repeatedly is the beauty of her face (Jdt 10:14,23; 11:21,23; 16:7). It is not until the recounting of Judith's deeds in the song of chapter 16 that it is said explicitly that she anointed her face with ointment (v 8).

description of the alteration of her countenance also follows immediately upon her prayer to God for power and protection. Finally, the Psalmist also recognizes that when one prays, i.e., seeks God and looks to God, the resultant freedom from fear is reflected by the joyful radiance of the face (Ps 34:5-6).

These various expressions describing a change of face shed light on the understanding of the phrase τὸ εἶδος τοῦ προσώπου αὐτοῦ ἕτερον in Luke 9:29. There is no indication in the Lucan text that the change was brought about by Jesus' own devices, as in the example of Judith. Nor would the sayings about wickedness changing the face, or about adversity altering the countenance to reveal one's true character be applicable to the change of Jesus' face in Luke's version of the transfiguration. However, the expressions that describe a change of face caused by an emotional or interior change provide a clue to the intepretation of Luke 9:29.

A further indication that the expression τὸ εἶδος τοῦ προσώπου αὐτοῦ ἕτερον may have to do with an inner change in Jesus, reflected on his face, is that numerous idiomatic expressions with πρόσωπον reflect the understanding that the face mirrors one's inner state. A face that falls is one that expresses anger or sadness (e.g., Gen 4:5, συνέπεσεν τῷ προσώπῳ; 1 Sam 1:18, τὸ πρόσωπον αὐτῆς οὐ συνέπεσεν ἔτι). But to fall on one's face, πίπτειν ἐπὶ πρόσωπον (e.g., 2 Sam 9:6; 14:4,22,33; Matt 17:6; 26:39; Luke 5:12; 17:16) is an act of obeisance. To set one's face, πρόσωπον στηρίζειν (Luke 9:51) or τάσσειν πρόσωπον (2 Kgs 12:17), is to show determination.[58] Adding the preposition ἐπὶ to στηρίζειν πρόσωπον means to set oneself against someone, connoting disfavor or even enmity (e.g., Jer 3:12; 21:10; Ezek 6:2; 13:17), as does ἐφιστάναι πρόσωπον (Lev 17:10; 20:3,5,6; 26:17). To turn one's face away, ἀποστρέφειν πρόσωπον (Deut 31:17,18; Ps 69:17), is another expression of displeasure. It can also mean "to overlook" (Ps 51:9). Expressions for fear are ὑποστέλλειν πρόσωπον (Deut 1:17) and ἐκκλίνειν ἀπὸ προσώπου (Deut 20:3). That the face reflects one's inner state or attitude is obvious from these expressions with πρόσωπον. Even more explicit on this point are statements such as: "When the heart rejoices, the countenance is cheerful, but when it is in sorrow, (the countenance) is sad" (Prov 15:13); "The mark of a happy heart is a cheerful face" (Sir 13:26); and "A sensible person is known by the look on his face" (Sir 19:29).

Against this background, Luke's expression τὸ εἶδος τοῦ προσώπου αὐτου ἕτερον can be understood as saying that a physical alteration of Jesus' facial expression took place that reflected a change in Jesus' inner being. This change was said to be visible to, and observable by, the three disciples who accompanied him to the hill country. The clues to the cause of this change in Jesus and its significance may be detected in the references to prayer in vv 28,29 and in the content of the conversation between Jesus, Moses, and Elijah in v 31.

The change in Jesus occurs in the context of prayer, a time when Jesus explicitly seeks communion with God. Often one's relationship with God is expressed in terms of God's face and the face of the one praying. God's face connotes God's presence (e.g., Ps 21:7, těhaddēhû běśimhâ 'et-pānêkā /

---

[58]See C. A. Evans, "'He Set His Face'" Luke 9,51 Once Again," *Bib* 68 (1987) 80-84 on the connotation of judgment in the expression πρόσωπον στηρίζειν.

εὐφρανεῖς αὐτὸν ἐν χαρᾷ μετὰ τοῦ προσώπου σου). Prayer itself is referred to as seeking the face of God: biqqēš pānîm / ζητεῖν τὸ πρόσωπον (Ps 27:8; 105:4), and also as turning one's face to God: nātān pānîm 'el / διδόναι τὸ πρόσωπον πρός (Dan 9:3). Entreating God's favor in prayer is expressed as δέεσθαι τὸ πρόσωπον or even more colorfully in Hebrew, "softening God's face," hillâ pānîm (e.g., 1 Sam 13:12; 2 Kgs 13:4; Zech 8:21), i.e., flattering or putting God in a gentler mood.

God's response of showing favor is formulated as "lifting up of the face," λαμβάνειν πρόσωπον (Gal 2:6) or ἐπαίρειν πρόσωπον (Num 6:26), or looking upon the face, ἐπιβλέπειν ἐπὶ τὸ πρόσωπον (Ps 84:9), or making God's face shine upon one, ἐπιφαίνειν τὸ πρόσωπον ἐπὶ (Num 6:25; Pss 67:1; 80:3,7). God's face being hidden (Gen 4:14; Deut 31:17,18) or turned away (Pss 21:25; 101:3) connotes divine displeasure and the absence of the divine protective presence. Worship of God is expressed by "falling on the face," πίπτειν ἐπὶ πρόσωπον (Num 20:6; Josh 5:14).

Seeing God face to face is an expression that is used to describe intense encounters with the divine, such as those of Jacob at Peniel (Gen 31:30) and Moses on Mount Sinai (Deut 5:4; 34:10). The psalmist expresses longing for God's presence as a desire to see God's face (Ps 41:3; 94:2). However, seeing God's face also involves great peril, as in Exod 33:20-23, where God's face cannot be seen though the divine presence is manifest. According to Rev 22:4 (also 2 Esdr 7:98), seeing God's face is a favor that will be reserved to the final consummation. In sum, expressions involving God's face or the face of the one praying are often used to describe one's relationship with God.

The examples from the OT and early Jewish literature that juxtapose a change of face with prayer give an interpretive clue for understanding the phrase τὸ εἶδος τοῦ προσώπου αὐτοῦ ἕτερον in Luke 9:29. As in the examples of Moses (Exod 34:29-30) and Hannah (1 Sam 1:18) and in the description of the psalmist (Ps 34:5-6), it is likely that Luke also is indicating that the alteration in Jesus' countenance reflected something that transpired between himself and God during his prayer.[59] The subject of the exchange between Jesus and God in Luke's transfiguration story is not made explicit,[60] although the context of 9:28-36 and the content of the conversation between Jesus, Moses, and Elijah in v 31 provide clues as to what Luke supposed it to be. The location of the episode, as the hinge between Jesus' Galilean and Jerusalem ministries, is an indication that Luke considered Jesus' mission to be the subject of his prayer at the transfiguration. Like the accounts of his baptism and agony, this time of prayer is depicted at a critical moment of transition in Jesus' mission.

The story does not elaborate on precisely what was the change in Jesus' face.

---

[59]Wand (Transfiguration, 24) has a similar understanding of this detail: ". . . if one's face can 'light up' on seeing a beloved person, it would be natural for one who was truly in love with God to exhibit an even more transforming joy when deeply engaged in prayer."

[60]Of all the times that Jesus is shown to be at prayer in Luke (3:21; 5:16; 9:18,28-29; 10:21-22; 11:1; 22:32,41-42; 23:46) only in 10:21-22; 22:32,41-42 and 23:46 is the content of Jesus' prayer given.

But in the final form of the story, with its Mosaic and apocalyptic overtones, the references to δόξα, and the description of Jesus' clothing becoming flashing white, the phrase τὸ εἶδος τοῦ προσώπου αὐτοῦ ἕτερον evokes an image of a radiant change in Jesus' countenance. The notion that the perfected righteous will have radiant faces (the ultimate change of countenance) occurs frequently in apocalyptic literature. 2 Esdr 7:97 says of those who have kept the ways of the Most High, "Their face is to shine like the sun." Dan 10:6 speaks of a man clothed in linen whose face is like lightning, τὸ πρόσωπον αὐτοῦ ὡσεὶ ὅρασις ἀστραπῆς. In a vision similar to that of Daniel, the seer in Rev 1:16 beholds one whose face is described as shining like the sun, ἡ ὄψις αὐτοῦ ὡς ὁ ἥλιος φαίνει.

That this radiance on the faces of the righteous is a reflection of the divine glory is made explicit in *1 Enoch* 18:4, "They shall not be able to look on the faces of the righteous because the Lord of spirits shall cause his light to shine on the faces of the saints and the elect righteous." Similarly, the Lucan description of the changed face of Jesus at the transfiguration, in the final form of the story, elicits the image of Jesus as God's righteous one.

It is not only the face of the righteous one that shines with the radiance of God, but the whole being, as in Dan 12:3, "And those who are wise shall shine like the brightness of the firmament, and those who turn many to righteousness, like the stars for ever and ever." Similarly, *2 Apoc. Bar.* 51:10 says: "They shall be changed . . . from beauty to splendor, from light to the radiance of glory." In *1 Enoch* 104:2, the righteous are assured, "You shall shine like the lights of heaven." And in the NT, Matt 13:43 says, "the righteous shall shine like the sun," οἱ δίκαιοι ἐκλάμψουσιν ὡς ὁ ἥλιος.

The extension of the radiance goes even further to include the clothing. *1 Enoch* 62:15 asserts, "The righteous and elect ones . . . shall wear the garments of glory." And in *2 Enoch* 22:8, where Enoch is taken up to the tenth heaven, God directs that his earthly garments be taken from him and that he be clothed in "the clothes of my glory." The connection between the glory of the righteous and the divine glory is made explicit here.

It is possible that Luke had these apocalyptic notions in mind when he connected the phrase καὶ ὁ ἱματισμὸς αὐτοῦ λευκὸς ἐξαστράπτων to τὸ εἶδος τοῦ προσώπου αὐτοῦ ἕτερον. Part of Luke's intent, then, would be to portray Jesus as God's righteous one, with a changed face and garments of glory. In the final form of the story, the joining of these two phrases creates an aura of an event that is not merely natural. In this respect, Luke's final form of the narrative is like that of Mark.

There are many references to garments in Luke and at times they have a symbolic meaning. The noun ἱματισμὸς, used in 9:29, occurs one other time in Luke's Gospel, in 7:25 (from Q), where it is part of a saying about those who dress in lovely apparel. It is also found in Acts 20:33, where Paul asserts to the Ephesians that he has not coveted anyone's money or clothing. Luke's more frequently used term for clothing is ἱμάτιον.[61] In the Gospel, it is found in

---

[61]Luke 5:36; 6:29; 7:25; 8:27,44; 9:29; 19:35,36; 22:36; 23:34; Acts 7:58; 9:39; 12:8; 14:14; 16:22; 18:6; 22:20,23.

sayings and instructions of Jesus (5:36 [2x]; 6:29; 7:25; 22:36) and in the description of the Gerasene demoniac who was unclothed (8:27). In the pericope of Jesus' entry into Jerusalem, garments are thrown on the colt (19:35) and spread on the road (19:36) as gestures of homage. In two instances, Jesus' clothes are mentioned: in 8:44, where the woman with the flow of blood touches the hem of his cloak and is healed, and in 23:34, where the soldiers cast lots to divide Jesus' garments.

One other term used in Luke-Acts for clothing is ἐσθής (Luke 23:11; 24:4; Acts 1:10; 10:30; 12:21). In each instance ἐσθής is part of a description of dazzling apparel. This noun is used of the robe in which Herod adorns Jesus in 23:11 and of Herod's own royal robes in Acts 12:21. Three times ἐσθής is used of the apparel of heavenly messengers: Luke 24:4; Acts 1:10; 10:30. In all three instances it is the dazzling, white apparel that identifies the "men" as heavenly beings.

The adjective λευκός occurs twice in Luke's writings, in Luke 9:29 and Acts 1:10. In both instances it is used of clothing in a description of a supernatural sort. In the OT and early Judaism, white clothing has various meanings.[62] Fine linen, bleached white, βύσσος, was used for priestly vestments[63] as well as for royal robes.[64] White clothing was worn on joyous occasions[65] and is spoken of in Prov 31:22 as the attire of the ideal wife. In Isa 3:23; Ezek 16:10; 27:7, fine, white linen is part of the lavish adornment that will be taken away from Jerusalem and Tyre. Similarly, it is the attire of the rich and fashionable in Luke 16:19.[66] In Eccl 9:8, the white clothing that one is exhorted to wear always is a symbol of purity.[67] Likewise, the Essenes' habitual wearing of white (λευχειμονεῖν διαπαντός) was most probably meant as a symbol of their sanctity.[68]

Several Greek inscriptions and rabbinic texts indicate that the dead were buried in white,[69] perhaps as a sign of their purity or as a preparation for entrance

---

[62]See W. Michaelis, "λευκός," *TDNT* 4 (1967) 241-50.

[63]Exod 28:5,6,8,15,29,35; 36:9,10,12,32,36,37; Jos. *Ant.* 3.7.2 §153-54.

[64]Esth 8:15; Jos. *Ant.* 8.7.3 §186.

[65]Philo, *Vit. Cont.*, 8 §66; Horace, *Sat.* 2.2 §59-61.

[66]In Jas 2:2,3 the bright clothing designated by ἐν ἐσθῆτι λαμπρᾷ carries the same connotation of honor and riches as the examples with βύσσος.

[67]Although clothing is not specifically mentioned in Ps 51:7; Isa 1:18; Dan 11:35; 12:10, the process of whitening is used in these examples as an analogy for purification from sinfulness.

[68]Josephus (*J.W.* 2.8.3 §123) does not give their motive for wearing white, but one can surmise from his description of the Essenes' cultivation of sanctity (*J.W.* 2.8.2 §119-20) that such was their motive. Their wearing of white was definitely not intended to be a mark of distinction, since they despised riches and held their goods in common (*J.W.* 2.8.3 §123).

[69]See W. Dittenberger, *Sylloge Inscriptionum Graecarum* (4 vols.; Lipsiae: Hirzelium, 1920) 3. 1218.2,3 for a 5th century B.C.E. inscription; 1219.9 for one from the 3d century B.C.E.; and 736.13,15,24 for inscriptions dated to 92 B.C.E. Rabbinic texts that indicate burial in white are *b. Sabb.* 114a; *y. Kil.* 32b,7.

into the heavenly world, where white was the proper color.[70] From its association with the divine world, the step to having white become the eschatological color *par excellence* was a simple one, and in the NT this is its predominant connotation. Thus in Rev 3:4,5,18; 4:4; 6:11; 7:9,13, those who endure are clad in white robes, which signifies their membership in the heavenly world, their purity, victory, and joy.[71] Other examples in which white clothing is the mark of a heavenly figure are found in 2 Macc 11:8; Mark 16:5; Matt 28:3; John 20:12; and Acts 1:10.

The participial adjective ἐξαστράπτων modifying λευκός in Luke 9:29 is the only occurrence of the compound verb ἐξαστράπτω in the NT. However, in Luke 17:24; 24:4, the related verb ἀστράπτω occurs as a participial adjective. In the first instance, it is part of a saying about the flashing of lightning, and in the second, it is used to describe the clothing of the two heavenly figures at the empty tomb. The compound verb περιαστράπτω is used twice in Acts (9:3; 22:6) of the light from heaven that flashed around Paul in his call experience. The noun ἀστραπή is found three times: in Luke 10:18; 17:24, in sayings about lightning; in 11:36 it denotes the bright rays of a lamp. Accordingly, in 9:29 ἐξαστράπτων connotes "flashing," or "gleaming like lightning." This participial adjective is at home in apocalyptic imagery, as its use in Ezek 1:4,7; Hab 3:3; Dan 10:6 (LXX) shows.

What Luke says about Jesus' clothes in the Gospel carries important symbolism about his person.[72] The Gospel opens with Jesus being wrapped in swaddling clothes (2:7,12). At his entrance into this world, Jesus is clothed in the manner of any ordinary infant, symbolizing that he is assuming the ordinary nature of all humanity. In the episode where the woman with the flow of blood touches Jesus' garment (8:43-48), the identification of his clothing with his very person is explicit. In v 44, it is said that she touched the fringe of his garment, ἥψατο τοῦ κρασπέδου τοῦ ἱματίου αὐτοῦ. But in the following verse, Jesus' question is, "Who was it that touched *me*?" τίς ὁ ἁψάμενός μου, and again in v 46, "Someone touched *me*," ἥψατό μού τις, and in v 47, "she had touched *him*," ἥψατο αὐτοῦ.[73]

In 23:11, where Herod arrays Jesus in gorgeous apparel, ἐσθῆτα λαμπρὰν, the robe's brightness may be symbolic of Jesus' guiltlessness, which Herod mocks. The adjective λαμπρός may also be a clue to Jesus' heavenly status, since in Acts

---

[70]In Dan 7:9, the Ancient of Days himself is robed in white.

[71]On the symbolism of white clothing in the Book of Revelation, see further G. B. Caird, *The Revelation of St. John the Divine* (2d ed.; London: Black, 1984) 85-86; 101-3; Collins, *Apocalypse*, 25, 31, 53.

[72]On clothing in Luke, see further, R. Karris, *Luke, Artist and Theologian* (New York: Paulist, 1985) 85-87.

[73]Luke is not the only one to employ clothing in such a symbolic way. Zech 3:3-5 equates filthy garments with iniquity and clean clothes with purity. Paul uses the bold metaphor of "clothing oneself with the Lord Jesus Christ" in Rom 13:14. Similarly, he speaks of "putting on" virtues in Col 3:12-14 and of attiring oneself with an imperishable nature in 1 Cor 15:53. Likewise, 2 Esdr 2:45 speaks of putting off mortal clothing and putting on immortal.

10:30; Rev 15:6; 19:8 λαμπρός is used to describe the clothing of heavenly beings.[74] In 23:34, the soldiers cast lots for Jesus' clothing. The garments of his earthly existence are removed, and the last apparel given him is the linen shroud in which his body is wrapped for burial (23:53). If 24:12 is included in the original text,[75] then the Gospel closes with the leaving behind of the linen cloth in the tomb, the last trappings of earthly existence.[76]

In such a schema, one may expect that the flashing, white clothing of Jesus in 9:29 also carries important symbolism that is revelatory of his person. The primary symbolism conveyed by Jesus' white clothing in 9:29 is that he is a heavenly being. Although it is no secret in Luke that Jesus is the Son of God (e.g., 1:32; 3:22), the meaning of this must be worked out in the course of the Gospel. In the context of Luke 9:21-22 and 9:43-45, where Jesus speaks to the disciples about his coming death, the white clothing is a confirmation of his heavenly status, his righteousness and purity, and his ultimate victory over death. The apocalyptic associations with white clothing introduce a future dimension to the understanding of Jesus' victory and heavenly status. And yet, the transfiguration is narrated in the context of a happening during Jesus' earthly ministry. In this way, Luke conveys the message that Jesus' heavenly status and glory are both present and yet to come.

In the final form of Luke 9:28-36, there is a parallelism between the dazzling white clothing of Jesus (v 29) and the glorious appearance of the two heavenly interpreters (v 31). It has been demonstrated that heavenly figures that appear in human form are identified as divine messengers by their glorious apparel. Jesus, shown here as a man in dazzling white clothing, is portrayed as God's ultimate interpreter. That his life is the pinnacle of divine communication with human beings is the message given in v 35: "listen to him."

## Luke 9:30

With a favorite formula of introduction, καὶ ἰδού + ἀνήρ, Luke introduces the originally anonymous angels. In the Lucan narrative such figures emphasize the significance of the key stages of Jesus' life: the birth of his predecessor (1:5-23); Jesus' birth (1:26-38; 2:8-15), his resurrection (24:1-11), his ascension (Acts 1:6-

---

[74]The suggestion that kingly clothing is implied in Luke 23:11 is to read Mark 15:1-17 into Luke's account. In Luke there is no suggestion of royal robes. Furthermore, when Luke wishes to convey "kingly clothing," he does so with ἐσθῆτα βασιλικὴν as in Acts 12:21. Karris (*Artist*, 87) understands ἐσθῆτα λαμπρὰν of 23:11 to be the white garment worn by a candidate for office, as described in Polybius, *The Histories*, X 4.9-5.1. This would make the irony of the choice of Barabbas in 23:18 all the more forceful. However, the color of the garment in 23:11 is not given, and λαμπρός does not necessarily mean white.

[75]It is attested by P[75] ℵ A B K L W X Δ Θ II Ψ 063 079 0124 f[1] f[13] 28 33 565 700 892 1009 1010 1071 1079 1195 1216 1230 1241 1242 1253 1344 1365 1546 646 228 2174 Byz Lect l[185m] it[9aur,c,f,ff2] vg syr[c,s,p,h,pal MSS] cop[sa,bo] arm eth geo Eusebius Cyril, but is omitted by D it[a,b,d,e,l,r1] syr[pal (MSS)] Mcion Diat.

[76]Jos., *Ant.* 3.7.7. §183 says that linen typifies the earth because the flax springs from it. Philo (*Cong. Erud. Grat.* 21 §117) also mentions linen as a symbol of the earth.

12); and the extension of his mission to the Gentiles (Acts 10:1-8). In the transfiguration episode the heavenly figures highlight a crucial point for the understanding of Jesus' mission: his "exodus" is the very fulfillment of his mission. These angelophanies, along with the angels mentioned in Acts 5:19; 7:30,35,38; 8:26; 10:3,7,22; 11:13; 12:6-19,23; 23:8-9; 27:23 give Luke's two volumes an aura of constant communication between God and God's chosen ones. They make it clear that God orchestrates the drama of salvation history.

Luke frequently uses the device of reporting conversations among characters to show how participants in the Gospel story came to grips with Jesus and to invite the readers into the process of working out their own understanding of Jesus and coming to faith in him. In the prelude to Jesus' baptism and ministry, people are waiting in expectation for the Messiah (3:15). When they hear John the Baptist's message, they carry on an interior dialogue, διαλογιζομένων πάντων ἐν ταῖς καρδίαις αὐτῶν, as to whether he is the expected one. This sets the stage for 4:36, where, at the beginning of Jesus' ministry, the people in Capernaum are amazed at Jesus' teaching and healing and converse with one another, συνελάλουν, to try to understand what they have heard and seen. The conversations of the scribes and Pharisees with one another contrast sharply with those of disciples or would-be followers. The dialogues of the former reflect their decision against Jesus. In 6:11 they discuss with one another, διελάλουν πρὸς ἀλλήλους what they might do to Jesus, and from then on their talking with one another about him is not in open conversation but rather murmuring, διεγόγγυζον, to one another against him (15:2). Similarly, Judas' conference with the chief priests in 22:4 (another instance in which συνλαλέω is used) is one of sinister betrayal.

By contrast, the disciples' conversations with one another reflect continued efforts to understand and come to belief in Jesus. In 8:25, after the calming of the storm, the disciples asked one another, λέγοντες πρὸς ἀλλήλους, who Jesus could be. At the end of the Gospel, in 24:14, disciples were still talking with each other, ὡμίλουν πρὸς ἀλλήλους, about all that had happened concerning Jesus; they were still trying to comprehend and believe. Only after the resurrection and Jesus' opening up of the scriptures for them did their understanding and faith become complete, as indicated in the last reference to disciples' speaking among themselves, εἶπαν πρὸς ἀλλήλους, in 24:32.

In this framework, the conversation between Jesus and the two figures in 9:30 also conveys an attempt to understand Jesus and his mission. In other instances where συνλαλέω, διαλαλέω, διαλογίζομαι, or λέγω/ὡμιλέω πρὸς ἀλλήλους are used, the conversation involves other characters' responses to Jesus and their striving to come to grips with him. In this instance, Jesus himself is in dialogue with two heavenly beings about his identity and mission.

When Luke conflated his sources for the transfiguration narrative, the two figures in 9:30, originally cast as predicting angels in the L source, took on the identities of Moses and Elijah as in the Marcan tradition. This adoption of Moses and Elijah by Luke may have been theologically motivated. Since Luke portrays Jesus as the ultimate envoy of God, interpreting the good news of salvation to humankind (4:18-19, etc.), he may have deemed it inappropriate for Jesus to be the recipient of an angelic interpretation. It is important to note that in Luke-Acts angels predict and interpret before Jesus is born (1:5-23,26-38; 2:8-15) and after

Two witnesses

his resurrection (Luke 24:1-9; Acts 1:6-12). But during Jesus' earthly sojourn he is the divine interpreter *par excellence.*

Futhermore, in the context of the gospel story, just before the transfiguration, the Lucan Jesus has already explained to his disciples that he must "suffer greatly and be rejected by the elders, the chief priests, and the scribes, and be killed and the the third day be raised" (9:22). To have such an understanding of his mission portrayed as a revelation to Jesus by predicting angels after he has already disclosed this to the disciples would not make narrative sense. Luke walks a fine line between being faithful to the traditions he has received, even when they are conflicting, and using his own creative artistry to achieve his own purposes.

By identifying the two men as Moses and Elijah, there is a further overlay of theological meaning. The significance of these two OT figures at the transfiguration has been variously interpreted. There are other explicit references to each of the two elsewhere in Luke, and there are several passages that allude to one or the other of them. In order to understand their role at the transfiguration, it is important to survey the part that each plays in Lucan writings and how that is related to the person of Jesus.

The explicit references to Moses in Luke's Gospel, besides 9:30,33, all refer to Moses' role as mediator of the Law. At the outset of the Gospel, Jesus is presented as belonging to a family who dutifully fulfills the Law of Moses (2:22). In his ministry, Jesus continues to direct people to do what Moses commanded (5:14) and teaches from Moses' writings (20:28,37). Similarly, in Acts, the laws, customs, and writings of Moses are mentioned in 6:11,14; 13:39; 15:1,5,21; 21:21. As a summary way of referring to the whole of the Law, the expression "Moses and the prophets" is used in Luke 16:29,31; 24:27,44; Acts 26:22; 28:23.

In addition to the explicit references, there are numerous allusions to Moses in Luke.[77] A parallel between Jesus and Moses is that each is said to possess the spirit (Num 11:17,25; Luke 4:12,14). Each spends forty days in the wilderness as a time of testing (Deut 8:2; Luke 4:2; Acts 7:36). Both Jesus and Moses are portrayed as the mouthpiece of God (Exod 4:15-16; Luke 4:32,43; 5:1), and each selects a group of seventy to share in his mission (Num 11:17,25; Luke 10:1,17). In 4:16-30; 7:22, Jesus is presented as the eschatological prophet, the prophet like Moses (Acts 3:22) who was to come at the end time. Jesus' feeding of the multitude in the deserted countryside in Luke 9:10-17 has echoes of Moses' provision of manna in the desert for the Israelites (Exod 16:1-36). Jesus' laments in Luke 9:41; 13:34-35 have overtones of Moses' cries against his people in Deut 1:12; 32:5,20. Both Jesus and Moses endorse others to share in their work (Num 11:26-30; Luke 9:49-50).

The whole travel narrative (Luke 9:51-18:14) of Jesus' journey to Jerusalem has many parallels to Moses' journey to the promised land.[78] The term

---

[77]O'Toole, "Parallels," gives a thorough examination of each allusion, classifying each as either a clear or a probable Lucan parallel between Jesus and Moses.

[78]See especially C. F. Evans, "The Central Section of St. Luke's Gospel," *Studies in the Gospels* (ed. D. E. Nineham; Oxford: Blackwell, 1957) 37-53, who outlines the whole of Luke 9:51-18:14 as a "Christian Deuteronomy." Also, J. Drury, *Tradition and Design in Luke's Gospel: A Study in*

ἀναλήμψις used of Jesus in Luke 9:51 may be a parallel to the postbiblical tradition that Moses did not die but was taken miraculously up to heaven.[79] Both Moses and Jesus are said to do powerful deeds "by the finger of God" (Exod 8:15; Luke 11:20). Moses and Jesus both provide a summary of their teachings as they are about to leave their disciples (Deut 1:1; Luke 24:44). Each suffers the accusation before a non-Jewish ruler that he is perverting his nation (Exod 5:4; Luke 23:2).

In Acts, the connection between Jesus and Moses is made explicit in 3:22-23; 7:37, where Jesus is shown to be the "prophet like Moses" (Deut 18:15). Furthermore, the whole portrayal of Moses' life in Stephen's speech in Acts 7 makes the patterns of the lives of Moses and Jesus identical.[80] At the institution of the Eucharist (Luke 22:20), Jesus speaks of a new covenant in his blood, which is reminiscent of the covenant in blood mediated by Moses (Exod 24:8). Both Jesus and Moses are described as prophets mighty in deed and word (Luke 24:19; Acts 7:22,36).

Luke may have intended a parallel between Jesus and Moses when he placed the genealogy of Jesus (3:23-38) between the accounts of his baptism (3:21-22) and the beginning of his ministry (4:14). Moses' genealogy is also located between the account of his call and that of the beginning of his mission (Exod 6:14-25).[81] In fact, the whole of Luke's infancy narrative can be compared to Jewish midrash on the birth and infancy of Moses.[82]

These comparisons of Jesus with Moses are set alongside another whole set of parallels drawn in Luke-Acts between Jesus and his followers.[83] What these parallels all illustrate is the continuity of God's plan of salvation from Moses through Jesus and to his disciples. Jesus, the new and final prophet, mighty in word and deed, is to be heard and followed. He is the means of salvation that supersedes Moses and the Law.

There are a number of explicit references to Elijah in Luke's Gospel in addition to those in 9:30-33. In 1:17, John the Baptist is said to go before the Lord in the spirit and power of Elijah. In 4:25,26, Jesus compares his poor reception in Nazareth with that of Elijah in his own home territory. In 9:8,19 the opinion is relayed that some thought Jesus was Elijah reappeared.

The allusions to Elijah are quite numerous in Luke. In 1:76; 7:27 John the

---

*Early Christian Historiography* (London: Darton, Longman, and Todd, 1976) 138-64. D. P. Moessner ("Luke 9:1-50: Luke's Preview of the Journey of the Prophet Like Moses of Deuteronomy," *JBL* 102 [1983] 575-605) contends that Luke 9:1-50 recapitulates and consummates the Exodus drama, portraying Jesus as the prophet like Moses. In Moessner's schema, the transfiguration is at the apex of the section, with the four episodes on either side providing parallel Moses-Deuteronomy motifs.

[79] Jos., *Ant.* 4.8.48 §326; *b. Sota* 13b; *Midr.* Deut 34:5.

[80] O'Toole, "Parallels," 7-10, gives the details.

[81] R. E. Brown, etc., *Mary in the New Testament* (Philadelphia: Fortress, 1978) 163.

[82] Drury, *Design*, 47, 48. See, for example, Jos. *Ant.*, 2.9.3 §215 through 2.9.7 §237; *Jub.* 47.

[83] See O'Toole, *Unity*, 62-94.

Baptist is called the prophet who will prepare the way for the Lord. This is an allusion to Mal 3:1, which speaks of the coming of God's messenger, who is eventually identified as Elijah in Mal 3:23.[84] In 3:16; 7:19, the phrases ἔρχεται and ὁ ἐρχόμενος, "the one who is to come," also allude to Mal 3:1, but in these instances, they are applied to Jesus. In the second example, Jesus rejects the identification of himself with Elijah, saying rather that John the Baptist is the one to be so identified. A parallel between Jesus and Elijah can be seen in the forty days of Jesus' fasting in the wilderness (4:2), which is similar to Elijah's forty days and nights without eating (1 Kgs 19:8).

The programmatic statement of Jesus' mission in 4:16-30 is comparable to the mission of Elijah as seen in 1 Kings 17 and 2 Kings 5. Both Jesus and Elijah are sent to outcasts beyond the borders of Israel. The many miracles of Jesus can be compared to those of Elijah. The miraculous catch of fish in 5:1-11 and the feeding of the five thousand in 9:10-17 are comparable to Elijah's miraculous provision of food in 1 Kings 17. Jesus' raising of the widow's son at Nain (7:11-17) has many parallels to Elijah's resuscitation of the widow's son at Zarephath (1 Kgs 17:8-24). As Elijah was able to control the weather (1 Kgs 17:1; 18:41-45), so too was Jesus (8:22-25). In many cases, peoples' response to Jesus' deeds was to "fall on their face" in homage (5:12; 17:16). So too in 1 Kgs 18:7,39, people make this gesture of reverence to Elijah.

There is another similarity between Jesus and Elijah in that both are portrayed as men of prayer (Luke 3:21; 5:16; 6:12; 9:18,28,29; 10:21-22; 11:1-13; 22:3,32,41-42; 23:46; 1 Kgs 17:21-22; 18:36-37; 19:9). The statement in Luke 9:51 about Jesus' being "taken up," τῆς ἀναλήμψεως αὐτοῦ and the description of his ascension in Acts 1:9 call to mind the manner of Elijah's being taken up into heaven (2 Kgs 2:11). Another allusion to Elijah is found in 9:61-62. The saying about putting one's hand to the plow as a metaphor for discipleship is reminiscent of Elijah's call of Elisha while plowing (1 Kgs 19:19-21). Jesus' saying about casting a fire on earth in 12:49 and the desire of James and John to bid fire come down from heaven to consume the Samaritans that refused to accept Jesus (9:54) call to mind the two times Elijah called down fire from heaven to consume the delegations from King Ahaziah (1 Kgs 1:10,12).[85]

There is a parallel between Jesus and Elijah in that each visits Jericho during his final days on earth, while en route to his being "taken up" (Luke 19:1; 2 Kgs 2:4). Also, in their final days, each has a close disciple who promises to remain in his company (Luke 22:33; 2 Kgs 2:4). Finally, Jesus' promise to his disciples of being clothed with power from on high after he leaves them (24:49) has echoes of Elisha's taking up of Elijah's mantle after the latter's departure (2 Kgs 2:13). The picture painted of Elijah in Luke's Gospel is that of a mighty prophet,

---

[84]On the identity of the messenger in Mal 3:1, see further B. Malchow, "The Messenger of the Covenant in Mal 3:1," *JBL* 103 (1984) 252-55.

[85]Some MSS of Luke 9:54 explicitly add ὡς καὶ 'Ηλίας ἐποίησεν A C D K W X Δ Θ Π Ψ f[1.13] 28 33 565 700[mg] (892 omit καὶ) 1009 1010 1071 1079 1195 1216 1230 1242 1253 1344 1365 1546 1646 2148 2174 *Byz Lect* l[69s,m, 185s,m, 1127s,m,] it[a,b,c,d,f,q,rl] syr[p,h,pal] cop[bo MSS] goth eth Marcion Diatessaron[a,s] Ambrosiaster, Basil, Gaudentius Chrysostom Augustine Antiochus.

fiery reformer, and miracle worker, whose ministry was performed, for the most part, outside of his home territory because of rejection by his own people. Luke also portrays Elijah as the returning messenger to be sent before the great and awesome day of YHWH.

There is an ambiguity in Luke's Gospel, however, as to who it is that is cast in the role of the new Elijah. At times it is John the Baptist, and at times it is Jesus. In 1:17,76; 7:27, the part of Elijah as the precursor is clearly given to John the Baptist. The first two examples are found in peculiarly Lucan material; the last is retained from Mark (1:2). In other instances, however, Luke omits possible parallels between John the Baptist and Elijah.[86] In his initial description of John the Baptist (3:1-20), Luke does not include the details about the prophet's clothing that Mark has. Mark's description of the garment of hair and the leather girdle (Mark 1:6) recalls the portrayal of Elijah's attire in 2 Kgs 1:8. The Marcan sequel to the transfiguration (9:11-13) that expounds on Elijah's coming and implies that this coming has already occurred with John the Baptist is not taken up by Luke.

If Luke knew the tradition behind Matt 11:14, he has deliberately omitted another reference that explicitly identifies John the Baptist with Elijah. The Marcan account of the death of John the Baptist (6:14-29) contains a number of details that are evocative of Elijah's story. The intervention of John the Baptist in Herod's affairs is like Elijah's accusation of Ahab in 1 Kings 21. The persecution of Elijah by Jezebel is called to mind by John the Baptist's death that is brought about by Herodias. These resemblances of John the Baptist to Elijah are suppressed in Luke's short notices of the death of John the Baptist (3:19-20; 9:9). So Luke's portrayal is mixed: at times John is seen as the Elijah-like forerunner, but at others, this identification is downplayed.

The reason for Luke's toning down of John's identification with Elijah is that for him, Jesus is the one who is Elijah-come-again.[87] Luke retains allusions to Elijah in reference to Jesus when they are contained in Mark (Luke 3:16; 8:22-25; 9:8,10-17,19; 22:33,39). Twice Luke adds details to the Marcan story to highlight the parallel with Elijah (4:2; 5:12).[88] Many of the parallels between Jesus and Elijah are peculiarly Lucan (4:16-30; 6:12; 7:11-17; 9:51,54,61-62; 12:49; 17:16; 19:1; 24:49; Acts 1:9) and appear to be a deliberate effort on the part of Luke to elicit a comparison between the two.

There are three instances in which the Lucan Jesus rejects the role of Elijah. In 7:27, Luke retains Mark's portrayal of John as taking Elijah's role. In 9:54, where James and John want to call down fire from heaven as Elijah did, Jesus rejects this kind of action for himself and his followers. Another difference

---

[86]See M.-É. Boismard, "Elie dans le NT," *Études Carmélitaines* 35 (1956) 116-28; J. D. Dubois, "Lá figure d'Elie dans la perspective lucanienne," *RHPR* 53 (1973) 155-76; J. P. Meier, "John the Baptist in Matthew's Gospel," *JBL* 99 (1980) 383-405.

[87]Fitzmyer, *Luke*, 213-15; J. A. T. Robinson, "Elijah, John and Jesus: An Essay in Detection," *NTS* 4 (1957-58) 263-81; R. Swaeles, "Jésus, nouvel Elie, dans saint Luc," *AsSeign* 69 (1964) 41-66.

[88]In Luke 4:2 the detail of Jesus fasting makes the allusion to 1 Kgs 19:8 more explicit. In 5:12 Luke says the man with leprosy "fell on his face" rather than Mark's "kneeling" (1:40). In 1 Kgs 18:7,39 Obadiah and "all the people" fall on their faces before Elijah.

between Jesus and Elijah is found in 9:61-62, where there is an implicit comparison between the two regarding discipleship. To become a follower of Jesus, one is not allowed to put the hand to the plow and then look back, as Elisha was permitted to do when Elijah called him (1 Kgs 19:20).[89]

In sum, the equation of Jesus with Elijah is particularly highlighted by Luke. A conflicting minor theme of John the Baptist as Elijah is found in three instances, retained from Luke's sources, but downplayed in deference to his theme of Jesus as Elijah. Once again, Luke balances faithfulness to his sources with pursuit of his own theological design. In this instance, he sacrifices complete thematic consistency to faithfulness to his sources. The picture of Jesus that emerges is that he is equated with Elijah in his role of eschatological prophet and miracle worker. But certain aspects of that role (e.g., that of a fiery social reformer, and that of precursor) are rejected. As with the Mosaic parallels, Luke's comparison of Jesus with Elijah highlights the continuity of God's work of salvation from the prophets of old through Jesus. Jesus is a prophet like Elijah, yet greater than he.

The significance of the individual figures of Moses and Elijah for Luke has been examined. The question now is whether there is a meaning beyond their individual significance in the joint appearance here of the two OT figures.[90]

The most common interpretation of the juxtaposition of the two figures is that together they represent the Law and the Prophets.[91] Moses was the mediator of the first covenant and, in his time, Elijah brought its renewal. This is the significance of Moses and Elijah in the one other instance in scripture in which they are named together, Mal 3:22-23.[92] Thus, in the transfiguration story, these two witnesses to the first covenant signify the continuity with and fulfillment of the former covenant in the new. The disappearance of Moses and Elijah in v 33 show that they must now give way to Jesus as the new covenant supersedes the old. One difficulty with this interpretation is the role assigned to Elijah as representative of the prophets. Elsewhere in scripture, and in Luke-Acts in particular, the formulaic expression is "Moses and the prophets" (Luke 16:29,31; 24:27,44; Acts 26:22;

---

[89]Some (e.g., Conzelmann, *Luke*, 88) also see an elimination of Elijah typology in Luke's omission of Jesus' cry on the cross (Mark 15:35-36). However, if Luke is portraying Jesus as the new Elijah, he may have eliminated the cry so as not to have Jesus calling on the one he typifies at the time of death. Other explanations for the omission of the cry are that Luke made use of L material for this passage, which did not contain the citation from Ps 22:2 (Taylor, *Passion*, 95-96), or that Luke eliminated it because he was offended by the cry of dereliction and substituted more edifying words (Bultmann, *Geschichte*, 296).

[90]The order of their names in Luke probably reflects the historical order of their earthly ministries. This contrasts with the Marcan order, where Elijah is named first, perhaps to stress the importance of his role in view of Mark 9:11-13. So Best, "Redaction," 48; A. Feuillet, "Les Perspectives propres à chaque évangéliste dans les récits de la Transfiguration," *Bib* 39 (1958) 283-84; Horstmann, *Studien*, 85-88.

[91]E.g., Cranfield, *Mark*, 295; Marshall, *Luke*, 384; Plummer, *Luke*, 251; and many others.

[92]Another probable reference to Moses and Elijah together is Rev 11:3. Here, although the two witnesses are not named, the descriptions in Rev 11:5-6,12 recall the deeds of Moses and Elijah. See further Collins, *Apocalypse*, 70-72; Haugg, *Zeugen*, 16-17; Jeremias, "'Ηλ(ε)ίας," 939; Ladd, *Revelation*, 155.

28:23), not "Moses and Elijah."

Another interpretation of the joint appearance of Moses and Elijah is that they represent the unveiling of the heavenly world that Jesus experienced in prayer.[93] These two had had similar experiences atop Mount Sinai (Exodus 19; 1 Kgs 19:9-18). Their presence in the transfiguration story may be to call attention to the fact that Jesus too underwent a profound experience of God at this particular time of prayer atop a mountain. Or their appearance as two heavenly beings may be intended to point to Jesus' heavenly status.

Both Moses and Elijah were prophets who suffered rejection and persecution,[94] yet each was vindicated by God. Thus, another interpretation of the presence of Moses and Elijah at the transfiguration is to confirm Jesus' prediction of his own suffering (9:21-22), but also to assure his future vindication.[95] One difficulty with this interpretation is that the dimension of suffering is not the most immediate association that one makes with the figures of Moses and Elijah. If the image of a vindicated sufferer was what Luke desired, Job or Jeremiah would have served more readily.

Another interpretation of the appearance of Moses and Elijah is that both were eschatological figures who were expected to return. It was anticipated that Elijah would return at the end time to prepare the way of the Lord (Mal 3:1). His task included turning the hearts of parents to their children and the hearts of children to their parents (Mal 3:23 [4:6]; Sir 48:10; Luke 1:17). His ministry would also be to bring about repentance in the people (Rev 11:3).[96] The returning Elijah was also to purify the priesthood (Mal 3:2-4), restore the tribes of Israel (Sir 48:10), and mitigate the wrath of God (Sir 48:10). Later tradition attributes to the returning Elijah the functions of forerunner of the messiah (2 Esdr. 6:26; Just. Dial. 8,4),[97] one who accompanies the messiah(s) (Gen. Rab. on Gen 49:14),[98]

---

[93]L. Brun, "Engel und Blutschweiss Lc 22,43-44," ZNW 32 (1933) 271.

[94]E.g., Exod 14:11-12; 16:2-3; 17:2-4; 1 Kgs 19:2; Heb 11:24-27; Apoc. Elijah 4:7-19; T. Mos. 3:11; 12:7. On the theory that the suffering servant in Deutero Isaiah exemplifies a new Moses, see H. M. Teeple, The Mosaic Eschatological Prophet (JBLMS 10; Philadelphia: SBL, 1957) 56-63, 92-93.

[95]Jeremias, "Ἠλ(ε)ίας," 939; A. R. C. Leaney, "The Christ of the Synoptic Gospels," Supplement to The New Zealand Theological Review (1966) 22-25; M. Pamment, "Moses and Elijah in the Story of the Transfiguration," ExpTim 92 (1980-81) 338-39.

[96]Pirque R. El. 43 also speaks of the returning Elijah's ministry of repentance.

[97]There is considerable debate on when the notion of Elijah as the precursor of the messiah first appeared. For the position that the idea developed in very early Christian times, see M. Faierstein, "Why Do the Scribes Say That Elijah Must Come First?" JBL 100 (1981) 75-86; J. A. Fitzmyer, "The Aramaic 'Elect of God' Text from Qumran Cave 4," Essays on the Semitic Background of the New Testament (London: Chapman, 1971) 127-60; Luke, 327; 671-2; "More About Elijah Coming First," JBL 104 (1985) 295-96; J. L. Martyn, "We Have Found Elijah," Jews, Greeks and Christians (SJLA 21; ed. R. Hamerton-Kelly, R. Scroggs; Leiden: Brill, 1976) 181-219; Robinson, "Essay," 263-81. For the opinion that the notion is pre-Christian see D. C. Allison, "Elijah Must Come First," JBL 103 (1984) 256-58; Jeremias, "Ἠλ(ε)ίας," 931; J. Starcky, "Les Quatre étapes du messianisme à Qumrân," RB 70 (1963) 489-505.

the high priest of the messianic age (*Tg. Yer.* I on Exod 40:10; Deut 30:4), the one who will solve disputed questions on law and ritual (*b. Ber.* 24a), and the one who will defeat the antichrist (*Apoc. Elijah* 5:32-35).[99]

The belief in Moses' return arose from a widespread notion that the idyllic conditions of Moses' days would return in messianic times.[100] A necessary component of this hope was the return of Moses or a prophet like him (Deut 18:15). The notion of Moses' return also flowed from the belief that those who had not died, i.e., Enoch, Elijah, and later, Moses, would return in the messianic era.[101] The functions of the returning Moses or the prophet like Moses included acting as a forerunner[102] or companion to the messiah(s) (*Tg. Yer.* I on Exod 12:42; *b. Sukk.* 52a; *Zohar* 1:25b),[103] one who would lead the wilderness generation to receive their reward (*Midr.* Deut 33:21; *Tg. Onq.* Deut 33:21; *Num. Rab.* 19:13-14), one who would solve legal problems (1 Macc 4:41-50; 14:41).

In the NT, the belief in the return of Elijah and that of the coming of a prophet (like Moses) appear in Mark 6:15; 8:28; 9:11; Matt 16:14; 17:10; Luke 9:7-8,19; John 1:21,25.[104] As in Rev 11:3-13, where the two witnesses who are reminiscent of Moses and Elijah are eschatological figures, so too in the transfiguration story, Moses and Elijah can be interepreted eschatologically. Their presence can be understood to proclaim the inauguration of the end time.[105]

Other interpretations of Moses and Elijah in the transfiguration story have to do with the traditions about their deaths. Concerning Elijah, it was believed that he did not die, but was taken up to heaven in a chariot of fire (2 Kgs 2:11).

---

[98]M. Burrows ("The Messiahs of Aaron and Israel," *ATR* 34 [1952] 205) interprets the coming prophet who accompanies the messiah(s) in 1QS 9:11 as Elijah. L. H. Silberman ("The Two 'Messiahs' of the Manual of Discipline," *VT* 5 [1955] 77-82) and R. E. Brown ("The Messianism of Qumran," *CBQ* 19 [1957] 53-82) interpret the prophet as the Mosaic prophet.

[99]See further, Teeple, *Prophet*, 4-8.

[100]*Ibid.*, 29-41. In later Judaism the idea is attested in *Mek.* Exod 16:25,33; 20:18; *Exod. Rab.* 23:20; 31:2.

[101]*Ibid.*, 43-48.

[102]One late reference in *Deut. Rab.* 3,14 on Deut 10:1 speaks of a joint coming of Moses and Elijah as precursors of the messiah. Elsewhere (e.g., *Apoc. Elijah* 5:32-35) Enoch and Elijah are expected to come together.

[103]There is much debate about whether the returning Moses or the prophet like Moses was himself a messianic figure. See further W. Bousset, *Die Religion des Judentums in Späthellenistischen Zeitalter* (Tübingen: Mohr, 1926) 232-33; Jeremias, "Μωυσῆς," *TDNT* 4 (1967) 858-63; Teeple, *Prophet* 43-48. See also W. Meeks, *The Prophet-King. Moses Traditions and the Johannine Christology* (NovTSup 14; Leiden: Brill, 1967) on John's debt to Moses traditions for his portrayal of Jesus as prophet and king in his Gospel.

[104]Brown (*John*, 235) suggests that there may be an amalgamation of the two eschatological figures in John 6:14. See also R. Schnackenburg, "Die Erwartung des Prophetens nach dem Neuen Testament und den Qumran-Texten," *International Congress on "The Four Gospels in 1957," Oxford, 1957* (SE I; TU 73; Berlin: Akademie, 1959) 622-39.

[105]Fuller, *Foundations,* 172; Hahn, *Titles,* 336; Jeremias, "Ἠλ(ε)ίας," 939; Kee, "Transfiguration," 144-46; Lohmeyer, "Verklärung," 190-91; Ziesler, "Transfiguration," 266.

Similarly, a tradition developed that Moses did not die (contrary to Deut 34:5), but was also taken up to heaven.[106] The presence of these two at the transfiguration may be interpreted as a prefigurement of Jesus' entrance into the heavenly realm.[107] However, Moses and Elijah may also serve as a contrast to Jesus in their manner of death and ultimate status. If the transfiguration was a foreshadowing of the resurrection, then Jesus is seen to be greater than these two OT figures. They did not die, but were translated to heaven. Jesus would die, and then be raised from the dead, giving him a far superior status.[108]

There are a number of other parallels that can be drawn between Moses and Elijah,[109] but they do not have any particular bearing on the significance of the apparition of the two together at the transfiguration.

To conclude all that has been said about Moses and Elijah, what seems clear with regard to Luke 9:28-36 is as follows. Having received a tradition in which two angels predicted and interpreted the significance of Jesus' coming ἔξοδος, Luke transformed these figures into Moses and Elijah, in accordance with the Marcan tradition. This provided a contrast between Jesus and Moses and Elijah, that also served Luke's theological interests. In Luke's Gospel, Jesus is portrayed as combining in his person many characteristics of both Moses and Elijah.[110] Like them, he is a prophet mighty in deed and word whose prime work is the establishment of the divine covenant with God's people. The new covenant in Jesus is in continuity with the old. God's saving action is the same throughout history. Like Moses and Elijah, Jesus too would suffer persecution and rejection, but would be vindicated by God. In fact, the very completion of Jesus' mission is to be through his death and all that would happen in Jerusalem to fulfill God's saving plan.

The presence of Moses and Elijah as divine interlocutors both underscores the significance of Jesus' ἔξοδος and contrasts his death to theirs. Moses' death (Deut 34:1-12) is portrayed peacefully, at the end of a long life lived in the service of God. He was mourned properly for thirty days by the Israelites, and his appointed successor, Joshua, carries on his mission. One has a similar sense about Elijah from 2 Kgs 2:1-12. Although his age is not given, Elijah also appears to be an old man, completing his earthly mission with a sense of fulfillment, passing on his mantle to his successor, Elisha. The dramatic description of his being taken up in the flaming chariot bespeaks God's approval of him. Although Moses and Elijah endured suffering and persecution during their lives, this is not foremost at their deaths. Jesus' death, by contrast, will be violent, and at the end of a brief ministry. It will be the result of his deliberate choice to fulfill his mission: in 9:51 Jesus will "set his face" to journey to Jerusalem and on the Mount of Olives (22:39-

---

[106]Ios. Ant. 4.8.48 §326; b. Sota 13b; Midr. Deut 34:5.

[107]Weeden, Traditions, 120.

[108]Thrall, "Elijah and Moses," 305-17.

[109]See, for example, Sr. Jeanne d'Arc, "Elie dans L'Histoire du Salut," VSpir 87 (1952) 136-47.

[110]G. W. H. Lampe, "The Lucan Portrait of Christ," NTS 2 (1955-56) 160-75; Swaeles, "Jesus," 41.

45) he will reaffirm that decision.

Rather than being surrounded by his faithful followers, Jesus will die with "all the people who had gathered for this spectacle" looking on. Jesus' "acquaintances" will stand at a distance (23:48-49). At his death, divine approbation will be on the lips of a dubious witness, a centurion (23:47). The continuation of his mission by his followers will appear unlikely. His burial will be by a seeming stranger (23:50-53). It is his resurrection from such a death that gives Jesus a status far superior to that of Moses and Elijah. The disappearance of Moses and Elijah from the scene in v 33 connotes their having been superseded by Jesus. As eschatological figures, Moses and Elijah also are heralds that in Jesus the end time is inaugurated. It is Jesus in whom salvation is now to be found and he is the one to be heeded.

## Luke 9:31

The explanatory phrase οἳ ὀφθέντες ἐν δόξῃ, retained from the L source, referred originally to ἄνδρες δύο, making it clear that the two men were angels. In the final form it refers to Moses and Elijah. As elsewhere in Luke-Acts, ὤφθη is used of beings who make their appearance in a supernatural way. Their radiance indicates that they belong to the heavenly realm.[111]

That Jesus is the one to whom Moses and Elijah appeared in glory is implied by v 30, which says that they were talking to him, and by the rest of v 31, which gives the content of their conversation. Whether or not Moses and Elijah appeared in glory to the disciples is left ambiguous. On the one hand, v 32 says that Peter and his companions were sleeping. Then upon waking they saw Jesus' glory and the two men standing with him, whom Peter identifies as Moses and Elijah in v 33. The text does not say that the disciples saw Moses' and Elijah's glory, although it says they saw Jesus' glory. The impression Luke leaves is that Moses and Elijah appeared specifically to Jesus and that the disciples happened, by chance, to glimpse them upon awakening.

The remainder of v 31 relates the content of the conversation between Jesus, Moses, and Elijah. They were speaking of Jesus' ἔξοδος, which he was to fulfill in Jerusalem, ἔλεγον τὴν ἔξοδον αὐτοῦ, ἣν ἤμελλεν πληροῦν ἐν Ἰερουσαλήμ.

There are several interpretations of the noun ἔξοδος. It occurs in only two other places in the NT. In Heb 11:22, it refers to the exodus, the historic and prophetic saving event in which God brought the Israelites out of Egyptian bondage and into the promised land. And indeed, this is the most immediate connotation of ἔξοδος for one steeped in a scriptural mindset.

The noun ἔξοδος also denotes "death," and is so used in 2 Pet 1:15.[112] A difficulty with this interpretation for 9:31 is that in the context of 9:18-27, which contains very blunt speech about Jesus' coming death, the use of ἔξοδος as a

---

[111]See above, chapter two, on 9:31-33a for the occurrences of ὤφθη and the range of meanings of δόξα in Luke-Acts.

[112]So also in Wis 3:2; 7:6; Jos. *Ant.* 4.8.2 §189.

euphemism for death seems unlikely.[113]    Another suggestion is that ἔξοδος
connotes Jesus' "coming out" of the grave at the resurrection.[114]

Another meaning of ἔξοδος is "departure," and this is the one that best
explains ἔξοδος in 9:31. Taken in a broad sense, it includes the whole complex of
events that forms Jesus' transit to God: his passion, death, burial, resurrection, and
ascension/exaltation.[115] This interpretation fits well with Luke's whole concept
of salvation history and with his geographical perspective. Luke presents salvation
history as a course of events following a schedule of times set by God and moving
along a "way" leading to the gentiles.[116] Accordingly, Luke depicts Jesus' entire
life and ministry as a course or "way."[117] The beginning of Jesus' public
ministry is termed εἰσόδος in Acts 13:24, and the beginning of the final events of
that journey is signaled with ἔξοδος in Luke 9:31. Thus, ἔξοδος carries a double
connotation:[118] it denotes the whole complex of events of Jesus' passion, death,
resurrection, and ascension/exaltation, while at the same time it echoes the
paradigmatic saving event of the exodus.[119] The message from the two heavenly
figures is that Jesus' "exodus," his death and its attendant events will be the great
redeeming action for his people, just as was the exodus of old. The conclusion of
Jesus' life and work that is to come shortly in Jerusalem is all in fulfillment of
God's saving plan. Jesus is the one who will lead forth God's people on a new
journey of liberation.[120]

The phrase ἣν ἤμελλεν πληροῦν ἐν Ἰερουσαλήμ elaborates on the meaning
of ἔξοδος. The verb μέλλω used with a present infinitive has several
connotations.[121] It can mean "to be about to," as in Luke 7:2; 19:4; 21:7.[122]
This construction can also serve as a periphrasis for the future, as in Acts 13:34;
20:38.[123] It also denotes an intended action, as in Luke 10:1.[124]    A final

---

[113]Ziesler, "Transfiguration," 268.

[114]Mánek, "New Exodus," 12; T. Zahn, *Das Evangelium des Lucas* (Vol. 3; Kommentar zum Neuen Testament; Leipzig: Deichertsche, 1922) 3. 383.

[115]Fitzmyer, *Luke*, 167; Feuillet, "'L'exode' de Jésus," 181-206.

[116]W. C. Robinson, *Der Weg des Herrn* (TF 36; Hamburg-Bergstedt: H. Reich, 1964). See especially pp. 39-43.

[117]Marshall, *Luke*, 384-85. Luke uses ἡ ὅδος in Acts 9:2; 19:9,23; 22:4; 24:14,22 to designate Christianity as a way of life, a way that imitates the way of Jesus.

[118]It is therefore best to translate it as "exodus," preserving the double connotation.

[119]W. L. Liefield, "Theological Motifs in the Transfiguration Narrative," *New Dimensions in New Testament Study* (Ed. R. N. Longenecker and M. C. Tenny; Grand Rapids: Zondervan, 1974) 173; Murphy-O'Connor, "Transfiguration," 12.

[120]Moessner, "Preview," 595; Ringe, "Exodus," 94; Garrett, "Exodus from Bondage," 656-80.

[121]BAGD, 500-1.

[122]Also in Acts 3:3; 5:35; 16:27; 18:14; 21:27; 22:26; 23:27.

[123]BAGD, 501, also lists Luke 22:23; 24:21; Acts 28:6 as examples in which μέλλω with a present infinitive serves as a periphrasis for the future. However, they are less clear examples of this connotation than Acts 13:34 and 20:38 and also carry the sense of "about to."

meaning conveyed by μέλλω + a present infinitive is "must, will certainly, is destined," i.e., it denotes an action that necessarily follows a divine decree. This is the connotation in 9:31 and 9:44, which both speak of the divine necessity of Jesus' death.[125] In Acts 26:22-23, the two-fold use of μέλλω expands the connotation of divine necessity to include Jesus' death, resurrection, and the kerygmatic proclamation. The sense of μέλλω in 9:31 is that Jesus' "exodus" must certainly be fulfilled in Jerusalem by divine necessity.[126]

The verb πληροῦν is used in several ways by Luke.[127] In Luke 2:40; 3:5 (= Isa 40:4); Acts 2:2,28 (= Ps 15:11); 5:3,28; 13:52, πληροῦν conveys a notion of fullness or totality. In Luke 21:24; Acts 7:23,30; 9:23; 24:27, it connotes the completeness of a period of time that has been "filled up," or has reached its end. Similarly, it is used in Luke 7:1; Acts 12:25; 13:25; 14:26; 19:21 with the idea of completion, termination. Fulfillment of divine predictions or promises, especially as found in scripture,[128] is expressed with πληροῦν in Luke 1:20; 4:21; 22:16; 24:44; Acts 1:16; 3:18; 13:27. In 9:31, πληροῦν carries both the connotation of completion as well as that of fulfillment of divine promises. The note of fulfillment is sounded in 4:21 at the inauguration of Jesus' Galilean ministry and again in 9:31 at the outset of the Jerusalem mission. In using the verb πληροῦν, Luke conveys in 9:31 that the completion of Jesus' life and mission is seen to be in fulfillment with God's saving plan.[129]

The city of Jerusalem plays an important role in the geographical schema of Luke-Acts.[130] Jerusalem is portrayed as the pivotal point in the divine plan of salvation, the center of Luke's theological universe. At the beginning of the Gospel, Jerusalem is the place of God's revelation; there is harmony between Jerusalem and God. It is at the temple in Jerusalem that the revelation is made to Zechariah (1:5-23) and that Simeon and Anna bless the child Jesus and proclaim his saving role (2:25-38). Jerusalem is also the city of pilgrimage, whither Mary,

---

[124]Also in Acts 17:31; 20:3,7,13; 23:15; 26:2; 27:30.

[125]BAGD, 501; Plummer, *Luke*, 251. Matthew also uses formulations with μέλλω in reference to Jesus' suffering and death to show that these occurrences are according to divine decree: 17:12,22; 20:22.

[126]Luke also uses δεῖ to express divine necessity, e.g., Luke 2:49; 4:43; 9:22; 21:9; Acts 1:16; 3:21; 4:12.

[127]See BAGD, 671-72; G. Delling, "πληρόω," *TDNT* 6 (1968) 286-98.

[128]Luke does not use the same type of "fulfillment formula," however, that Matthew does, with πληρόω introducing an explicit OT citation, as in Matt 1:22-23; 2:15,17-18,23; 4:14-16; 8:17; 12:17-21; 13:35; 21:4-5; 27:9-10. See further Soares Prabhu, *Formula Quotations*, 59-60.

[129]See further C. H. Talbert, "Promise and Fulfillment in Lucan Theology," *Luke-Acts. New Perspectives from the Society of Biblical Literature Seminar* (New York: Crossroad, 1984) 91-103 for a description of the works of those who view the promise-fulfillment schema as the central theological idea of Luke-Acts. Talbert raises questions regarding the data used in such works, the use of the concept of fulfillment in Luke's cultural milieu, and the feasibility of subsuming all Lucan theology under one theme.

[130]See further Conzelmann, *Luke*, 17-94; B. E. Reid, "The Centerpiece of Salvation History: Jerusalem in the Gospel of Luke," *TBT* 29 (1991) 20-24.

Joseph, and Jesus journey to celebrate the feast of Passover (2:41) and where Jesus receives the first favorable response to his words (2:46-47). But an ominous note is struck in 4:9, where the pinnacle of the temple in Jerusalem becomes a site for Jesus' temptation. Throughout the Galilean ministry (4:14-9:50) Jesus' exclusive locus of activity is Galilee. The only reference made to Jerusalem is in 5:17, where some Pharisees and teachers from Jerusalem are present when Jesus heals the paralytic, and they join the crowd in glorifying God. So, too, people from Jerusalem form part of the audience for the Sermon on the Plain (6:17).

Jerusalem is not mentioned again in Luke until 9:31, when it becomes the city of destiny for Jesus' "exodus." He sets his face to go there (9:51) when the days draw near for him to be taken up. It is at this point that Jerusalem becomes the symbol of all who reject Jesus (9:53; 13:4),[131] all who are faithless in Israel. Jerusalem is the city that kills prophets (13:33,34) and the place where everything written of Jesus will be accomplished (18:31). When Jesus enters the city he weeps over it and foretells its destruction 19:41-44 and 21:20-24). The temple is no longer where faithful Israelites recognize God's revelation. It is characterized as a "den of thieves" (19:46) where the leaders of the people plot Jesus' death (19:47).

However, the positive portrayal of Jerusalem is resumed after Jesus' resurrection. In contrast to Mark and Matthew, Luke locates all his postresurrection stories in Jerusalem (24:1-53). The disciples are instructed to remain in the city until they are clothed with power from on high (24:49). And indeed, in Acts 2:1-13 they receive the power of the Spirit that impels them to preach the gospel to the "ends of the earth," beginning from Jerusalem (Luke 24:47; Acts 1:8). The remainder of Acts illustrates the missionary endeavor continually going forth from and returning to Jerusalem (Acts 8:4-8,14-17,25,26; 9:32; 11:2,22,27; 12:25; 13:13; 15:2,4,40; 19:21; 20:16,22; 21:15,17).

## Luke 9:32

In this verse, the presence of Peter and his companions is recalled. They were last mentioned in v 28 and have been peripheral to the story so far. Before reintroducing them into the narrative, Luke explains their lack of participation by their having been asleep.

The expression ὁ δὲ Πέτρος καὶ οἱ σὺν αὐτῷ singles Peter out as the representative of the small group of disciples. Other instances in Luke where Peter (or Simon) takes the role of leader or representative disciple are 5:1-11; 8:45; 9:20; 12:41; 18:28; 22:31-34,54-62; 24:34, and predominantly throughout the first half of Acts. An expression similar to ὁ δὲ Πέτρος καὶ οἱ σὺν αὐτῷ is found in Luke 5:9, where Peter and all who were with him, καὶ πάντας τοὺς σὺν αὐτῷ, are

---

[131]The listing of the elders, chief priests, and scribes, the members of the Jerusalem Sanhedrin, in the first passion prediction in 9:22, already intimates the role that Jerusalem will take on as Jesus approaches his death.

amazed at the miraculous catch of fish.[132]

The next phrase, ἦσαν βεβαρημένοι ὕπνῳ, is a puzzling detail on the level of story. Nothing in the narrative explains why the disciples should have been so tired.[133] On a symbolic level, the motif of sleep carries many connotations. There are three other times in Luke's Gospel when sleeping and awakening occur.[134] In 8:22-25 (= Mark 4:35-41), where Jesus falls asleep during the storm, his sleep portrays his assurance and his dominance over the forces of chaos.[135] His disciples, by awakening him, demonstrate their fear and lack of faith.

But this connotation of assurance and power is not what is conveyed by the disciples' sleep in 9:32. In Luke 8:49-56 (= Mark 5:35-43; Matt 9:23-26), where Jesus raises Jairus's daughter, her sleeping is taken for death by all who were witnesses. Jesus, however, perceives that she is only asleep, and he calls to her to arise. This incident reflects a common use of sleep as a metaphor for death.[136] If this connotation is what is operative in 9:32, then perhaps the "sleep" that weighs down the disciples is the death of Jesus that confronts them.

The closest parallel to the waking and sleeping in 9:32 is found in the agony scene (22:45-46) where the disciples also fall asleep in the face of Jesus' imminent death. In this instance, there is the connotation of sleep as spiritual inadequacy (as in Rom 13:11; 1 Thess 5:6; Eph 5:14; and possibly Acts 20:9), although Luke softens this with his explanation that it was sorrow that caused the disciples to sleep (22:45). It has already been noted that the detail of sleeping and waking in 9:32 is probably transplanted from an original context of the Gethsemane tradition. The presence of this detail in the transfiguration story would then create a uniform background between the transfiguration and agony narratives. By making such a connection between the two stories, Luke highlights the similarites and differences between these two times of Jesus' prayer. Both relate to his coming passion, death, and resurrection, but the one portrays the ultimate glory achieved through the passion, while the other depicts the depths of the struggle and sorrow it entails. In both instances, the disciples' sleep points up their frailty in the face of Jesus' suffering.

One other instance of sleeping and waking is found in Acts 12:1-24, where Peter is asleep in prison and is awakened and led out of bondage by an angel of the Lord. S. R. Garrett sees Peter's sleeping and awakening as symbolic of death and

---

[132]Some MSS of 8:45 (ℵ A C D L P W Θ Ξ f[1.13] 33 892 1009 1071 1195 1230 1241 1253 Lect M latt sy[p.h] bo) have the identical expression as 9:32, by adding καὶ οἱ σὺν αὐτῷ to ὁ Πέτρος. This addition may be due to scribal harmonization with Mark 5:31: καὶ ἔλεγον αὐτῷ οἱ μαθηταὶ αὐτοῦ. Or perhaps it is an attempt to have Peter share the blame of rebuking Jesus. See Metzger, Textual Commentary, 146.

[133]Fitzmyer (Luke, 800) says that in view of 9:37 there is the suggestion that the setting was nighttime. But this is not explicit in the narrative.

[134]The various verbs for sleeping used by Luke are: ἀφυπνόω in 8:23; καθεύδω in 8:52; 22:46; κοιμάω in 22:45.

[135]H. Balz, "ὕπνος," TDNT 8 (1972) 553.

[136]E.g., Dan 12:2; Acts 7:60; 13:36; 20:9; 1 Thess 5:10; 1 Enoch 49:3; 91:10; 92:3; 100:5.

resurrection. She links Acts 12:1-24 to Luke 9:31, showing that Jesus' "exodus," discussed with Moses and Elijah at the transfiguration, becomes "a new typological model for divine intervention in human history."[137] She argues that just as God led the Hebrews out of Egypt, so God leads Jesus out of bondage through his death, resurrection, and ascension, and continues to lead Christians from the bondage of Satan and death, as demonstrated in Peter's release in Acts 12. Following this interpretation, Peter's sleeping and awakening in Luke 9:32 prefigures that of Acts 12:1-24.

A common biblical motif is that of sleep as a time for God's communication with chosen human beings (e.g., Num 12:6; Deut 13:1; 1 Sam 3:2-15; 28:6; Matt 1:20,24; 2:12,13,19,22). But it is unlikely that this meaning is operative in 9:32, since it is not during their sleep but only after awakening, that the revelation from heaven to the disciples (v 35) takes place.

It has also been suggested that the sleep of the disciples in 9:32 is an apocalyptic stage prop.[138] However, the way sleep is used in apocalyptic literature does not fit the narrative in Luke 9:32. In apocalyptic literature, eschatological visions take place during sleep, e.g., Dan 10:9; 2 Enoch 1:5-6. It is unlikely that this connotation is intended in Luke 9:32. Again, what the disciples see at the transfiguration is perceived after they awaken, not in a vision during their sleep.

In the final form of the transfiguration story, the disciples' sleep functions as a means to keep the disciples on the periphery during the event described in vv 29-31. There is a similarity here to the way the sleep motif functions in Gen 2:21, where YHWH casts a deep sleep on the man, returning him to a state of inactivity to make it clear that it is YHWH who is doing the subsequent work of creating the woman.[139] Similarly, in Luke 9:32 sleep closes off the disciples' ability to perceive what transpires. The sleep of Peter and his companions also serves as an excuse for their lack of comprehension that is displayed in v 33. As in Sir 40:5, sleep confuses their minds.

Upon awakening, διαγρηγορήσαντες δὲ, the disciples begin to perceive what is happening. The phrase διαγρηγορήσαντες δὲ means "becoming fully awake."[140] The prefix δια- gives the intensive connotation "fully" and the aorist

---

[137]"Exodus from Bondage," 670.

[138]Fitzmyer, Luke, 800.

[139]See P. Trible, God and the Rhetoric of Sexuality (Philadelphia: Fortress, 1978) 45.

[140]Plummer (Luke, 252) interprets the phrase as "keeping awake." However, since this is a stative verb, the aorist participle is ingressive and should be translated "becoming fully awake." Also, when Luke wants to convey "keeping awake," or watchfulness, he uses the simple form of the verb γρηγορέω. This is found in Luke 12:37 as part of an admonition to watchfulness for the coming of the Son of Man. In Acts 20:31, γρηγορέω is part of a similar exhortation by Paul to the Ephesian elders before his departure to Jerusalem. Another verb used by Luke for watchfulness is ἀγρυπνέω, which appears in 21:36, where Jesus warns against the cares and excesses of life that weigh down the hearts of believers. The verb διαγρηγορέω, a hapax in the NT, does not convey in 9:32 the same connotation of watchfulness as γρηγορέω and ἀγρυπνέω, but rather that of "becoming fully awake."

is ingressive. On the level of the story, there is no evidence that the awakening of the disciples carries the figurative meaning of coming to consciousness or gaining insight on a spiritual level. Quite the contrary, in the remainder of the gospel the disciples continue to be portrayed as misunderstanding Jesus and his mission. On the level of the later reflection of the community who preserved this story, the transfiguration provided one more step in the awakening to the mystery revealed in the person of Christ.

What the disciples saw, εἶδον, at their awakening was the δόξα of Jesus and the two men standing with him, τοὺς δύο ἄνδρας τοὺς συνεστῶτας αὐτῷ. The act of seeing has an important connection with faith throughout Luke. From the very opening of the Gospel (1:2), Luke stresses the importance of the testimony of eyewitnesses, setting the tone for a theme of seeing that leads to faith and then to proclamation of the word. Characters in Luke who are said to see (ὁράω) Jesus or a deed of Jesus and come to believe in him and proclaim him include: the shepherds in 2:15; Simeon in 2:30; Simon Peter in 5:8; the leper in 5:12; the Gerasene demoniac in 8:28; the herdsmen in 8:34; the leper in 17:15; the multitude near Jericho in 18:43; Zacchaeus in 19:3; the multitude of disciples in 19:37; the centurion in 23:47; and the Galilean women in 23:49.[141] Accordingly, the seeing of the disciples at the transfiguration is important in their formation as witnesses and proclaimers of the word. Some, like Herod, in 9:9; 23:8, or Simon the Pharisee in 7:39, or the crowd in 19:7, see but do not come to faith. The eschatological fulfillment of the reign of God is also spoken of in terms of what will be seen: 3:6; 9:27; 13:28; 17:22; 21:27.[142] What the disciples see at the transfiguration gives a foretaste of what will be seen at the time of eschatological fulfillment.

In the final form of the story, what the disciples see when they perceive the δόξα of Jesus is the divine radiance that is his.[143] An important step is taken in the NT when δόξα, which had been used in relation to God (e.g., Luke 2:9; 7:55) is now used of Jesus. The phrase εἶδον τὴν δόξαν αὐτοῦ has echoes of Num 12:8, where it is said that Moses saw the glory of God, τὴν δόξαν κυρίου εἶδεν. The expression also calls to mind OT eschatological promises of seeing God's glory, e.g., ὄψεται τὴν δόξαν κυρίου (Isa 35:2); ὄψονται τὴν δόξαν μου (Isa 66:18). Against this background, εἶδον τὴν δόξαν αὐτοῦ in 9:32 can also be understood as a proleptic vision of Jesus' eschatological glory.[144] This interpretation agrees with Luke's use elsewhere of δόξα in reference to Jesus, where it is a future glory

---

[141]These are the examples in which the verb ὁράω is used. In the case of the Galilean women, they are introduced in 8:1-3, and are witnesses of Jesus' death (23:49). Luke 24:1-12 describes how they are the first to proclaim the word after the resurrection. On the importance of the theme of witness in Luke-Acts, see Conzelmann, *Luke*, 37-38; Fitzmyer, *Luke*, 26, 171, *passim*, and O'Toole, *Unity*, 43-46, *passim*.

[142]In each of these instances the future tense of ὁράω is used.

[143]See Ramsey, *Glory*, 101, for the interpretation that the whole transfiguration episode is the one instance during Jesus' earthly ministry in which he allows his disciples to glimpse him in his heavenly glory.

[144]Boobyer, *Transfiguration*, 23.

into which he will enter: 9:26; 21:27; 24:26.

There is another connotation for δόξα that may have been operative in the original form of the story contained in Luke's special source: that of "form" or "appearance."[145] This connotation of δόξα comes from the notion that something in the appearance of a person or thing attracts attention or commands recognition. This meaning borders closely on that of "splendor" or "glory," as is evident from Isa 11:3 (LXX): οὐ κατὰ τὴν δόξαν κρίνει. The Hebrew word that δόξα translates in this instance is mar 'eh, which denotes appearance.[146] In 2 Macc 3:26 δόξα is used to describe the pleasing appearance of the two young men: κάλλιστοι δὲ τὴν δόξαν. In several OT examples, the LXX translates δόξα for těmunâ, another Hebrew word for "form" or "representation." In Num 12:8: τὴν δόξον κυρίου εἶδεν; and Ps 17(16):15: ἐγὼ δὲ ἐν δικαιοσύνῃ ὀφθήσομαι τῷ προσώπῳ σου, χορτασθήσομαι ἐν τῷ ὀφθῆναι τὴν δόξαν σου. In this last example, it is notable that τὴν δόξαν is parallel with τῷ προσώπῳ, a possible indication of the proximate meaning of the two. Another example in which δόξα translates a Hebrew word for "form" or "appearance" is Isa 52:14, where δόξα is used for tō 'ar and is parallel with εἶδος (= mar 'eh): οὕτως ἀδοξήσει ἀπὸ ἀνθρώπων τὸ εἶδος σου καὶ ἡ δόξα σου ἀπὸ τῶν ἀνθρώπων. In the NT, another example that shows the close connection between δόξα and "form" or "representation" is 1 Cor 11:7, where εἰκὼν and δόξα are juxtaposed: ἀνὴρ . . . εἰκὼν καὶ δόξα θεοῦ ὑπάρχων.[147]

What these examples show is that in some cases δόξα connotes "form" or "appearance," and such a connotation is quite coherent for Luke 9:32 in its original form. Just as the meaning of εἶδος and δόξα are closely related in Isa 52:14, as are πρόσωπον and δόξα in Ps 17(16):15, so τὴν δόξαν αὐτοῦ in Luke 9:32 is understood in reference to τὸ εἶδος τοῦ προσώπου αὐτου in 9:29. There are several layers of meaning in 9:32. What the disciples saw upon awakening was Jesus' δόξα, his appearance, which had become altered during his prayer. The visible alteration may be understood as a natural radiance, δόξα, a "lighting up" of Jesus' countenance that was the result of his communion with God. In the final form of the narrative, the δόξα of Jesus comes to be understood in the sense of heavenly radiance or divine glory.

The disciples also see the two men standing with Jesus, τοὺς δύο ἄνδρας τοὺς συνεστῶτας αὐτῷ. This detail, preserved from the L source, originally referred to the two predicting angels. Such angels are almost always said to be standing with,

---

[145]Cremer, "δόξα," 207; E. C. E. Owen, "δόξα and Cognate Words," JTS 33 (1932) 132-50, 265-79. For numerous examples demonstrating the wide semantic range of δόξα, see L. H. Brockington, "The Septuagintal Background to the New Testament Use of δόξα," Studies in the Gospels in Memory of R. H. Lightfoot (ed. D. E. Nineham; Oxford: Blackwell, 1955) 1-8.

[146]KB, 563.

[147]Brockington ("Septuagintal Background," 1-8) also notes that in Rom 1:23; 9:4; 2 Cor 8:23; John 17:22,24 the connotation of δόξα may be close to what is suggested in 1 Cor 11:7: the concept of "God-likeness" in form or image.

before, or by the one to whom they appear,[148] This detail indicates that the messenger stands in place of God, whose message they bear.[149] In the final form, the two men are Moses and Elijah, standing with Jesus.

## Luke 9:33

Having been reintroduced in v 32, the disciples now become active participants in the story. As the two heavenly figures depart from the scene, καὶ ἐγένετο ἐν τῷ διαχωρίζεσθαι αὐτοὺς ἀπ' αὐτοῦ, the focus of the narrative shifts away from Jesus and his interlocutors and moves to the disciples. The construction ἐν τῷ + a present infinitive connotes contemporary action,[150] i.e., as the two were departing, Peter speaks.

Peter, acting as the mouthpiece for the trio, speaks to Jesus, εἶπεν ὁ Πέτρος πρὸς τὸν Ιησοῦν, addressing him as ἐπιστάτα, "master." This title of address is peculiar to Luke and is found five other times in the Gospel: 5:5; 8:24,45; 9:49; 17:13. In two of these instances (5:5; 8:45), it is found on the lips of Peter. The title ἐπιστάτα is used exclusively by disciples or followers of Jesus. The Marcan title in 9:5, 'ραββί, which Luke never uses,[151] is not exactly equivalent in meaning to ἐπιστάτα. Implicit in ἐπιστάτα is the notion of mastery or authority of any kind, not only that of a teacher. This connotation is clear in each instance that the title is used in Luke. It always occurs in a situation of complaint or distress, in which the one who addresses Jesus as ἐπιστάτα is calling for his mastery over the situation. When Luke wants to stress Jesus' teaching authority, he uses the title διδάσκαλος, a title that is more often found on the lips of nondisciples in Luke.[152] The substitution of ἐπιστάτα for Mark's 'ραββί emphasizes Jesus' mastery of the situation.

The next phrase, καλόν ἐστιν ἡμᾶς ὧδε εἶναι, "it is good that we are here," is best understood as Peter's enthusiastic estimation of the benefit for himself and

---

[148]Gen 18:2: εἱστήκεισαν ἐπάνω αὐτοῦ; Num 22:22: ἀνέστη ὁ ἄγγελος τοῦ θεοῦ; Num 22:24: ἔστη ὁ ἄγγελος; Num 22:26: ὁ ἄγγελος . . . ὑπέστη; Num 22:31: τὸν ἄγγελον κυρίου ἀνθεστηκότα; Josh 5:13: ἑστηκότα ἐναντίον αὐτοῦ; 1 Chr 21:15: ὁ ἄγγελος κυρίου ἑστὼς; 1 Chr 21:16: τὸν ἄγγελον κυρίου ἑστῶτα; Ezek 40:3: εἱστήκει ἐπὶ τῆς πύλης; Ezek 43:6: ὁ ἀνὴρ εἱστήκει ἐχόμενός μου; Dan 8:15: ἔστη κατεναντίον μου; Dan 8:17: ἔστη ἐχόμενός μου τῆς στάσεως; Zech 1:11: τῷ ἀγγέλῳ κυρίου τῷ ἐφεστῶτι ἀνὰ μέσον τῶν ὀρέων; Zech 3:5: ὁ ἄγγελος κυρίου εἱστήκει; 2 Macc 3:26: περιστάντες ἐξ ἑκατέρου μέρους; Luke 1:11: ἑστὼς ἐκ δεξιῶν τοῦ θυσιαστηρίου τοῦ θυμιάματος; 2:9: ἐπέστη αὐτοῖς; 24:4: ἐπέστησαν αὐταῖς; Acts 1:10: παρειστήκεισαν αὐτοῖς; 10:30: ἔστη ἐνώπιόν μου; 2 Enoch 1:5 (J): "They stood at the head of my bed;" 2 Enoch 1:5 (A): "The men were standing with me;" Jos. Ant. 5.6.2. §213: αὐτῷ παραστάντες.

[149]Mullins ("Commission Forms," 612) makes this observation with regard to persons who stand or who are commanded to stand in commision forms.

[150]Zerwick, Biblical Greek, §390.

[151]Recall that in vv 33b-35 Luke's source is the Marcan tradition.

[152]Luke 3:12; 7:40; 8:49; 9:38; 10:25; 11:45; 12:13; 18:18; 19:39; 20:21,28,39; 21:7; 22:11. See further Glombitza, "διδάσκαλος," 275-78; M. Hengel, "Jesus was not a 'rabbi,'" *The Charismatic Leader and His Followers* (New York: Crossroad, 1981) 42-50; Viviano, "Rabbouni," 207-18.

his companions of what they are witnessing. It is also possible to understand Peter's remark to mean, "It is good for you that we are here," i.e., to make the tents for you,[153] and that part of Peter's mistake is in thinking that Jesus, Moses, and Elijah would have need for tents.

In Peter's proposition καὶ ποιήσωμεν σκηνὰς τρεῖς, μίαν σοὶ καὶ μίαν Μωϋσεῖ καὶ μίαν 'Ηλίᾳ, the subject of ποιήσωμεν is not made explicit, but is most likely meant to be Peter, John, and James, the same referents for the preceding ἡμᾶς. As in Luke 5:5; 8:45; 9:20; 12:41; 18:28, Peter speaks on behalf of himself and his companions.

There are several interpretations of the significance of σκηνή in 9:33. On a literal level, Peter's proposal to erect tents, or temporary dwellings, atop the mountain has been understood as a suggestion to prolong their stay so as to extend their experience there.[154] Or, a very simple explanation is that Peter wants to show proper respect for the unexpected visitors. His desire to fulfill the requirements of hospitality is what prompts him to suggest the building of tents. And what more appropriate dwelling for two men of the desert than σκηναί?[155]

On the symbolic level, the σκηνάς of 9:33 recall the tent of meeting, σκηνή ('ōhel mô 'ēd) in which God would speak[156] with representative Israelites during the period of wilderness wandering (Num 11:16-17,24-30; Exod 27:21).[157] Similarly, σκηνή was also used to refer to the tabernacle (miškān) of God's dwelling, the portable sanctuary made by the Israelites (Exodus 25-30; 35-40) and used during the wilderness period. Against this background, Peter would be suggesting the mountain of the transfiguration as a new locus for God's encounter with human beings. A problem with this interpretation is the number of tents.

Another association with σκηνή is the feast of Tabernacles, a joyous harvest feast that was a seven-day pilgrimage feast to Jerusalem in the time of Jesus (Deut 16:13; John 7:1-14). During the feast, participants would dwell in booths (sukkôt) as a commemoration of God's protection of Israel during the wilderness wanderings. With this connection in mind, Peter may be relating his enthusiasm over the transfiguration experience to the joy of the feast of Tabernacles.[158] Another aspect of the feast is that it also looked forward to the end time, when all

---

[153]E.g., Easton, Luke, 144.

[154]E.g., Trocmé (Formation, 125) who sees behind Mark 9:4 a sharp thrust by the evangelist at certain leaders of the church of his day whom he accuses of wasting time in vain contemplation instead of facing the real problems posed for the community by its encounter with people from the outside, such as those in Mark 9:14.

[155]M. D. Hooker, "'What Doest Thou Here, Elijah?' A Look at St. Mark's Account of the Transfiguration," The Glory of Christ in the New Testament. Studies in Christology (Ed. L. D. Hurst and N. T. Wright; Oxford: Clarendon, 1987) 65-66.

[156]God was not thought to reside there permanently, but rather the divine presence was manifest there whenever Moses entered to speak with God.

[157]Ziesler, "Transfiguration," 266-67.

[158]Some commentators (e.g., Riesenfeld, Transfiguré, 265-80; Stanley, Apostolic Church, 134-45) have taken the mention of σκηνάς as an indication that the historical setting of the transfiguration was the feast of Tabernacles.

nations would join Israel in celebrating the feast (Zech 14:16-21). Peter's proposition, then, would indicate that he thought this consummation was at hand.[159]

Another eschatological interpretation is that σκηνάς refers to the eschatological dwelling of the Messiah. Thus, Peter's suggestion would indicate that he believes the end of the age has arrived and that the time of God's eschatological visit and eternal dwelling with the people has come.[160] A difficulty with this interpretation is the number of tents proposed. If σκηνάς denotes the eschatological dwelling of the Messiah, only one is needed.[161] Also, it is questionable whether the idea of the Messiah dwelling in a tent was a widespread notion.[162]

There is one other reference to σκηνάς in Luke's Gospel that may help in understanding the notion present in 9:33. In 16:9, there is a saying of Jesus about being received into heavenly habitations, αἰωνίους σκηνάς. The connotation here is that σκηνή is the place where the presence of God dwells forever, and it is akin to the first interpretation of σκηνή presented.

The phrase μὴ εἰδὼς ὃ λέγει is an aside to the reader that indicates the inappropriateness of what Peter has proposed. How one understands Peter's mistake depends on how his proposition is interpreted. If Peter intended the tents as new tents of meeting, or places of encounter between God and human beings, then his mistake may be that he does not understand that the σκηνή, the dwelling of God with humans, is already present in Jesus.[163] However, this interpretation seems to be reading a Johannine theme (e.g., John 1:14) into Luke. Peter's misunderstanding may simply be that he does not comprehend that God does not abide in humanly constructed dwellings. This interpretation would be consonant with what Luke says in Acts 7:44-50, that God does not dwell in "houses made with hands."

If the connotation of σκηνάς in 9:33 is understood as eschatological, then Peter's misunderstanding is in thinking that the end time itself actually had come. The correct understanding would be that the end time was only prefigured at the transfiguration.[164] First, the whole complex of events that make up Jesus' "exodus" must be fulfilled. Another interpretation is that Peter's mistake may be in the number of tents he proposes. If by suggesting one each for Jesus, Moses, and Elijah he is placing all three on the same plane, then his error consists in his

---

[159]So Schürmann, Lukasevangelium, 560.

[160]Léon-Dufour, "Transfiguration," 102.

[161]Dabrowski ("Transfiguration," 96) responds to this objection with the explanation that there was an eschatological expectation that all the just would dwell in tents with the Messiah. However, the rabbinic texts he gives in support of the notion are all of a later date than the Gospel. Furthermore, the tents are proposed for Jesus, Moses, and Elijah, not for Peter, John, and James, who might hope to be among the just who could dwell in tents with the Messiah.

[162]See W. Michaelis, "σκηνή," TDNT 7 (1971) 372-73, who asserts that there is no OT reference to the Messiah dwelling in a tent.

[163]Caird, "Transfiguration," 292-93; Ziesler, "Transfiguration," 267.

[164]Boobyer, Transfiguration, 78-79.

failure to recognize Jesus' unique status.[165] ~~This mistake would then be addressed by the voice in v 35, which emphasizes the person and message of Jesus. This~~ interpretation is the one that best fits the flow of events in the story.

## Luke 9:34

The expression ταῦτα δὲ αὐτοῦ λέγοντος at the beginning of v 34 links closely the preceding comments of Peter with the next event, the coming of the cloud. While Peter is speaking, there appears a cloud, ἐγένετο νεφέλη, that overshadows the group, ἐπεσκίαζεν αὐτούς.

There are several ways of interpreting the significance of the cloud in v 34. With the presence of other motifs from the exodus/wilderness experience, the cloud calls to mind the pillar of cloud that was a symbol of the presence of YHWH during the wilderness wandering. The pillar of cloud pointed the way during the exodus (Exod 13:21-22) and accompanied the Israelites in all their journeyings (Num 14:14; Exod 40:38). It also formed a protective shield between the Israelites and the pursuing Egyptians at the crossing of the Reed Sea (Exod 14:19-20). The cloud also signaled when they should move onward (Exod 40:36-37). YHWH descended in the cloud at moments of special revelation (Exod 34:5; Num 11:25), and the cloud also rested on the tent of meeting when YHWH appeared there (Exod 33:9-11; 40:34-35; Deut 31:15).

This same symbolism is operative in 1 Kgs 8:10-11, where the cloud, God's presence, fills the temple at its dedication in the days of Solomon. And 2 Macc 2:8 recalls this significance of the cloud in the days of Moses and Solomon. In Isa 4:5 the portrayal of the restoration of Jerusalem includes a cloud, i.e., God's presence, covering Mt. Zion and its assemblies. In Luke's transfiguration story, the cloud is readily interpreted as one more symbol for the presence of God, along with the details of prayer on a mountaintop, altered facial expression, white clothing, heavenly figures, and tents.[166] As a symbol of the mysteriousness of divine manifestation, the cloud represents both God's self-revelation and self-veiling.[167]

Clouds also appear frequently as an apocalyptic motif. In addition to the symbolism of divine manifestation, which is found in Ezek 1:4; 10:3-4; 1 Thess 4:17, clouds also function as a kind of vehicle of transport. Such is the image in Luke 21:27, where Jesus speaks of the coming of the Son of Man in a cloud with power and great glory, τὸν υἱὸν τοῦ ἀνθρώπου ἐρχόμενον ἐν νεφέλῃ μετὰ δυνάμεως καὶ δόξης πολλῆς, an echo of Dan 7:13, found also in Rev 1:7. So too in Acts 1:9, at Jesus' ascension, a cloud is said to have taken him, νεφέλη ὑπέλαβεν αὐτὸν, out of the sight of the disciples. Also similar is Rev 11:12, where the two witnesses (implied to be Moses and Elijah) go up to heaven in a cloud, ἀνέβησαν εἰς τὸν οὐρανὸν ἐν τῇ νεφέλῃ. And in Rev 14:14, the one like a son of man is

---

[165]Ellis, "Composition," 122; Thrall, "Elijah and Moses," 305-17; Hooker, "Elijah," 64.

[166]So Fitzmyer, *Luke*, 802; Léon-Dufour, "Transfiguration," 104-5; Liefield, "Motifs," 170; Marshall, *Luke*, 387; Ziesler, "Transfiguration," 267.

[167]A. Oepke, "νεφέλη," *TDNT* 4 (1967) 905.

seated on a white cloud at the time of judgment. However, in 9:34 the cloud is not a vehicle of transport unless one interprets it as being the means by which Moses and Elijah depart from the scene. But this interpretation neglects the fact that at the beginning of v 33, Moses and Elijah are already said to be departing, before any mention of a cloud is made. The more prevalent symbolism of νεφέλη connoting God's presence is the more likely intention of Luke for 9:34.

There is an ambiguity over the referents of the pronouns both times that αὐτούς appears in v 34.[168] The text says that a cloud came and overshadowed them, αὐτούς, and that they became afraid, ἐφοβήθησαν, as they, αὐτούς, entered into the cloud. The question is whether αὐτούς means Jesus, Moses, and Elijah each time, or whether it includes the disciples.

Those who understand the referents of αὐτούς as Jesus, Moses, and Elijah, but not the disciples,[169] say that v 35 implies that the voice speaks from the cloud to those outside, i.e., the disciples. However, the exclusion of the disciples is not a necessary inference from the phrase ἐκ τῆς νεφέλης, as Exod 24:15-18 illustrates. In that instance, it is said that Moses and Joshua went up the mountain and the cloud covered the mountain, and that YHWH called Moses out of the midst of the cloud, ἐκ μέσου τῆς νεφέλης. This text implies that Moses was enveloped in the cloud that covered the mountain and there he heard God's voice from the midst of the cloud.

In light of this example, especially if there is a parallelism intended with it in 9:34, it is better to understand the pronouns in v 34 as including the disciples. In addition, v 33 has already indicated that Moses and Elijah were in the process of departing. Therefore, it would make little sense to say that then they start to enter the cloud which has just arrived. Furthermore, there is a question as to what would be the significance of the cloud enveloping Jesus, Moses, and Elijah, while leaving out the disciples. It has already been shown that the cloud is not a means of transport for them. If the cloud is meant to symbolize the manifestation of God's presence to Jesus, Moses, and Elijah, then it arrives a bit belatedly in the narrative. Signs of the divine presence involving these three are already visible in the change of Jesus' facial expression, his glistening garments, and the glory ascribed to all three.

It is not Jesus, Moses, and Elijah who are drawn into the divine presence at this point of the narrative, but rather the disciples. Having first been sleepy bystanders, Peter, John, and James are just at the point of entering into the mystery of what is transpiring at the transfiguration. They have awakened, but in their first look at the externals, Jesus' appearance and the two men standing with him, they do not entirely grasp the situation, as Peter's proposition in v 33 reveals. It is the disciples, then, who are drawn into interaction with the divine by the overshadowing cloud. Both pronouns include them.

The verb used of the cloud, ἐπισκιάζω, is comparatively rare in the NT.

---

[168]Variants in some MSS try to resolve the difficulty. P[75] omits the second αὐτούς to convey that it was the disciples who entered the cloud. Others, (P[45] A D R W Θ Ψ f[1.13] M sy[h] sa) read ἐκείνους εἰσελθεῖν for εἰσελθεῖν αὐτούς, making it Jesus, Moses, and Elijah who entered the cloud.

[169]E.g., Goguel, "Notes," 151; Oepke, "νεφέλη," 908.

Aside from its occurrence in all three synoptic accounts of the transfiguration, it is found in only two other instances: Luke 1:35; Acts 5:15. The basic meaning of ἐπισκιάζω is "overshadow." This is the same notion that is found in Exod 40:34-35 (LXX), where the cloud overshadows, ἐπεσκίαζεν, the tent of meeting. In Luke 1:35 ἐπισιάζω is used of the power of the Most High that will overshadow Mary for the birth of Jesus. In Acts 5:15, the sick are laid in the streets so that Peter's shadow might fall on some of them, ἡ σκιὰ ἐπισκιάσῃ τινὶ αὐτῶν. This action implies an flow of divine healing power from Peter. In each of these examples, as well as in 9:34, ἐπισκιάζω conveys the notion of emanation of divine power.

The implied subject of the verb ἐφοβήθησαν is the disciples. Luke has taken the detail of fear from Mark, where the disciples are clearly the ones who are afraid. A fearful response on the part of one to whom a manifestation of the divine is made is a constant motif, especially in Lucan writings. At the apparition of an angel of God to Zechariah (1:13), Mary (1:30), the shepherds (2:9-10), and the women at the tomb (24:5), their first reaction in each instance is fear. Jesus' deeds, as manifestations of God's power, also provoke fear in disciples or followers (5:10; 8:25,35,50). So too, in 9:34, the disciples are fearful when confronted with the divine. While uncomprehending onlookers, their response was "It is good that we are here" (v 33). But direct involvement with God, which is indicated in v 35, is a fear-producing phenomenon. By moving the element of fear to this place in his narrative, Luke conveys the idea of initial fear at divine manifestation.[170]

One further observation is that the echoes of Exod 40:34-35 found in Luke 9:34 create a contrast between the former covenant and the new. In Exodus, the cloud overshadowed, ἐπεσκίαζεν, the tent of meeting, and the glory, δόξα, of God filled it so that Moses could not enter, εἰσελθεῖν. By contrast, in the age of the new covenant, Peter and his companions do enter, εἰσελθεῖν, into the presence of God.

## Luke 9:35

With the symbolism of the overshadowing cloud in v 34, the disciples have been drawn into the encounter with the divine. In v 35 Peter and his companions remain those for whom the action is intended, as the message of the voice from the cloud is specifically directed to them. The voice that comes from the cloud, καὶ φωνὴ ἐγένετο ἐκ τῆς νεφέλης, is one of many voices that punctuate Luke's Gospel. His whole account of the good news is orchestrated by voices that come, ἐγένετο + φωνή, voices that are raised, (ἐπ)αίρειν + φωνὴν and voices that cry out, ἀνακράζειν + φωνῇ μεγάλῃ. In the overture to the Gospel, Mary's voice of greeting to Elizabeth (another example of ἐγένετο + φωνὴ) is an initial herald of the good news (1:44), which next is taken up by Elizabeth's son, John, as the voice preparing the way for the Lord (3:4 = Isa 4:3). At his baptism (3:22), a voice from heaven proclaims Jesus as God's beloved Son.

Throughout the course of Jesus' ministry, people in need cry out with a mighty voice to Jesus, e.g., the man with the unclean spirit in 4:33; the Gerasene

---

[170]Mark, by contrast, uses the disciples' fear (9:6) as an excuse for their lack of comprehension, and Matthew postpones it until after the voice from the cloud speaks (17:6).

demoniac in 8:28; the lepers in 17:13. People also raise their voices in blessing, e.g., the woman in 11:27, and in exuberant praise to God for Jesus' saving works, e.g., the healed leper in 17:15; and the multitude of disciples at Jesus' triumphal entry into Jerusalem in 19:37. In the climax of the Gospel, the chorus of voices that demand Jesus' crucifixion prevail (23:23) until the cry of Jesus' commendation of his spirit into the hands of God (23:46) strikes the final chord. This voice of God's faithful one is the voice that resounds through the ages.

In this chorus of voices, the voice from the cloud in 9:35 is substantially a reprise of the voice in 3:22. The theme of Jesus' special status as God's Son is replayed, but in a different key. In 9:35 the voice is directed to the disciples (οὗτός ἐστιν ὁ υἱός μου is in the third person), whereas at the baptism scene (3:22) Jesus is the one to whom it is directed (σὺ εἶ ὁ υἱός μου is in the second person). The message for the disciples is both a confirmation of Peter's declaration of Jesus' messiahship (9:20) and a corrective of his misunderstanding of what that entails (9:33). Peter and his companions must understand Jesus' divine sonship in the way it will be played out: as the servanthood of God's chosen one whose exodus will bring salvation. It is with this understanding that they must listen to and obey him.

As the voice of God, the phrase ἐγένετο φωνὴ occurs not only in Luke's accounts of Jesus' baptism (3:22) and transfiguration (9:35) but also in Acts 7:31, which recalls the voice that came to Moses from the burning bush (Exod 3:4), and in Acts 10:13,15, which tells of the voice that came to Peter in his vision. In Acts 9:4,7; 11:7; 22:7,9; 26:14, Paul repeatedly tells of the voice that he heard, ἤκουσεν φωνήν, during his conversion experience. God's self-revelation by means of a voice is consistently found in the OT as well. The voice of the Lord, ἡ φωνὴ κυρίου, is said to have spoken to Moses whenever he entered the tent of meeting (e.g., Num 7:89). The prophets, e.g., Isaiah (6:8) and Ezekiel (2:1) receive their calls by means of the voice of God. Although the word φωνή (qôl) is not always used, divine communication with God's chosen instruments is most frequently expressed in terms of God speaking to the person or the word of God coming to them (e.g., Gen 15:1; Jer 1:2; Jonah 1:1; Mic 1:1; Zech 1:1). Accordingly, "hearing the voice of the Lord," (ὑπ)ακούω τῆς φωνῆς κυρίου, becomes the quintessential expression of worship of God and true obedience (e.g., Deut 26:17; Josh 24:24; Jer 3:13,25).

In 9:35, hearing the voice of God is equated with hearing and heeding Jesus. The directive is given to the disciples: αὐτοῦ ἀκούετε.[171] Faithful following is put in terms of hearkening and heeding (ἀκούω) God's word. A new note is struck by emphasizing that Jesus is the one to whom disciples must listen and whom disciples must heed. He is the word of God for them. This emphasis on the person of Jesus is evident in v 35 by Luke's inversion of Mark's word order, with the placement of αὐτοῦ, the personal pronoun referring to Jesus, before the imperative ἀκούετε.

In Luke's transfiguration story, as elsewhere in his Gospel, both seeing and

---

[171]There is no connection in 9:35 between the voice from the cloud and the rabbinic notion of *bat qôl* as B. W. Bacon ("Jesus Voice From Heaven," *AJT* 9 [1905] 451-73) proposed. The two concepts are essentially different and that of *bat qôl* is a later product of rabbinic Judaism. See further, Dabrowski *(Transfiguration*, 181-84). See also Brown *(John*, 467) on John 12:28.

hearing are involved in the process of coming to fuller faith that then leads to proclamation of the gospel. In 2:20, the shepherds praise God for all they had heard and seen, πᾶσιν οἷς ἤκουσαν καὶ εἶδον. When John's disciples inquire of Jesus whether he is the "one who is to come," he directs them to tell John what they have seen and heard, ἃ εἴδετε καὶ ἠκούσατε (7:22). Although the process of faith is circumvented in Herod, he is anxious not only to hear of Jesus but to see him as well (9:9; 23:8). The resurrected Jesus capitalizes on both sight and hearing in bringing the disciples to the necessary faith in him as risen. With the two on the road to Emmaus, he both speaks to interpret all that concerns him in the scriptures (24:25-27) and opens their eyes in recognition (24:31). When he appears to the eleven in Jerusalem, he stresses that they both see him (24:39) and understand his words (24:44) so that they may become fearless witnesses (24:48).

This Lucan emphasis on seeing and hearing is reiterated in Acts as well. In Paul's retelling of his conversion experience in Acts 22:14-15, he recounts that he saw the Just One and heard a voice from his mouth so as to be a witness to all people of what he had seen and heard. In Acts 28:26-28, Paul's final estimation of the response of the Romans to his preaching is formulated in terms of hearing and seeing for understanding and perceiving God's salvation (echoing Isa 6:9). So too at the transfiguration, the faith response of the disciples is determined by what they see (v 32) and what they hear (v 35).

The identification of Jesus as "my chosen Son," gives the justification for the disciples' allegiance to Jesus as the unique agent of God's saving actions. The phrase ὁ υἱός μου conveys Jesus' special divine filiation. The expression ὁ υἱός μου is one of three forms that the title "Son of God" takes in Lucan writings.[172] In 9:35, as in 3:22, ὁ υἱός μου is the proclamation of the heavenly voice, God's identification of Jesus. Jesus himself takes up this title in 10:22, where three times he refers to himself as ὁ υἱός. At the annunciation, Jesus is first called "Son of the Most High," υἱὸς ὑψίστου (1:32), and then, "Son of God," υἱὸς θεοῦ (1:35). From the first, Jesus is identified in Luke's Gospel as the unique divine Son. In the temptation account, Satan seizes on this identification of Jesus (4:3,9), εἰ υἱὸς εἶ τοῦ θεοῦ, as also do the demons in 4:41. The Gerasene demoniac combines both phrases, calling Jesus υἱὲ τοῦ θεοῦ τοῦ ὑψίστου (8:28). The title is not used again in Luke's Gospel until the interrogation of Jesus by the high priest, σὺ οὖν εἶ ὁ υἱὸς τοῦ θεοῦ (22:70). In Acts, Paul proclaims Jesus the Son of God in 9:20, οὗτός ἐστιν ὁ υἱὸς τοῦ θεοῦ, and in 13:33 applies the title "Son" to him from Ps 2:7, υἱός μου εἶ σύ.

There is a long history to the title "Son of God" in the ancient Near East, from its application to Egyptian pharaohs, to Hellenistic and Roman rulers, to mythical heroes (e.g., θεῖοι ἄνδρες), to famous historical people.[173] In the OT,

---

[172]See Fitzmyer, *Luke*, 205-7.

[173]For bibliography on the traditions behind the "Son of God" title, see Fitzmyer, *Luke*, 205-6. For the development in Christian understanding of the meaning of Jesus as the Son of God see "The Son of God," chap. 2, pp. 12-64 in J. D. G. Dunn, *Christology in the Making. A New Testament Inquiry into the Origins of the Doctrine of the Incarnation*. Philadelphia: Westminster, 1980. See also "Did Jesus Claim to be the Son of God?" in J. D. G. Dunn, *The Evidence for Jesus*. Philadelphia:

the title has diverse nuances. It is used of angels (e.g., Gen 6:2; Job 1:6; 2:1; Ps 29:1; Dan 3:25) and of Israel in a collective sense (e.g., Exod 4:22; Deut 14:1; Isa 1:2). "Son of God" is also a title of adoption for a Davidic king (e.g., 2 Sam 7:14; Ps 2:7) and for an upright individual (e.g., Wis 2:18). There is no clear example from the OT or from Palestinian Jewish tradition that attests to a messianic understanding of "Son of God."[174] In later Judaism (e.g., 4 Ezra 7:28-29; 13:32), "my son" was applied to the messiah. It cannot be proved that this nuance was operative in pre-NT times. The connotations of special divine favor and divine power that are found in the use of this title in Palestinian Judaism and in the Hellenistic world are carried over into its use with regard to Jesus. The "Son of God" title for Jesus is recognized as an element of the early kerygma.[175]

The further designation of Jesus as ὁ ἐκλελεγμένος brings into greater relief the direct relationship between Jesus' special status as God's Son and his election by God to follow the path of suffering to glory. It is likely that Luke intended ὁ ἐκλελεγμένος as an allusion to Isa 42:1, where the servant of God is called ὁ ἐκλεκτός.[176] This title would further clarify the meaning of the content of the conversation between Jesus, Moses, and Elijah in v 31. The phrase ὁ ἐκλελεγμένος also forms a link with Luke 23:35, where the scoffers at the cross taunt Jesus as ὁ ἐκλεκτός. Together the allusion back to Isa 42:1 and forward to Luke 23:35 produce the idea of a suffering servant.

Unlike Mark's account, Luke's voice from the cloud does not repeat the same message as at Jesus' baptism. In that instance (Luke 3:22) the voice was directed to Jesus and its import was the designation of Jesus as one in special filial relationship with God. In Luke 9:35 the voice is directed to the disciples and Luke advances the previous understanding of Jesus as ὁ ἀγαπητός to that of Jesus as suffering servant conveyed by ὁ ἐκλελεγμένος. Ironically, it is precisely because Jesus is God's unique Son that he is chosen to undergo the passion. The scoffers at the cross in 23:35 do not understand this. They expect that if Jesus were indeed the Messiah of God, the Chosen One, ὁ χριστὸς τοῦ θεοῦ ὁ ἐκλεκτός, then he would save himself from the cross. In Luke 24:26 the connection between suffering and the Messiah (uniquely Lucan) is reaffirmed as the risen Christ asks the two journeying to Emmaus, οὐχὶ ταῦτα ἔδει παθεῖν τὸν Χριστὸν καὶ εἰσηλθεῖν εἰς τὴν δόξαν αὐτοῦ. Finally, the election of Jesus by God, like the election of disciples

---

Westminster, 1985, pp. 30-52.

[174]See J. A. Fitzmyer, "The Contribution of Qumran Aramaic to the Study of the New Testament, *A Wandering Aramean* (SBLMS 25; Chico, CA: Scholars, 1979) 92-93, 105-7. D. Barthélemy and J. T. Milik (*Qumran Cave I* [DJD 1; Oxford: Clarendon, 1955] 108-18) question this assertion in view of the text 1QSa 2:11-12, which can be rendered, "If God begets the Messiah." However, see the response of Fitzmyer in "The Son of David Tradition and Mt 22:41-46 and Parallels," *Essays on the Semitic Background of the New Testament* (London: Chapman, 1971) 115-19, and in "The Aramaic 'Elect of God' Text," 153.

[175]See Conzelmann, *Theology*, 76-82; M. Hengel, *The Son of God: The Origin of Christology and the History of Jewish Hellenistic Religion* (Philadelphia: Fortress, 1976).

[176]These two terms share the same semantic range.

by Jesus, is fulfilled only in obedience.[177]

When used eschatologically, as in Mark 13:19-27 (= Matt 24:22-31) and Luke 18:7, the chosen, οἱ ἐκλεκτοί, are those who faithfully serve and are vindicated at the end time. As ὁ ἐκλελεγμένος, so Jesus too is the faithful servant, like that of Isa 42:1, who will ultimately be vindicated by God.

The adjective ἐκλεκτός (from the same verb ἐκλέγομαι as the perfect participle passive ἐκλελεγμένος) is used in the OT for particular individuals of God's choosing who are to fulfill specific tasks.[178] It is not until later apocalyptic literature that "the Elect One" takes on messianic connotations (e.g., *1 Enoch* 39:6; 40:5; 45:3).[179] In Luke 9:35, although ὁ ἐκλεκτός is used of the Messiah, this title is not itself a messianic designation in the strict sense.

**Luke 9:36**

The conclusion to the story tells that, when the voice had spoken, Jesus was found alone. The aorist passive εὑρέθη may carry the same connotations of "be" or "prove to be" as the Hebrew passive *nimṣā'*; see also Luke 17:18.

In its original context, as the conclusion to v 33a, εὑρέθη 'Ιησοῦς μόνος followed logically the departure of the two heavenly interpreters. The incident retold in the account contained in Luke's special source focused only on Jesus. After the two heavenly figures serve their function, Jesus is left alone to begin the ἔξοδος on which he will embark. The disciples' presence in the story found in the L source is purely peripheral. They function only as witnesses that can testify to the event afterward. In the final form of the Lucan story, v 36b brings the emphasis back to the person of Jesus. He alone remains; he is the one to be heeded; it is his way that the disciples must follow.

**V. CONCLUSION**

The preceding analyses have intended to answer the question of how Luke understood the two traditions that he joined to create his account of the transfiguration, and what meaning he conveyed through this composite narrative. The examination of the context of Luke 9:28-36 show the transfiguration to be a turning point in the Gospel. It functions as a hinge between the two phases of Jesus' ministry, that which takes place in Galilee, and that which is carried out in Jerusalem. Situated in Luke 9, the transfiguration is one of a series of episodes that

---

[177]Matthew emphasizes this in 22:14, where it is clear that election is an invitation that demands a decision and carries with it a corresponding responsibility of obedience. See further G. Schrenk, "ἐκλεκτός," *TDNT* 4 (1967) 186-92.

[178]E.g., it is used of Moses in Ps 106:23; of David in Ps 89:19; of Jacob/Israel in Isa 42:1.

[179]In the Qumran Aramaic text designated as 4QMess ar. by J. Starcky, ("Un texte messianique araméen de la grotte 4 de Qumrân," *École des langues orientales anciennes de l'Institut Catholique de Paris: Mémorial du cinquantenaire 1914-1964* [Travaux de l'Institut Catholique de Paris 10; Paris: Bloud et Gay, 1964] 51-66) that contains a reference to the "Elect of God," *bĕḥîr 'ĕlāhā'*, it is doubtful that the title refers to a messiah. See further Fitzmyer, "Elect of God," 127-60.

answers the question posed in 9:9, "Who is this?" An explicit answer is given by the voice from the cloud: Jesus is God's chosen Son. A further implicit answer is given: Jesus is one who stands in continuity with the OT figures of Moses and Elijah, but supersedes them as the one in whom God's saving action is now manifest. The pericope both affirms Peter's recognition of Jesus as the Messiah and corrects the disciples' understanding of what that messiahship entails: an "exodus" through suffering and death into glory. For followers of Jesus, the path is the same as his, and it is he alone that disciples must heed and follow.

# CHAPTER FOUR

# CONCLUSIONS AND IMPLICATIONS

This study of the Lucan account of the transfiguration set out to investigate the history of the tradition behind Luke 9:28-36 and to determine the meaning that Luke intended to convey in his specific version of the story. The intent was to test the hypothesis that another source in addition to the Marcan tradition could be detected for Luke 9:28-36. A further aim was to determine whether information about a historical event in the life of Jesus could be discerned from the proposed special Lucan source. In chapter one were outlined the various approaches of exegetes to the synoptic accounts of the transfiguration. Included were the historical approach, the resurrection-appearance approach, the mythological approach, the approach from the Jewish background of the OT and apocalyptic literature, and the redaction-critical approach. It became evident that with the advent of redaction criticism there was a shift in the starting point of scholarly investigations of the transfiguration narratives. The earlier question of how to understand the transfiguration event became the question of how to understand Mark's account as an interpretation of his sources and how to understand the versions of Matthew and Luke as interpretations of Mark.

It was noted that almost all scholars begin with the presupposition that the Lucan account is simply a redaction of Mark's, and that all the differences between the two versions can be explained in terms of Lucan composition and redaction. Taking up the suggestion of several scholars that Luke had at his disposal two separate traditions, that of Mark as well as one unique to him, this study set out to do a detailed investigation of Luke 9:28-36 by means of source and redaction criticism.

In chapter two an analysis of the internal consistency of Luke's narrative revealed several tensions in the story and led to the formulation of the hypothesis that Luke 9:28-36 is a composite of two originally separate pieces of tradition. A verse-by-verse examination of Luke 9:28-36 vis-à-vis Mark 9:2-8 confirmed this hypothesis. Behind Luke 28-33a,36b is a uniquely Lucan source that contained a story about an incident that focused on Jesus. To this, Luke joined the Marcan tradition that stands behind Luke 9:33b-35 and relates an event directed to the disciples. Verse 32b, the detail about the disciples' sleepiness, is an element from the Gethsemane tradition that Luke inserted into the transfiguration story. Verses 29c, the description of Jesus' clothing, and 30b, the identification of the two men as Moses and Elijah, were inspired by the Marcan tradition and composed by Luke to interweave the two separate sources. Also attributable to Lucan composition is v 36a.

A form-critical analysis of the pericope revealed the inadequacy of past attempts at form classification. It was shown that 9:28-33a,36b is in the form of a predictive angelophany, which underscored the importance of the transfiguration as a saving event. In its final form, 9:28-36 becomes a pronouncement story.

The question was then posed whether Luke's two sources represent two different stages of development of the same underlying tradition, or whether they were entirely unrelated on a literary level before they were brought together by Luke. The conclusion was drawn that the latter was the case.

The agreements between the Matthean and the Lucan versions against the Marcan account were then examined. These supposed agreements were shown to be very few and only superficial. It was concluded that they can best be explained as coincidental similarities that resulted in the process of independent redaction by Matthew and Luke of their respective sources.

Chapter three was devoted to the question of how Luke understood the traditions he combined and what meaning he conveyed in his formulation of the transfiguration story. A study of the context of Luke 9:28-36 showed that the pericope is situated at a turning point in the Gospel. It is the hinge between two phases of Jesus' ministry: that which pertained to Galilee, and that which was carried out in Jerusalem. In the context of chapter nine, the transfiguration episode is fourth in a series of scenes that give an answer to the question posed by Herod in 9:9, "Who is this?" The christological affirmation of Jesus as God's chosen Son is made explicitly in v 35. There is also given an implicit identification of Jesus as one who stands in continuity with the OT figures, but who supersedes them as the one in whom God's saving action is manifest in the new age. With regard to the disciples, it was demonstrated that the transfiguration confirms Peter's declaration of Jesus as the Messiah but also illustrates the way in which that messiahship is to be understood, i.e., as a way that leads through suffering and death to glory. The final point evident in Luke's account is that the path for disciples can be no different from the one taken by Jesus.

This study has several implications concerning the synoptic source relationships, Luke's particular redactional methodology, the determination of the historicity of the transfiguration event, and insights into Luke's theology, especially with regard to christology and discipleship. First, from the analysis of the transmission of the tradition of the transfiguration story some assertions can be made regarding the synoptic source relationships. It is clear that the source relationship among the synoptic gospels for any given pericope that they have in common is often more complex than the solution provided by the two-document theory. In the case of the transfiguration accounts, the relationship between Matthew and Mark is as the two-source hypothesis asserts: Matthew was dependent on Mark and redacted this tradition in accord with his own stylistic and theological tendencies.

The relationship between Luke and Mark with regard to this pericope proved to be more complex. This is not the only Lucan passage about which this can be said. A Lucan passage that has a Marcan parallel is not always a simple reworking of the Marcan source by Luke. In a number of instances, Luke has combined material from a source peculiar to him with redacted Marcan material. Such was shown to be the case in the example of Luke 9:28-36. The analysis of the so called agreements in the transfiguration story between Matthew and Luke against Mark affirmed the tenet of the two-source theory that there was no direct relationship between Matthew and Luke.

At the beginning of this study, the approach of earlier exegetes who began with presuppositions about the historicity of the transfiguration event was criticized on the grounds that conclusions about historicity must stand at the end of an exegetical study, not at the beginning. The question then is posed here whether the preceding analysis of the history of the tradition of the Lucan transfiguration narrative provides any information for determining the historicity of the event. In other words, how far back has this study taken us toward discerning a preresurrection event in the life of Jesus? The answer to this question must involve a recognition of the nature of the evidence, the stages of the transmission of the gospel tradition, and the purpose for which the gospel stories were written.

The form in which the Luke 9:28-36 is preserved is that of a predictive angelophany converted into a pronouncement story. The primary intent of such a narrative is to convey a theological statement. The purpose is not to deliver historical or biographical information about Jesus. Rather, stories of this sort are faith statements intended for the building up of the early Christian communities. A historical tradition lies behind the synoptic gospel stories, but what is preserved in these stories is a stage of the tradition that is twice-removed from the actual events in the life of Jesus. Intervening between the historical events of Jesus' life and the written accounts of them was a stage of preaching by the early Christians, in which their postresurrection understanding and faith colored the handing on of Jesus' words and deeds. It is questionable whether the results of this study can supply further information about the first stage of the tradition, that of the historical events of Jesus' life. Because of the fragmentary nature of the evidence, the methods of historical criticism cannot provide scientifically certain results. It was acknowledged throughout the above analyses that many of the conclusions regarding the assignation of material to one source or another or to Luke's own composition are based on what has been perceived to be the evangelist's usual tendencies and result only in probability.

Recognizing these limitations, the most that can be said with certainty about the historicity of the transfiguration event, then, is that the disciples had a revelation concerning Jesus' identity and mission, in which Jesus' passion, death, and resurrection were understood as mandated by God in accord with the divine plan of salvation. All three evangelists present this as an event that occurred at the end of Jesus' Galilean ministry. If the uniquely Lucan piece of the tradition is closer to the historical incident as Murphy-O'Connor asserts,[1] then it preserves for us a glimpse into the process by which the earthly Jesus came to understand more completely God's intent for his "exodus" to be the fulfillment of his mission.

Important implications about Luke's theology can be gained from the study of his transfiguration narrative. By examining Luke's method of selection and redaction of his sources, a clearer understanding of his theological intent is gained. In the area of christology, Luke 9:28-36 is a key passage. It contains an important affirmation of Jesus' messiahship, but also clarifies the way that messiahship is to be understood: as one entailing suffering and death leading to glory. Jesus is proclaimed God's unique chosen Son whose "exodus" will be the saving event of the new age. By juxtaposing Jesus, Moses, and Elijah, Luke emphasizes that Jesus stands in continuity with the OT figures, but also supersedes them. In placing the transfiguration in the context of Jesus' prayer, Luke brings to the fore one of his

---

[1] "Transfiguration," 18.

favorite themes: the importance of prayer. By depicting Jesus at prayer at the pivotal moments of his life, Luke intimates that the source of Jesus' power for his mission was his prayerful union with God.

In terms of discipleship, Luke shows in the transfiguration story that it is in following Jesus that disciples are drawn into encounter with God, and that Jesus is the one who is to be listened to and obeyed. Luke also stresses the importance of seeing and hearing for disciples so that they may respond in faith to what they perceive. Finally, Luke shows that disciples are fallible people who do not always comprehend God's way or its manifestation in the life of Jesus. But Luke would have them embark on the same path as Jesus, a path that necessarily entails suffering and death leading to glory.

# BIBLIOGRAPHY

Albright, W. F. and C. S. Mann. *Matthew*. AB 26. Garden City, NY: Doubleday, 1971.

Allen, W. C. *A Critical and Exegetical Commentary on the Gospel According to S. Matthew*. ICC. New York: Scribner, 1907.

Allison, D. C. "Elijah Must Come First," *JBL* 103 (1984) 256-58.

Alsup, J. E. *The Post-Resurrection Appearance Stories of the Gospel Tradition. A History-of-Tradition Analysis*. Calwer theologische Monographien 5. London: SPCK, 1975.

Andersen, F. I. "2 (Slavonic Apocalypse of) Enoch," *The Old Testament Pseudepigrapha*. 2 vols. Ed. J. H. Charlesworth. Garden City, NY: Doubleday, 1983. Pp. 1.94-97.

Apuleius. *Metamorphoses*. Greek-French. tr. P. Vallette. 3 vols. Paris: Société d'édition "Les Belles lettres," 1940-45.

d'Arc, Sr. Jeanne. "Elie dans L'Histoire du Salut," *VSpir* 87 (1952) 136-47.

Bacon, B. W. "After Six Days: A New Clue for Gospel Critics," *HTR* 8 (1915) 94-121.

_____. "Jesus Voice From Heaven," *AJT* 9 (1905) 451-73.

Badcock, F. J. "The Transfiguration," *JTS* 22 (1921) 321-26.

Bailey, J. A. *The Traditions Common to the Gospels of Luke and John*. Leiden: Brill, 1963.

Baldacci, P. R. *The Significance of the Transfiguration Narrative in the Gospel of Luke: A Redactional Investigation*. Ph.D. Diss. Marquette University, Milwaukee, 1974.

Baltensweiler, H. *Die Verklärung Jesu. Historisches Ereignis und synoptische Berichte*. ATANT 33. Zurich: Zwingli, 1959.

Baltzer, K. "Considerations Regarding the Office and Calling of the Prophet," *HTR* 61 (1968) 567-91.

Balz, H. "ὕπνος, ktl.," *TDNT* 8 (1972) 545-56.

Barrett, C. K. *The New Testament Background: Selected Documents*. New York: Harper & Row, 1961.

Barthélemy, D. and J. T. Milik. *Qumran Cave I*. DJD 1. Oxford: Clarendon, 1955.

Bartlet, J. V. "The Sources of St. Luke's Gospel," *Studies in the Synoptic Problem by Members of the University of Oxford*. Ed. W. Sanday. Oxford: Clarendon, 1911. Pp. 313-63.

Bauer, W., F. W. Gingrich, and F. W. Danker, *A Greek-English Lexicon of the New Testament and Other Early Christian Literature*. 2d ed. Chicago/London: University of Chicago, 1979.

Beare, F. W. *The Gospel According to Matthew*. San Francisco: Harper & Row, 1981.

Behm, J. "μορφή, μορφόω, μόρφωσις, μεταμορφόω," *TDNT* 4 (1967) 742-59.

Bernardin, J. B. "The Transfiguration," *JBL* 52 (1933) 181-89.

Bertram, G. "Die Himmelfahrt Jesu von Kreuz und der Glaube an seine Auferstehung," *Festgabe für Adolf Deissmann*. Tübingen: Mohr, 1927. Pp. 187-217.

Best, E. *Disciples and Discipleship: Studies in the Gospel According to Mark.* Edinburgh: Clark, 1986.

_____. *Following Jesus: Discipleship in the Gospel of Mark.* JSNTSup 4. Sheffield: JSOT, 1981.

_____. "Mark's Preservation of the Tradition," *L'Évangile selon Marc.* Ed. M. Sabbe. BETL 34. Gembloux: Duculot, 1974. Pp. 21-34.

_____. "The Marcan Redaction of the Transfiguration," *International Congress on Biblical Studies.* Ed. E. A. Livingstone. SE 7. TU126. Berlin: Akademie, 1982. Pp. 41-53.

Betz, H. D. "Jesus as Divine Man," *Jesus and the Historian.* Philadelphia: Fortress, 1968.

Beyer, H. W. "ἕτερος," *TDNT* 2 (1964) 702-4.

Beyer, K. *Semitische Syntax im Neuen Testament.* Band 1. Satzlehre Teil 1. SUNT 1. 2d ed. Göttingen: Vandenhoeck & Ruprecht, 1968.

Bieler, L. *ΘΕΙΟΣ ANHP: Das Bild des 'Göttlichen Menschen' in Spätantike und Frühchristentum.* Darmstadt: Wissenschaftliche Buchgesellschaft, 1967.

Bigg, C. *The Epistles of St. Peter and St. Jude.* ICC. Edinburgh; Clark, 1902.

Binet-Sanglé, C. *La folie de Jésus.* Paris: Maloine, 1909.

Black, M. *An Aramaic Approach to the Gospels and Acts.* 3d ed. Oxford: Clarendon, 1967.

Blass, F. and A. Debrunner. *A Greek Grammar of the New Testament and Other Early Christian Literature.* tr. R. W. Funk. Chicago: University of Chicago, 1961.

Blinzler, J. *Die neutestamentlichen Berichte über die Verklärung Jesu.* NTAbh 17/4. Münster: Aschendorff, 1937.

Blomberg, C. L. "Midrash, Chiasmus, and the Outline of Luke's Central Section," *Gospel Perspectives III: Studies in Midrash and Historiography.* Ed. R. T. France and D. Wenham. Sheffield: JSOT, 1983. Pp. 217-61.

Bode, E. L. *The First Easter Morning: the Gospel Accounts of the Women's Visit to the Tomb of Jesus.* Rome: Biblical Institute, 1970.

Boismard, M.-É. "Elie dans le NT," *Études Carmélitaines* 35 (1956) 116-28.

_____. "Le réalisme des récits évangéliques," *LumVie* 109 (1972) 31-41.

_____. *Synopse des quatre évangiles en français.* 2 vols. Paris: Cerf, 1972.

_____. "The Two-Source Theory at an Impasse," *NTS* 26 (1980) 1-17.

Boismard, M.-É. and A. Lamouille. *Les Acts des Deux Apôtres.* 3 vols. EBib 12,13,14; Paris: Gabalda, 1990.

Boobyer, G. H. "St. Mark and the Transfiguration," *JTS* 41 (1940) 119-40.

_____. *St. Mark and the Transfiguration Story.* Edinburgh: Clark, 1942.

Bostock, D. G. "Jesus as the New Elisha," *ExpTim* 92 (1980) 39-41.

Bousset, W. *Kyrios Christos; Geschichte des Christusglaubens von den Anfängen des Christentums bis Irenaeus.* FRLANT 21. Göttingen: Vandenhoeck & Ruprecht, 1913.

_____. *Die Religion des Judentums in Späthellenistischen Zeitalter.* Tübingen: Mohr, 1926.

Bouyer, L. *La Bible et l'évangile.* Paris: Cerf, 1953.

Bovon, F. *Luc le théologien: vingt-cinq ans de recherches (1950-75)*. Neuchâtel/Paris: Delachaux & Niestlé, 1978.

Braithwaite, W. C. "The Teaching of the Transfiguration," *ExpTim* 17 (1905-6) 372.

Bretscher, P. G. "Exodus 4.22-23 and the Voice from Heaven," *JBL* 87 (1968) 301-11.

Brockington, L. H. "The Septuagintal Background to the New Testament Use of ΔΟΞΑ," *Studies in the Gospels in Memory of R. H. Lightfoot*. Ed. D. E. Nineham. Oxford: Blackwell, 1955. Pp. 1-8.

Brodie, T. L. "Greco-Roman Imitation of Texts as a Partial Guide to Luke's Use of Sources," *Luke-Acts. New Perspectives from the SBL Seminar*. Ed. C. H. Talbert. New York: Crossroad, 1984. Pp. 17-46.

_____. "Jesus as the New Elisha: Cracking the Code," *ExpTim* 93 (1981) 39-42.

_____. "The Departure for Jerusalem (Luke 9,51-56) as a Rhetorical Imitation of Elijah's Departure for the Jordan (2 Kgs 1,1-2,6)," *Bib* 70 (1989) 96-109.

Brown, R. E. *The Birth of the Messiah: A Commentary on the Infancy Narratives in Matthew and Luke*. Garden City, NY: Doubleday, 1977.

_____. *The Gospel According to John I-XII*. AB 29. Garden City, NY: Doubleday, 1966.

_____. *The Gospel According to John XIII-XXI*. AB 29a. Garden City, NY: Doubleday, 1970.

_____. "Incidents That are Units in the Synoptic Gospels but Dispersed in St. John," *CBQ* 23 (1961) 143-48.

_____. "The Messianism of Qumran," *CBQ* 19 (1957) 53-82.

Brown, R. E. and R. F. Collins. "Canonicity," *NJBC*, art. 66 §68 p. 1048.

Brown, R. E., K. P. Donfried, *et al*. *Mary in the New Testament*. Philadelphia: Fortress, 1978.

Brun, L. "Engel und Blutschweiss Lc 22,43-44," *ZNW* 32 (1933) 265-76.

Bultmann, R. *Die Geschichte der synoptischen Tradition*. 3d ed.; Göttingen: Vandenhoeck & Ruprecht, 1957.

_____. *The Gospel of John*. Philadelphia: Westminster, 1971.

Bultmann, R. and D. Lührmann. "ἐπιφαίνω, κτλ.," *TDNT* 9 (1974) 7-10.

Burkill, T. A. *Mysterious Revelation*. Ithaca: Cornell University Press, 1963.

Burrows, M. "The Messiahs of Aaron and Israel," *ATR* 34 (1952) 202-6.

Butler, B. C. *The Originality of St. Matthew: A Critique of the Two-Document Hypothesis*. Cambridge: University, 1951.

_____. "St. Luke's Debt to St. Matthew," *HTR* 32 (1939) 237-308.

Cadbury, H. J. *The Making of Luke-Acts*. London: SPCK, 1961.

_____. "The Relative Pronouns in Acts and Elsewhere," *JBL* 42 (1923) 150-57.

_____. *The Style and Literary Method of Luke*. HTS 6. Cambridge, MA: Harvard University, 1920.

Caird, G. B. *The Revelation of St. John the Divine*. 2d ed. London: Black, 1984.

_____. "The Transfiguration," *ExpTim* 67 (1955-56) 291.

Carlston, C. E. "Transfiguration and Resurrection," *JBL* 80 (1961) 233-40.

Cartlidge D. "Transfigurations of Metamorphosis Traditions in the Acts of John, Thomas, and Peter," *The Apocryphal Acts of Apostles*. Semeia 38. Ed. D. MacDonald. Decatur, GA: Scholars, 1986. Pp. 53-66.

Cerfaux, L. "Les Unités littéraires antérieures aux trois premiers évangiles," *La Formation des évangiles, problème synoptique et Formgeschichte*. RechBib 2. Bruges: Desclée, 1957. Pp. 24-33.

Cerfaux, L., J. Coppens, B. Dehandschutter. *L'évangile de Luc*. Gembloux: Duculot, 1973.

Charlesworth, J. H., ed. *The Old Testament Pseudepigrapha*. 2 vols. Garden City, NY: Doubleday, 1983.

Chilton, B. D. "The Transfiguration: Dominical Assurance and Apostolic Vision," *NTS* 27 (1981) 115-24.

Collins, A. Y. *The Apocalypse*. New Testament Message 22. Wilmington, DE: Glazier, 1979.

Collins, J. J. "Old Testament Apocalypticism and Eschatology," *NJBC* art. 19. Pp. 298-304.

Conzelmann, H. *An Outline of the Theology of the New Testament*. New York: Harper & Row, 1969.

_____. *The Theology of St. Luke*. Philadelphia: Fortress, 1961.

Corney, R. W. "Colors," *IDB* 1 (1962) 657-58.

_____. "White," *IDB* 4 (1962) 841.

Coune, M. "Baptême, Transfiguration et Passion," *NRT* 92 (1970) 165-79.

_____. "L'Évangile de la transfiguration," *Paroisse et liturgie* 52 (1970) 157-70.

_____. "La Transfiguration dans l'exégèse des sept premiers siècles," *AsSeign* 28 (1963) 64-80.

Cranfield, C. E. B. *The Gospel According to St. Mark*. CGTC. Cambridge: University Press, 1966.

Creed, J. M. "'L' and the Structure of the Lucan Gospel. A Study of the Proto-Luke Hypothesis," *ExpTim* 46 (1934-35) 101-7.

Cremer, H. *Biblisch-theologisches Wörterbuch des neutestamentlichen Griechisch*. Rev. J. Kögel. Stuttgart: Perthes, 1923.

Dabeck, P. "Siehe es erschienen Moses und Elias (Matt 17.3)," *Bib* 23 (1942) 175-89.

Dabrowski, E. *La transfiguration de Jésus*. Scripta Pontificii Instituti Biblici 85. Rome: Biblical Institute, 1939.

Daniélou, J. "Le Christ Prophète," *VSpir* 78 (1948) 154-70.

Danker, F. *Jesus and the New Age. A Commentary on St. Luke's Gospel*. Philadelphia: Fortress, 1988.

Daube, D. *The New Testament and Rabbinic Judaism*. New York: Arno, 1973.

Davies, J. G. "The Prefigurement of the Ascension in the Third Gospel," *JTS* 6 (1955) 229-33.

Davies, J. H. "The Purpose of the Central Section of St. Luke's Gospel," *Papers Presented to the Second International Congress on New Testament Studies held at Christ Church, Oxford, 1961. Part 1: The New Testament Scriptures.* SE 2. TU 87. Berlin: Akademie, 1964. Pp. 164-69.

Delling, G. "πληρόω," *TDNT* 6 (1968) 286-98.

Denis, A. M. "Une Théologie de la rédemption. La transfiguration chez Saint Marc," *VSpir* 101 (1959) 136-49.

Derrett, J. D. M. "Peter and the Tabernacles," *DRev* 108 (1990) 37-48.

Dibelius, M. *Die Formgeschichte des Evangeliums.* 5th ed. Tübingen: Mohr, 1966.

_____. *From Tradition to Gospel.* tr. B. L. Woolf. New York: Scribner, 1934.

Dietrich, W. *Das Petrusbild der lukanischen Schriften.* BWANT 5. Stuttgart: Kohlhammer, 1972.

Dillon, R. J. *From Eye-Witnesses to Ministers of the Word. Tradition and Composition in Luke 24.* AnBib 82. Rome: Biblical Institute, 1978.

Dittenberger, W. *Sylloge Inscriptionum Graecarum.* 4 vols. Lipsiae: Hirzelium, 1920.

Dodd, C. H. "The Appearances of the Risen Christ: an Essay in Form-Criticism of the Gospels," *Studies in the Gospels: Essays in Memory of R. H. Lightfoot.* Ed. D. E. Nineham. Oxford: Blackwell, 1957. Pp. 9-35.

_____. "Some Johannine 'Herrnworte' with Parallels in the Synoptic Gospels," *NTS* 2 (1955) 75-86.

Donaldson, T. L. *Jesus on the Mountain: A Study in Matthean Theology.* JSNTSup 8. Sheffield: JSOT, 1985.

Driver, S. and G. B. Gray. *A Critical and Exegetical Commentary on the Book of Job.* ICC. Edinburgh: Clark, 1950.

Drury, J. *Tradition and Design in Luke's Gospel: A Study in Early Christian Historiography.* London: Darton, Longman, and Todd, 1976.

Dubois, J. D. "La figure d'Elie dans la perspective lucanienne," *RHPR* 53 (1973) 155-76.

Dunn, J. D. G. *Christology in the Making. A New Testament Inquiry into the Origins of the Doctrine of the Incarnation.* Philadelphia: Westminster, 1980.

_____. *The Evidence for Jesus.* Philadelphia: Westminster, 1985.

Dupont, J. *The Sources of Acts. The Present Position.* London: Darton, Longman & Todd, 1964.

Easton, B. S. *The Gospel According to St. Luke. A Critical and Exegetical Commentary.* Edinburgh: Clark, 1926.

Ehrman, B. D. and M. A. Plunkett. "The Angel and the Agony: The Textual Problem of Luke 22:43-44," *CBQ* 45 (1983) 401-16.

Elliott, J. K. "Jerusalem in Acts and in the Gospels," *NTS* 23 (1976-77) 462-69.

_____. "The Use of ἕτερος in the New Testament," *ZNW* 60 (1969) 140-41.

Ellis, E. E. "La composition de Luc 9 et les sources de sa christologie," *Jésus aux Origines de la Christologie.* Ed. J. Dupont. BETL 11. Gembloux: Leuven University, 1975.

_____. *The Gospel of Luke.* NCB. London: Nelson, 1966.

Evans, C. A. "'He Set His Face': Luke 9:51 Once Again," *Bib* 68 (1987) 80-84.

Evans, C. A. "Luke's Use of the Elijah/Elisha Narratives and the Ethic of Election," *JBL* 106 (1987) 75-83.

Evans, C. F. "The Central Section of St. Luke's Gospel," *Studies in the Gospels. Essays in Memory of R. H. Lightfoot*. Ed. D. E. Nineham. Oxford: Blackwell, 1957. Pp. 37-53.

Evans, D. "Academic Scepticism, Spiritual Reality and Transfiguration," *The Glory of Christ in the New Testament. Studies in Christology*. Ed. L. D. Hurst and N. T. Wright. Oxford: Clarendon, 1987. Pp. 175-86.

Faierstein, M. "Why Do the Scribes Say That Elijah Must Come First?" *JBL* 100 (1981) 75-86.

Farmer, W. R. *The Synoptic Problem: A Critical Analysis*. New York: Macmillan, 1964. Rev. ed. Dillsboro, NC: Western North Carolina Press, 1976.

Farrer, A. "On Dispensing With Q," *Studies in the Gospels. Essays in Memory of R. H. Lightfoot*. Ed. D. E. Nineham. Oxford: Blackwell, 1955. Pp. 55-86.

Feuillet, A. "'L'exode' de Jésus et le déroulement du mystère rédempteur d'après S. Luc et S. Jean," *RevThom* 77 (1977) 181-206.

_____. "Les Perspectives propres à chaque évangéliste dans les récits de la Transfiguration," *Bib* 39 (1958) 281-301.

Fiedler, P. *Die Formel "und siehe" im Neuen Testament*. STANT 20. Munich: Kösel, 1969.

Fitzmyer, J. A. "The Aramaic 'Elect of God' Text from Qumran Cave 4," *Essays on the Semitic Background of the New Testament*. London: Chapman, 1971. Pp. 127-60.

_____. "The Composition of Luke, Chapter 9," *Perspectives on Luke-Acts*. Ed. C. H. Talbert. Special Studies Series 5. Danville, VA: Association of Baptist Professors of Religion, 1978. Pp. 139-52.

_____. "The Contribution of Qumran Aramaic to the Study of the New Testament, *A Wandering Aramean*. SBLMS 25. Chico, CA: Scholars, 1979. Pp. 85-113.

_____. *The Genesis Apocryphon of Qumran Cave I*. 2d ed. BibOr 18A. Rome: Biblical Institute, 1971.

_____. *The Gospel According to Luke I-IX*. AB 28. Garden City, NY: Doubleday, 1981.

_____. *The Gospel According to Luke X-XXIV*. AB 28a. Garden City, NY: Doubleday, 1985.

_____. "More About Elijah Coming First," *JBL* 104 (1985) 295-96.

_____. "Papyrus Bodmer XIV: Some Features of our Oldest Text of Luke," *CBQ* 24 (1962) 170-79.

_____. "The Priority of Mark and the 'Q' Source in Luke," *To Advance the Gospel*. New York: Crossroad, 1981. Pp. 3-40.

_____. "The Son of David Tradition and Mt 22:41-46 and Parallels," *Essays on the Semitic Background of the New Testament*. London: Chapman, 1971. Pp. 113-26.

_____. "The Use of *Agein* and *Pherein* in the Synoptic Gospels," *Festschrift to Honor F. W. Gingrich*. Ed. E. H. Barth and R. E. Cocroft. Leiden: Brill, 1972. Pp. 147-60.

da Fonseca, A. G. *Quaestio Synoptica*. 3d ed. Institutiones biblicae. Rome: Biblical Institute, 1952.

Forster, A. H. "The Meaning of Δόξα in the Greek Bible," *ATR* 12 (1929-30) 311-16.

Friedrichsen, T. A. "The Matthew-Luke Agreements against Mark. A Survey of Recent Studies: 1975-1989," *L'Évangile de Luc*. Ed. F. Neirynck. BETL 32. Leuven: University, 1989. Pp. 335-91.

Fryer, A. T. "The Purpose of the Transfiguration," *JTS* 5 (1904) 214-17.

Fuchs, A. "Die Verklärungserzählung des Mc-Ev. in der Sicht moderner Exegese," *TPQ* 125 (1977) 29-37.

Fuller, R. H. *The Formation of the Resurrection Narratives*. New York: MacMillan, 1971.

_____. *The Foundations of New Testament Christology*. New York: Scribner, 1965.

_____. "The 'Thou Art Peter' Pericope and the Easter Appearances," *McCQ* 20 (1967) 309-15.

Garrett, S. R. "Exodus from Bondage: Luke 9:31 and Acts 12:1-24," *CBQ* 52 (1990) 656-80.

Gaster, T. H. "Angel," *IDB* 1 (1962) 128-34.

Gause, R. H. *The Lukan Transfiguration Account: Luke's Pre-Crucifixion Presentation of the Exalted Lord in the Glory of the Kingdom of God*. Ph.D. Diss. Atlanta: Emory University, 1975.

Geldenhuys, N. *Commentary on the Gospel of Luke*. NIC. Grand Rapids. Eerdmans, 1968.

George, A. "Le Sens de la mort de Jésus pour Luc," *RB* 80 (1973) 186-217.

_____. "Tradition et rédaction chez Luc. La Construction du troisième évangile," *De Jésus aux évangiles: Tradition et rédaction dans les évangiles synoptiques*. Ed. I. de la Potterie. BETL 25. Gembloux: Duculot, 1967. Pp. 100-29.

_____. "La Transfiguration (Luc 9:28-36)," *BVC* 33 (1960) 21-25.

Gerber, W. "Die Metamorphose Jesu, Mark 9.2f. par.," *TZ* 23 (1967) 385-95.

Gils, F. *Jésus prophète d'après les évangiles synoptiques*. Orientalia et biblica lovaniensia 2. Louvain: Publications universitaires, 1957.

Glasson, T. F. *Moses in the Fourth Gospel*. SBT 40. London: SCM, 1963.

Glombitza, O. "Die Titel διδάσκαλος und ἐπιστάτης für Jesus bei Lukas," *ZNW* 49 (1958) 275-78.

Goetz, K. G. *Petrus*. Leipzig: Hinrichs, 1927.

Goguel, M. "Notes d'histoire évangélique. Esquisse d'une interprétation du récit de la transfiguration," *RHR* 81 (1920) 145-57.

Grässer, E. *Das Problem der Parusieverzögerung in den synoptischen Evangelien und in der Apostelgeschichte*. BZNW 22. Berlin: Töpelmann, 1957.

Grundmann, W. *Das Evangelium nach Lukas*. THKNT 3. Berlin: Evangelische Verlagsanstalt, 1974.

Gruppe, O. "Verwandlung," *Griechische Mythologie und Religionsgeschichte*. 2 vols. Munich: Beck, 1906. Pp. 2. 1920-21.

Guillaume, J.-M. *Luc interprète des anciennes traditions sur la résurrection de Jésus*. EBib. Paris: Gabalda, 1979.

Gundry, R. *Matthew: A Commentary on his Literary and Theological Art*. Grand Rapids: Eerdmans, 1982.

Habel, N. "The Form and Significance of the Call Narratives," *ZAW* 77 (1965) 297-323.

Haenchen, E. *The Acts of the Apostles*. Philadelphia: Westminster, 1971.

Hahn, F. *The Titles of Jesus in Christology*. New York: World, 1969.

von Harnack, A. "Die Verklärungsgeschichte Jesu, der Bericht des Paulus (1 Kor 15,3ff) und die beiden Christusvisionen des Petrus," *SBAW* (1922) 62-80.

Haugg, D. *Die zwei Zeugen. Eine exegetische Studie über Apk. 11,1-13*. NTAbh 17,1. Münster: Aschendorff, 1937.

Hawkins, J. C. *Horae Synopticae. Contributions to the Study of the Synoptic Problem*. 2d ed. Oxford: Clarendon, 1968.

_____. "The Limitations to St. Luke's Use of St. Mark's Gospel," *Studies in the Synoptic Problem by Members of the University of Oxford*. Ed. W. Sanday. Oxford: Clarendon, 1911. Pp. 27-94.

Hengel, M. *The Charismatic Leader and His Followers*. New York: Crossroad, 1981.

_____. *The Son of God: The Origin of Christology and the History of Jewish Hellenistic Religion*. Philadelphia: Fortress, 1976.

Hennecke, E. *New Testament Apocrypha*. 2 vols. Ed. W. Schneemelcher and R. McL. Wilson. Philadelphia: Westminster, 1965.

Herr, D. "Variations of a Pattern: 1 Kings 19," *JBL* 104 (1985) 292-93.

Holladay, C. R. ΘΕΙΟΣ ΑΝΗΡ *in Hellenistic-Judaism: A Critique of the Use of This Category in New Testament Christology*. SBLDS 40. Missoula: Scholars, 1977.

Höller, J. *Die Verklärung Jesu. Eine Auslegung der neutestamentlichen Berichte*. Freiburg: Herder, 1937.

Holmes, R. "The Purpose of the Transfiguration," *JTS* 4 (1903) 543-47.

Holzmeister, U. "Einzeluntersuchungen über das Geheimnis der Verklärung Christi," *Bib* 21 (1940) 200-10.

Hooke, S. H. *The Resurrection of Christ as History and Experience*. London: Darton, Longman & Todd, 1967.

Hooker, M. D. "'What Doest Thou Here, Elijah?' A Look at St. Mark's Account of the Transfiguration," *The Glory of Christ in the New Testament. Studies in Christology*. Ed. L. D. Hurst and N. T. Wright. Oxford: Clarendon, 1987. Pp. 59-70.

Horstmann, M. *Studien zur markinischen Christologie: Mk 8:27-9:13 als Zugang zum Christusbild des zweiten Evangeliums*. NTAbh 6. Münster: Aschendorff, 1969.

Hubbard, B. J. "Commissioning Stories in Luke-Acts," *Semeia* 8 (1977) 103-26.

_____. *The Matthean Redaction of a Primitive Apostolic Commissioning: An Exegesis of Matthew 28:16-20*. SBLDS 19. Missoula, MT: Scholars, 1974.

Hull, W. E. "A Structural Analysis of the Gospel of Luke," *RevExp* 64 (1967) 421-25.

Jeremias, J. *Das Evangelium nach Lukas*. Chemnitz/Leipzig: Müller, 1930.

_____. "'Ηλ(ε)ίας," *TDNT* 2 (1964) 928-41.

_____. "'ΙΕΡΟΥΣΑΛΗΜ/'ΙΕΡΟΣΟΛΥΜΑ," *ZNW* 65 (1974) 273-76.

_____. "Μωϋσῆς," *TDNT* 4 (1967) 848-73.

_____. *Die Sprache des Lukasevangeliums. Redaktion und Tradition im Nicht-Markusstoff des dritten Evangeliums*. Göttingen: Vandenhoeck & Ruprecht, 1980.

Johannessohn, M. "Das biblische καὶ ἐγένετο und seine Geschichte," *Zeitschrift für vergleichende Sprachforschung* 53 (1925) 161-212.

Johnson, L. T. *The Writings of the New Testament*. Philadelphia: Fortress, 1986.

Jones, D. R. "The Background and Character of the Lukan Psalms," *JTS* 19 (1968) 19-50.

Karris, R. *Luke, Artist and Theologian*. New York: Paulist, 1985.

Keck, L. E. and J. L. Martyn, eds. *Studies in Luke-Acts*. Philadelphia: Fortress, 1966, 1980.

Kee, H. C. "The Transfiguration in Mark: Epiphany or Apocalyptic Vision?" *Understanding the Sacred Text*. Ed. J. Reumann. Valley Forge, PA: Judson, 1972. Pp. 137-52.

Kelber, W. *Mark's Story of Jesus*. Philadelphia: Fortress, 1979.

_____. *The Oral and the Written Gospel*. Philadelphia: Fortress, 1983.

_____. *The Passion in Mark*. Philadelphia: Fortress, 1976.

Kennedy, H. A. A. "The Purpose of the Transfiguration," *JTS* 4 (1903) 270-73.

Kenny, A. "The Transfiguration and the Agony in the Garden," *CBQ* 19 (1957) 444-52.

Kittel, G. "ἄγγελος," *TDNT* 1 (1964) 74-87.

_____. "δόξα," *TDNT* 2 (1964) 233-53.

_____. "εἶδος, εἰδέα," *TDNT* 2 (1964) 373-75.

Klein, G. "Die Berufung des Petrus," *ZNW* 58 (1967) 1-44.

Knox, W. L. *The Sources of the Synoptic Gospels*. Ed. H. Chadwick. 2 vols. Cambridge: University, 1957.

Koehler, L. and W. Baumgartner. *Lexicon in Veteris Testamenti libros*. 2d ed. Leiden: Brill, 1958.

Koester, H. *Introduction to the New Testament*. Vol. 1. *History, Culture, and Religion of the Hellenisitic Age*. Philadelphia: Fortress, 1982.

Kuby, A. "Zur Konzeption des Markus-Evangeliums," *ZNW* 49 (1958) 52-64.

Kümmel, W. G. *Introduction to the New Testament*. Nashville: Abingdon, 1973.

_____. *The Theology of the New Testament*. Nashville: Abingdon, 1973.

Kuntz, J. K. *The Self-Revelation of God*. Philadelphia: Westminster, 1967.

Ladd, G. E. *A Commentary on the Revelation of John*. Grand Rapids: Eerdmans, 1972.

Lafontaine, R. and P. M. Beernaert. "Essai sur la structure de Marc 8.27-9.13," *RSR* 57 (1969) 543-61.

Lagrange, M.-J. *Évangile selon Saint Luc*. 2d ed. EBib. Paris: Gabalda, 1921.

_____. *Évangile selon Saint Marc*. EBib. Paris: Gabalda, 1947.

_____. "Les Sources du troisième évangile," *RB* 4 (1895) 5-22; *RB* 5 (1896) 5-38.

Lampe, G. W. H. "The Lucan Portrait of Christ," *NTS* 2 (1955-56) 160-75.

Lane, W. "*THEIOS ANĒR* Christology and the Gospel of Mark," *New Dimensions in New Testament Study*. Ed. R. Longenecker and M. Tenney. Grand Rapids: Zondervan, 1974. Pp. 144-61.

LaVerdiere, E. *Luke*. New Testament Message 4. Wilmington, DE: Glazier, 1980.

Leaney, A. R. C. "The Christ of the Synoptic Gospels," *Supplement to The New Zealand Theological Review* (1966) 22-25.

_____. *The Gospel According to St. Luke*. Black's New Testamtent Commentaries. London: Black, 1958.

_____. "Jesus and Peter: The Call and Post-Resurrection Appearance (Luke v.1-11 and xxiv.34)," *ExpTim* 65 (1953-54) 381-82.

LeDéaut, R. "Actes 7.48 et Matthieu 17.4 (par.) à la lumière du Targum Palestinien," *RSR* 52 (1964) 85-90.

Legault, A. "An Application of the Form-Critique Method to the Anointings in Galilee (Lk 7,36-50) and Bethany (Mt 26,6-13; Mk 14:,3-9; Jn 12:1-8)," *CBQ* 16 (1954) 131-45.

Léon-Dufour, X. *Concordance of the Synoptic Gospels*. Paris: Desclée, 1956.

_____. "La Transfiguration de Jésus," *Études d'évangile*. Parole de Dieu 2. Paris: Editions du Seuil, 1965. Pp. 83-122.

Liddell, H. G. and R. Scott. *A Greek-English Lexicon*. Rev. H. S. Jones. 2 vols. Oxford: Clarendon, 1925.

Liefield, W. L. "Theological Motifs in the Transfiguration Narrative," *New Dimensions in New Testament Study*. Ed. R. N. Longenecker and M. C. Tenny. Grand Rapids: Zondervan, 1974. Pp. 162-79.

Lindars, B. *The Gospel of John*. NCB. London: Oliphants, 1972.

Lohmeyer, E. *Das Evangelium des Markus*. MeyerK 2; Göttingen: Vandenhoeck & Ruprecht, 1938.

_____. "Die Verklärung Jesu nach dem Markus-Evangelium," *ZNW* 21 (1922) 185-215.

Lohse, E. "πρόσωπον," *TDNT* 6 (1968) 768-78.

Long, B. O. "Prophetic Call Traditions and Reports of Visions," *ZAW* 84 (1974) 494-500.

McCurley, F. R. "'And After Six Days' (Mark 9.2): A Semitic Literary Device," *JBL* 93 (1974) 67-81.

McLoughlin, S. "Les accords mineurs Mt-Lc contre Mc et le problème synoptique: Vers la théorie de deux sources," *De Jésus aux évangiles: Tradition et rédaction dans les évangiles synoptiques*. BETL 25. Ed. I. de la Potterie. Gembloux: Duculot, 1967. Pp. 17-40.

McNeile, A. H. *The Gospel According to St. Matthew*. London: McMillan, 1952.

Malchow, B. "The Messenger of the Covenant in Mal 3:1," *JBL* 103 (1984) 252-55.

Mánek, J. "The New Exodus of the Books of Luke," *NovT* 2 (1957) 8-23.

Mann, C. S. *Mark*. AB 27. Garden City, NY: Doubleday, 1986.

Manson, T. W. *The Teaching of Jesus*. London/New York: Cambridge University, 1935.

Manson, W. *The Gospel of Luke*. New York: Harper, 1930.

Marshall, I. H. *Commentary on Luke*. New International Greek Testament Commentary 3. Grand Rapids: Eerdmans, 1978.

_____. "Son of God or Servant of Yahweh?—A Reconsideration of Mark 1.11," *NTS* 15 (1969) 326-36.

Martin, R. "Semitic Traditions in Some Synoptic Accounts," *SBL Seminar Papers* 26. Ed. K. Richards. Atlanta: Scholars, 1987. Pp. 295-335.

_____. *Syntax Criticism of the Synoptic Gospels*. New York: Mellen, 1987.

Martyn, J. L. "We Have Found Elijah," *Jews, Greeks and Christians*. SJLA 21. Ed. R. Hamerton-Kelly and R. Scroggs. Leiden: Brill, 1976. Pp. 181-219.

Masson, C. "La Transfiguration de Jésus," *RTP* 14 (1964) 1-14.

Mauser, U. *Christ in the Wilderness*. London: SCM, 1963.

Meeks, W. *The Prophet-King. Moses Traditions and the Johannine Christology*. NovTSup 14. Leiden: Brill, 1967.

Meier, J. P. "John the Baptist in Matthew's Gospel," *JBL* 99 (1980) 383-405.

_____. *Matthew*. New Testament Message 3. Wilmington: Glazier, 1980.

_____. *The Vision of Matthew: Christ, Church, and Morality in the First Gospel*. Theological Inquiries. New York: Paulist, 1979.

Metzger, B. *A Textual Commentary on the Greek New Testament*. New York: UBS, 1971.

Meyer, E. *Ursprung und Anfänge des Christentums*. 3 vols. Stuttgart & Berlin: Cotta'sche, 1921.

Michaelis, W. "λευκός, λευκαίνω," *TDNT* 4 (1967) 241-50.

_____. "σκήνη," *TDNT* 7 (1971) 368-81.

Miller, R. J. "Elijah, John, and Jesus in the Gospel of Luke," *NTS* 34 (1988) 611-22.

Moessner, D. P. "Jesus and the 'Wilderness Generation': The Death of the Prophet Like Moses According to Luke," *SBL Seminar Papers*. Ed. K. H. Richards. Chico, CA: Scholars, 1982. Pp. 319-40.

_____. "Luke 9:1-50: Luke's Preview of the Journey of the Prophet Like Moses of Deuteronomy," *JBL* 102 (1983) 575-605.

_____. "'The Christ Must Suffer': New Light on the Jesus-Peter, Stephen, Paul Parallels in Luke-Acts," *NovT* 28 (1986) 220-56.

Moiser, J. "Moses and Elijah," *ExpTim* 96 (1984-85) 216-17.

Mowinckel, S. *The Psalms in Israel's Worship*. 2 vols. New York: Abingdon, 1967.

Müller, H.-P. "Die Verklärung Jesu: Eine motivgeschichtliche Studie," *ZNW* 51 (1960) 56-64.

Mullins, T. Y. "New Testament Commission Forms, Especially in Luke-Acts," *JBL* 95 (1976) 603-14.

Muñoz-Iglesias, S., "Los Evangelios de la Infancia y las infancias de los héroes," *EstBib* 16 (1957) 329-83.

Murphy-O'Connor, J. "What Really Happened at the Transfiguration?" *Bible Review* 3 (1987) 8-21.

Murray, G. "Did Luke Use Mark?" *DRev* 104 (1986) 268-71.

Neirynck, F. *Duality in Mark. Contributions to the Study of the Markan Redaction*. BETL 31. Leuven: Leuven University, 1972.

Neirynck, F. "La materière marcienne dans l'évangile de Luc," *L'Évangile de Luc. Problèmes littéraires et théologiques*. Gembloux: Duculot, 1973. Pp. 157-201.

_____. "Minor Agreements Matthew-Luke in the Transfiguration Story," *Orientierung an Jesus. Zur Theology der Synoptiker*. Für Josef Schmid. Ed. P. Hoffmann. Freiburg: Herder, 1973. Pp. 253-65.

_____. *The Minor Agreements of Matthew and Luke Against Mark With a Cumulative List*. BETL 37. Leuven: Leuven University, 1974.

Neyrey, J. "The Apologetic Use of the Transfiguration in 2 Peter 1:16-21," *CBQ* 42 (1980) 504-19.

_____. *The Passion According to Luke. A Redaction Study of Luke's Soteriology*. Theological Inquiries. New York: Paulist, 1985.

_____. "Synoptic Problem," *NJBC*, art. 40. Pp. 587-95.

Nickelsburg, W. E. "Enoch, Levi and Peter: Recipients of Revelation in Upper Galilee," *JBL* 100 (1981) 575-600.

Nilsson, M. P. *A History of Greek Religion*. Oxford: Clarendon, 1925.

Nineham, D. E., ed. *Studies in the Gospels. Essays in Memory of R. H. Lightfoot*. Oxford: Blackwell, 1955.

Nützel, J. M. *Der Verklärungserzählung im Markusevangelium. Eine redaktionsgeschichtliche Untersuchung*. FB 6. Würzburg: Echter, 1973.

O'Callaghan, J. "Discusión crítica en Mt 17,4," *Bib* 65 (1984) 91-93.

_____. "Mt 17,7: revisión crítica," *Bib* 66 (1985) 422-23.

Oepke, A. "ἐπιστάτης," *TDNT* 2 (1964) 622-23.

_____. "νεφέλη, νέφος," *TDNT* 4 (1967) 902-10.

O'Rourke, J. J. "The Construction with a Verb of Saying as an Indication of Sources in Luke," *NTS* 21 (1975) 421-23.

Osiek, C. *Rich and Poor in the Shepherd of Hermas*. CBQMS 15. Washington, DC: CBA, 1983.

O'Toole, R. "Luke's Message in Luke 9:1-50," *CBQ* 49 (1987) 74-89.

_____. "The Parallels Between Jesus and Moses," *BTB* 20 (1990) 22-29.

_____. *The Unity of Luke's Theology. An Analysis of Luke-Acts*. Good News Studies 9. Wilmington, DE: Glazier, 1984.

Owen, E. C. E. "*Doxa* and Cognate Words," *JTS* 33 (1932) 132-50, 265-79.

Pamment, M. "Moses and Elijah in the Story of the Transfiguration," *ExpTim* 92 (1980-81) 338-39.

Paretsky, J. A. *Jewish Eschatological Expectation and the Transfiguration of Christ*. Diss. Rome: Pontifical University of St. Thomas Aquinas, 1985.

Paulus, H. E. G. *Exegetisches Handbuch über die drei ersten Evangelien*. 3 vols. Heidelberg: Winter, 1842.

Peabody, D. B. *Mark as Composer*. New Gospel Studies 1. Macon, GA: Mercer University, 1987.

Pedersen, S. "Die Proklamation Jesu als des eschatologischen Offenbarungsträgers (Mt 17.1-13)," *NovT* 17 (1975) 241-64.

Pelletier, A. "Les apparitions du Ressuscité en termes de la Septante," *Bib* 51 (1970) 76-79.

Perkins, P. *Resurrection: New Testament Witness and Contemporary Reflection*. Garden City, NY: Doubleday, 1984.

Perrin, N. "The Christology of Mark: A Study in Metholodogy," *JR* 51 (1971) 173-87.

Perry, A. M. *The Sources of Luke's Passion-Narrative*. Chicago: University of Chicago, 1919.

Pesch, R. *Das Markusevangelium*. 2 vols. HTKNT. Freiburg: Herder,1976.

_____. *Der reiche Fischfang: Lk 5,1-11/Jo 21,1-14: Wundergeschichte—Berufungserzählung—Erscheinungs-bericht*. Düsseldorf: Patmos, 1969.

Plummer, A. *The Gospel According to St. Luke*. ICC. NewYork: Scribner, 1903.

Propp, W. H. "The Skin of Moses' Face—Transfigured or Disfigured?" *CBQ* 49 (1987) 375-86.

Ramsay, W. M. "The Time of the Transfiguration," *Expositor* 6 (1908) 557-62.

Ramsey, A. M. *The Glory of God and the Transfiguration of Christ*. London/New York: Longmans, Green, 1945.

Ravens, D. A. S. "Luke 9,7-62 and the Prophetic Role of Jesus," *NTS* 36 (1990) 119-29.

Rehkopf, F. *Die lukanische Sonderquelle: Ihr Umfang und Sprachgebrauch*. WUNT 5. Tübingen: Mohr, 1959.

Reicke, B. *The Epistles of James, Peter, and Jude*. AB 37. Garden City, NY: Doubleday, 1964.

_____. *The Roots of the Synoptic Gospels*. Philadelphia: Fortress, 1986.

Reid, B. "The Centerpiece of Salvation History: Jerusalem in the Gospel of Luke," *TBT* 29 (1991) 20-24.

Reiser, M. *Syntax und Stil des Markusevangeliums im Licht der hellenistischen Volksliteratur*. WUNT 11. Tübingen: Mohr, 1984.

Reitzenstein, R. *Hellenistic Mystery Religions: Their Basic Ideas and Significance*. PTMS 15. Pittsburgh: Pickwick, 1978.

Rengstorf, K. H. *Das Evangelium nach Lukas*. NTD 3. Göttingen: Vandenhoeck & Ruprecht, 1958.

Richard, E. "Luke—Writer, Theologian, Historian: Research and Orientation of the 1970's," *BTB* 13 (1983) 3-15.

Riesenfeld, H. *Jésus transfiguré. L'arrière-plan du récit évangélique de la transfiguration de Notre-Seigneur*. ASNU 16. Copenhagen: Munksgaard, 1947.

Ringe, S. "Luke 9:28-36: The Beginning of an Exodus," *The Bible and Feminist Hermeneutics*. Semeia 28. Ed. Mary Ann Tolbert. Chico, CA: Scholars, 1983. Pp. 83-99.

Ringgren, H. "Luke's Use of the Old Testament," *Christians Among Jews and Gentiles*. Ed. G. Nichelsburg and G. MacRae. Philadelphia: Fortress, 1986. Pp. 227-35.

Rivera, L. F. "Interpretatio Transfigurationis Jesu in redactione evangelii Marci," *VD* 46 (1968) 99-104.

Robbins, V. "Classifying Pronouncement Stories in Plutarch's *Parallel Lives*," *Semeia* 20 (1981) 29-52.

Robinson, J. A. T. "Elijah, John and Jesus: An Essay in Detection," *NTS* 4 (1957-58) 263-81.

Robinson, J. M. "Jesus: From Easter to Valentinus (or to the Apostles' Creed),"
    *JBL* 101 (1982) 5-37.

_____. The *Gattung* of Mark (and John)," *Jesus and Man's Hope*. 2 vols.
    Pittsburgh: Pittsburgh Theological Seminary, 1970.

Robinson, W. C. *Der Weg des Herrn*. TF 36. Hamburg-Bergstedt: H. Reich, 1964.

Sabbe, M. "La Rédaction du récit de la transfiguration," *La venue du Messie*.
    RechBib 6. Bruges: Desclée, 1962. Pp. 65-100.

Sanday, W. *Studies in the Synoptic Problem*. Oxford: Clarendon, 1911.

Sanders, E. P. *The Tendencies of the Synoptic Tradition*. Cambridge: University,
    1969.

Schillebeeckx, E. "The Transfiguration of the Suffering Son of God (Mark 9.2-9),"
    *God Among Us*. New York: Crossroads, 1983. Pp. 78-82.

Schmid, J. *Matthäus und Lukas: Eine Untersuchung der Verhältnisse ihrer
    Evangelien*. Freiburg: Herder, 1930.

Schmiedel, P. W. "Simon Peter," *Encyclopedia Biblica*. 4 vols. Ed. T. K. Cheyne.
    New York: Macmillan, 1903. Pp. 4. 4570-71.

Schmithals, W. "Der Markusschluss, die Verklärungsgeschichte und die
    Aussendung der Zwölf," *ZTK* 69 (1972) 379-411.

Schnackenburg, R. "Die Erwartung des Prophetens nach dem Neuen Testament und
    den Qumran-Texten," *International Congress on "The Four Gospels in 1957,"
    Oxford, 1957*. SE I. TU 73. Berlin: Akademie, 1959. Pp. 622-39.

_____. *The Gospel According to St. John*. 3 vols. New York: Seabury, 1968,
    1980, 1982.

Schneider, G. "Das Problem einer vorlukanischen Passionserzahlung," *BZ* 16
    (1972) 222-44.

Schneider, J. "ἀναβαίνω," *TDNT* 1 (1964) 519-22.

Schnellbächer, E. L. "ΚΑΙ ΜΕΤΑ 'ΗΜΕΡΑΣ 'ΕΞ (Markus 9,2)," *ZNW* 71 (1980)
    252-57.

_____. *The Tradition about the Transfiguration of Jesus and its Function in
    the New Testament Gospels*. M.Phil. Diss. University of Hull, 1979.

Schniewind, J. *Die Parallelperikopen bei Lukas und Johannes*. 2d ed. Hildesheim:
    Olms, 1958.

Schramm, T. *Der Markus-Stoff bei Lukas: Eine literarkritische und
    redaktionsgeschichtliche Untersuchung*. SNTSMS 14. Cambridge: Cambridge
    University, 1971.

Schrenk, G. "ἐκλεκτός," *TDNT* 4 (1967) 181-92.

Schulz, S. *Die Stunde der Botschaft. Einführung in die Theologie der vier
    Evangelisten*. Hamburg: Furche, 1967.

Schürmann, H. *Das Lukasevangelium*. HTKNT 3. Freiburg: Herder, 1969.

Schweizer, E. *The Good News According to Luke*. Atlanta: John Knox, 1984.

_____. *The Good News According to Matthew*. Atlanta: John Knox, 1975.

_____. "Eine hebraisierende Sonderquelle des Lukas?" *TZ* 6 (1951) 161-85.

_____. *Jesus*. Richmond: John Knox, 1971.

Seidensticker, P. *Die Auferstehung Jesu in der Botschaft der Evangelisten. Ein traditionsgeschichtlicher Versuch zum Problem der Sicherung der Osterbotschaft in der apostolischen Zeit.* SBS 27. Stuttgart: Katholisches Bibelwerk, 1967.

Senior, D. *1 & 2 Peter.* New Testament Message 20. Wilmington, DE: Glazier, 1980.

Sidebottom, E. M. *James, Jude, and 2 Peter.* Century Bible London: Nelson, 1967.

Silberman, L. H. "The Two 'Messiahs' of the Manual of Discipline," *VT* 5 (1955) 77-82.

Smith, M. "The Origin and History of the Transfiguration Story," *USQR* 36 (1980) 39-44.

Soards, M. L. *The Passion According to Luke. The Special Material of Luke 22.* JSNTSup 14; Sheffield: JSOT Press, 1987.

Soares Prabhu, G. *The Formula Quotations in the Infancy Narrative of Matthew.* AnBib 63. Rome: Biblical Institute, 1976.

Sparks, H. F. D. "The Semitisms of St. Luke's Gospel," *JTS* 44 (1943) 129-38.

Spitta, F. "Die evangelische Geschichte von der Verklärung Jesu," *ZWT* 53 (1911) 121-23.

Stanley, D. *The Apostolic Church in the New Testament.* Westminster: Newman, 1967.

Starcky, J. "Les Quatre étapes du messianisme à Qumrân," *RB* 70 (1963) 489-505.

_____. "Un Texte messianique araméen de la grotte 4 de Qumrân," *École des langues orientales anciennes de l'Institut Catholique de Paris: Mémorial du cinquantenaire 1914-1964.* Travaux de l'Institut Catholique de Paris 10. Paris: Bloud et Gay, 1964. Pp. 51-66.

Steenberg, D. "The Case Against the Synonymity of *MORPHĒ* and *EIKŌN*," *JSNT* 34 (1988) 77-86.

Stegner, W. R. "Lucan Priority in the Feeding of the Five Thousand," *BR* 21 (1976) 19-28.

_____. *Narrative Theology in Early Jewish Christianity.* Louisville, Westminster/John Knox, 1989.

_____. "The Transfiguration," in *Narrative Theology in Early Jewish Christianity.* Louisville: Westminster/John Knox, 1989.

Stein, R. H. "Is the Transfiguration (Mark 9:2-8) a Misplaced Resurrection Account?" *JBL* 95 (1976) 79-96.

Strack, H. L. and P. Billerbeck. *Kommentar zum Neuen Testament aus Talmud und Midrasch.* 6 vols. Munich: Beck, 1922, 1924, 1926, 1928, 1956, 1961.

Strauss, D. F. *The Life of Jesus Critically Examined.* Philadelphia: Fortress, 1972.

Streeter, B. H. *The Four Gospels: A Study in Origins.* London: Macmillan, 1964.

Swaeles, R. "Jésus, nouvel Elie, dans saint Luc," *AsSeign* 69 (1964) 41-66.

Synge, F. C. and D. Baly. "The Transfiguration Story," *ExpTim* 82 (1970-71) 82-83.

Talbert, C. H. *Literary Patterns, Theological Themes and the Genre of Luke-Acts.* SBLMS 20. Missoula, MT: Scholars, 1974.

Talbert, C. H. "The Lukan Presentation of Jesus' Ministry in Galilee, Lk 4:31-9:50," *RevExp* 64 (1967) 485-97.

_____. ed. *Luke-Acts. New Perspectives from the Society of Biblical Literature Seminar.* New York: Crossroad, 1984.

_____. ed. *Perspectives on Luke-Acts.* Edinburgh: Clark, 1978.

Tannehill, R. C. *The Narrative Unity of Luke-Acts.* Philadelphia: Fortress, 1986.

_____. "Introduction: The Pronouncement Story and Its Types," *Semeia* 20 (1981) 1-13.

_____. "Varieties of Synoptic Pronouncement Stories," *Semeia* 20 (1981) 101-19.

Taylor, V. *Behind the Third Gospel.* Oxford: Oxford University, 1926.

_____. *The Formation of the Gospel Tradition.* London: Macmillan, 1964.

_____. *The Gospel According to Mark.* 2d ed. London: Macmillan, 1966.

_____. *The Passion Narrative of St. Luke.* SNTSMS 19. Cambridge: University, 1972.

Teeple, H. M. *The Mosaic Eschatological Prophet.* JBLMS 10. Philadelphia: SBL, 1957.

Thrall, M. "Elijah and Moses in Mark's Account of the Transfiguration," *NTS* 16 (1969-70) 305-17.

Tiede, D. L. *Charismatic Figure as Miracle Worker.* Missoula, MT: Scholars, 1972.

_____. *Prophecy and History in Luke-Acts.* Philadelphia: Fortress, 1980.

Trémel, B. "Des Récits apocalyptiques: Baptême et transfiguration," *LumVie* 119 (1974) 70-83.

Trible, P. *God and the Rhetoric of Sexuality.* Philadelphia: Fortress, 1978.

Trites, A. A., "The Prayer Motif in Luke-Acts," Ed. C. H. Talbert. Danville, VA: Association of Baptist Professors of Religion, 1978. Pp. 168-86.

_____. "The Transfiguration in the Theology of Luke: Some Redactional Links," *The Glory of Christ in the New Testament. Studies in Christology.* Ed. L. D. Hurst and N. T. Wright. Oxford: Clarendon, 1987. Pp. 71-81.

_____. "The Transfiguration of Jesus: The Gospel in Microcosm," *EvQ* 51 (1979) 67-79.

Trocmé, E. *The Formation of the Gospel According to Mark.* London: SPCK, 1975.

Turner, C. H. "Marcan Usage: Notes, Critical and Exegetical, on the Second Gospel," *JTS* 26 (1925) 12-20.

Turner, N. "The Minor Verbal Agreements of Matthew and Luke against Mark," *International Congress on "The Four Gospels in 1957," Oxford, 1957.* SE 1. TU 73. Berlin: Akademie, 1959. Pp. 223-34.

Tyson, J. B. "The Blindness of the Disciples in Mark," *JBL* 80 (1961) 261-68.

Underhill, E. *The Mystic Way.* London/New York: Dent, 1913.

van Unnik, W. C. "Eléments Artistiques dans l'évangile de Luc," *ETL* 46 (1970) 401-12.

Vaganay, L. *Le Problème Synoptique: une hypothèse de travail.* Tournai: Desclée, 1954.

de Vaux, R. *Ancient Israel, Its Life and Institutions*. New York: McGraw-Hill, 1965.

Viviano, B. T. "Rabbouni and Mark 9:5," *RB* 97 (1990) 207-18.

Wand, J. W. C. *Transfiguration*. London: The Faith Press, 1967.

Weeden, T. J. *Mark—Traditions in Conflict*. Philadelphia: Fortress, 1971.

Weiss, B. *Die Evangelien des Markus und Lukas*. MeyerK 1 part 2. Göttingen: Vandenhoeck & Ruprecht, 1901.

_____. *Die Quellen des Lukasevangeliums*. Stuttgart/Berlin: Cotta, 1907.

Wellhausen, J. *Das Evangelium Marci*. Berlin: Reimer, 1909.

Wilke, C. G. *Der Urevangelist, oder exegetisch-kritische Untersuchung über das Verwantschaftsverhältnis der drei ersten Evangelien*. Dresden: Fleischer, 1838.

Williams, W. H. "The Transfiguration—A New Approach?" *International Congress on New Testament Studies*. Ed. E. A. Livingstone. SE 6. TU 112. Berlin: Akademie, 1973. Pp. 635-50.

Wink, W. "Mark 9:2-8," *Int* 36 (1982) 63-67.

Winn, A. C. "Worship as a Healing Experience. An Exposition of Matthew 17.1-9," *Int* 29 (1975) 68-72.

Zahn, T. *Das Evangelium des Lucas*. Vol. 3 Kommentar zum Neuen Testament. Leipzig: Deichertsche, 1922.

Zerwick, M. *Biblical Greek*. Scripta Pontificii Instituti Biblici 114. Rome: Biblical Institute, 1963.

Ziesler, J. A. "The Transfiguration Story and the Markan Soteriology," *ExpTim* 81 (1969/70) 263-68.

# INDEX

# I. CITATIONS OF SCRIPTURE AND OTHER ANCIENT SOURCES

## HEBREW SCRIPTURES

### Genesis

| | |
|---|---|
| 1:31 | 59n. |
| 2:21 | 130 |
| 3:4 | 78 |
| 3:18 | 56n. |
| 4:5 | 110 |
| 4:8 | 45n.55n. |
| 4:14 | 56n.111 |
| 4:16 | 56n. |
| 6:2 | 141 |
| 6:7 | 56n. |
| 8:13 | 56n. |
| 15:1 | 139 |
| 15:17 | 59n. |
| 16:1-16 | 84 |
| 16:1-6 | 84 |
| 16:7-12 | 85n. |
| 16:7 | 84 |
| 16:10-12 | 84 |
| 16:11 | 78 |
| 16:13 | 78.84 |
| 16:14 | 84 |
| 16:15 | 84 |
| 17:1-21 | 85n. |
| 17:3 | 56n. |
| 17:12 | 100n. |
| 17:17 | 56n. |
| 18-19 | 79 |
| 18:1-16 | 84 |
| 18:1-12 | 85n. |
| 18:1 | 79.84 |
| 18:2 | 79.84.133n. |
| 18:10 | 84 |
| 18:12 | 84 |
| 18:14 | 84 |
| 18:16 | 84 |
| 18:18 | 84 |
| 18:33 | 79 |
| 19:1-22 | 80 |
| 19:1 | 79 |
| 19:1a | 80 |
| 19:1b | 80 |
| 19:1c | 80 |
| 19:5 | 79 |
| 19:10 | 79 |
| 19:12-13 | 81 |
| 19:12 | 79 |
| 19:14 | 81 |
| 19:15 | 79.81 |
| 19:16 | 79.81 |
| 19:17 | 81 |

| | |
|---|---|
| 19:29 | 55n. |
| 21:4 | 100n. |
| 21:17-19 | 80n. |
| 22:1 | 47n. |
| 22:9-14 | 80n. |
| 22:13 | 59n. |
| 23:17 | 56n. |
| 24:7 | 80n. |
| 24:40 | 80n. |
| 24:55 | 48n. |
| 25:18 | 56n. |
| 29:17 | 106 |
| 31:2 | 108.109 |
| 31:5 | 108.109 |
| 31:13 | 80n. |
| 31:30 | 111 |
| 32:31 | 106 |
| 39:6 | 106 |
| 39:7 | 47n. |
| 40:1 | 47n. |

### Exodus

| | |
|---|---|
| 1:8 | 106n. |
| 2:15 | 56n. |
| 3:1-4:16 | 78 |
| 3:1-12 | 81.85n. |
| 3:2 | 78 |
| 3:4 | 139 |
| 4:15-16 | 117 |
| 4:22 | 141 |
| 5:4 | 118 |
| 6:14-25 | 118 |
| 8:15 | 118 |
| 13:21-22 | 136 |
| 14:11-12 | 122n. |
| 14:19-20 | 136 |
| 14:19 | 80n. |
| 15:13 | 89 |
| 16:1-36 | 117 |
| 16:2-3 | 122n. |
| 16:10 | 9.89 |
| 17:2-4 | 122n. |
| 19 | 122 |
| 19:9 | 9.89 |
| 19:20 | 103n. |
| 19:34 | 89 |
| 22:29-30 | 100 |
| 23:20-23 | 80n. |
| 23:20 | 56n. |
| 24 | 19.26 |

# II. AUTHORS CITED

ACHEVÉ D'IMPRIMER
EN AVRIL 1993
PAR L'IMPRIMERIE
DE LA MANUTENTION
A MAYENNE
N° 138-93